P9-CBL-679

DISCARDED

THE HARLEY LYRICS

THE WARD BEQUEST

The late Sir Adolphus William Ward, successively Professor of History and English, Principal of Owens College and Vice-Chancellor of the University of Manchester, bequeathed one thousand pounds to the University. By the decision of the Council of the University, the income from this sum is to be devoted to the advancement of research in History and in English. It will normally be used to assist the publication by the University Press of approved works of scholarship, and all works of which the cost of publication has been wholly or partially defrayed from the fund will be issued with the imprint of ' The Ward Bequest '.

This is the ninth volume published under the terms of the fund.

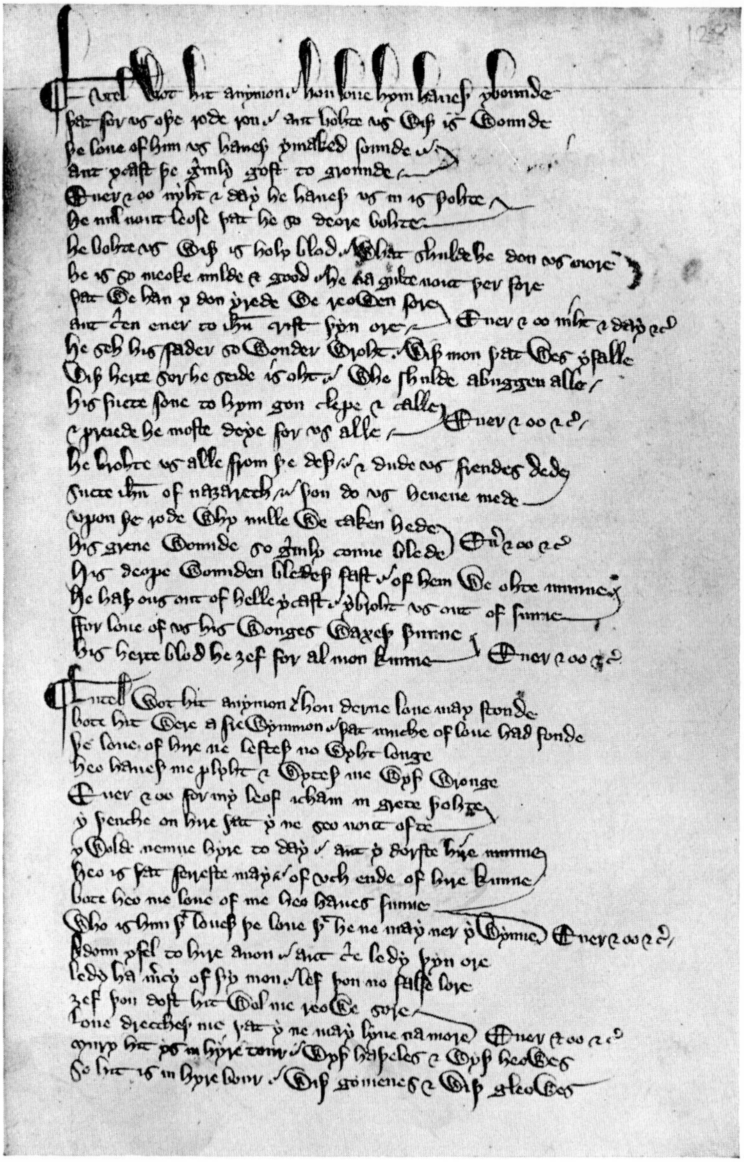

OLD AND MIDDLE ENGLISH TEXTS
GENERAL EDITOR: G. L. BROOK

THE HARLEY LYRICS

THE MIDDLE ENGLISH LYRICS
OF MS. HARLEY 2253

EDITED BY

G. L. BROOK

MANCHESTER UNIVERSITY PRESS

© 1956 G. L. Brook

Published by the University of Manchester at

THE UNIVERSITY PRESS

316-324 Oxford Road, Manchester, 13

First Edition 1948
Second Edition 1956
Third Edition 1964
Fourth Edition 1968

GB SBN 7190 0116 1

Printed and bound in Great Britain by
Butler and Tanner, Ltd., Frome and London

To
THE MEMORY OF
MY MOTHER

OLD AND MIDDLE ENGLISH TEXTS

GENERAL EDITOR : G. L. BROOK

PREFACE

The excellence of the Middle English lyrics of MS. Harley 2253 has long been recognized. W. P. Ker, for example, gave them a prominent place in his *English Literature : Mediæval*, and said that the manuscript contained ' everything best worth remembering in the old lyrical poetry '. Unfortunately the lyrics have not been very easily accessible. The most recent complete edition is that of Böddeker, which was published seventy years ago. It has a full linguistic introduction and glossary, but the edition suffers from the editor's fondness for unnecessary emendations. Many of the lyrics have been printed by Carleton Brown in his *Religious Lyrics of the Fourteenth Century* and *English Lyrics of the Thirteenth Century*, but his labours, valuable though they were, have not rendered a new edition unnecessary. Carleton Brown's chief contribution to the study of the Middle English lyric was the collection of material from a wide variety of sources. He was content to leave many difficulties in the lyrics unexplained, and some of the interpretations which he suggested seem unconvincing.

It has to be admitted that the text of the lyrics contains many difficulties, and I cannot claim to have solved all of them. Fortunately the textual difficulties are for the most part confined to a few of the lyrics. The reader who is not already familiar with the *Harley Lyrics* is recommended to omit Nos. 2, 3, 6, 8, and 30 on a first reading of the present edition.

I owe a very great debt to the late Professor E. V. Gordon and to Professor Bruce Dickins for encouragement and help ungrudgingly given. My thanks are due too to the Trustees of the British Museum for allowing me to make use of the manuscript, and to Professor J. W. H. Atkins, Professor F. W. Baxter, Professor H. B. Charlton, the Rev. C. W. Dugmore, Mrs. I. L. Gordon, Professor Simeon Potter, Professor T. B. W. Reid, Dr. A. H. Smith, and Dr. F. Whitehead for help and advice on many points. Finally, I should like to acknowledge my indebtedness to the Manchester University Press for undertaking the publication of the book, to its officials for their co-operation, and to the administrators of the Ward Bequest for bearing part of the cost.

G. L. BROOK

February, 1948.

PREFACE TO THE SECOND EDITION

In preparing this edition I have not made any major changes. The revision has consisted in the main of the correction of errors and the re-wording of a few sentences which now seem to me badly expressed. The most thorough revision has been that of the Bibliography. A good deal of work on the medieval lyric has been published during recent years, and the Bibliography, though still selective, is a good deal fuller than that of the first edition. I should like to thank the reviewers and colleagues who have pointed out errors and omissions. I am conscious that the Notes, with their frequent expressions of disagreement with earlier writers on the lyrics, may sometimes disguise the large number of occasions when I am in agreement with them. I have tried to mention the sources of all important contributions to the interpretation of the lyrics, but I have not tried to produce a variorum edition, and I have quoted no source for interpretations which are likely to have occurred independently to many readers. I should like here to make acknowledgement to Mr. G. V. Smithers, whose reading and interpretation *sully* at 2.57 and 14.6.(*English and Germanic Studies* III, p. 81) seem to me completely convincing ; I have adopted his interpretation in the present edition.

G.L.B.

July, 1955.

PREFACE TO THE THIRD EDITION

The only significant additions to the present edition are in the Bibliography, which has been brought up to date. Since the edition is planned on the same lines as the volumes in the series of Old and Middle English Texts, it has seemed reasonable to add the new edition to that series.

G.L.B.

February, 1964.

PREFACE TO THE FOURTH EDITION

The changes in the new edition have for the most part been made to take account of the suggestions of Professors J. A. W. Bennett and G. V. Smithers in their *Early Middle English Verse and Prose* (second edition, Oxford, 1968).

G.L.B.

August, 1968.

CONTENTS

FACSIMILE

INTRODUCTION

One of the chief obstacles in the way of the study of medieval literature is the disappearance of valuable material. The total bulk of Middle English writings that have been preserved is considerable, but among those writings religious and didactic works preponderate enormously. Such a lack of balance is the natural result of the part played by the monasteries in the preservation of manuscripts and does not necessarily reflect contemporary taste. It would be rash to assume that the monks who compiled the manuscript miscellanies had no knowledge of love lyrics or other secular literature, but it is natural that such versions as they possessed should not normally find their way into monastic libraries to be copied and preserved as a sacred duty. Hence large numbers of religious lyrics have been preserved but not many secular lyrics. More than half the secular lyrics that have come down from before the end of the fourteenth century are preserved in a single manuscript, MS. Harley 2253, in the British Museum. Although other Harleian manuscripts contain lyrics, the term *The Harley Lyrics* has come to be applied to the lyrics of this manuscript.

THE MANUSCRIPT

MS. Harley 2253 is a parchment folio of 141 leaves, 11¼ inches by 7½ inches. Two leaves have been cut out after f. 52 and six after f. 140. The first 48 leaves contain Anglo-Norman religious pieces written in a late thirteenth-century hand. The rest of the manuscript, with the possible exception of a few recipes on f. 52 v., is in the same early fourteenth-century hand, which closely resembles that used in a Chronicle of England in MS. Royal 12 C xii, ff. 62 r. to 68 v.[1] The editors of the publications of the New Palaeographical Society [2] and Hall [3] say that the present manuscript consists of two manuscripts bound together, the second one beginning at f. 49, where the second hand begins. This view cannot be correct, since ff. 47 to 52 belong to the same gathering of leaves.

The contents of the manuscript are very miscellaneous. There are religious pieces in Latin prose and verse and saints' lives, fabliaux, and miscellaneous poems in Anglo-Norman ; and the English poems include versions of such well-known works as *King*

---

[1] As pointed out by Hall, *King Horn* (Oxford, 1901), p. viii.
[2] Vol. II. plate 241.   [3] *King Horn*, p. vii.

Horn, The Proverbs of Hendyng, and *The Sayings of Saint Bernard,* as well as some of the earliest English political songs and the lyrics in this volume. The present edition does not include the political songs, but contains all the other short poems which can properly be described as lyrics. It is not easy to draw the line between lyrical and non-lyrical religious poems. The lyric exerted an influence on other forms of verse, and in the poems of this manuscript it is possible to see the lyric gradually merging into other literary forms. For example, *The Sayings of Saint Bernard* and *Maximion* are written in stanzas similar to those used in lyrics and deal with similar themes, but they are too long and too impersonal to be regarded as lyrics. The translation of the Latin poem, *Dulcis Jesu Memoria,* is not included because of its length and because the type to which it belongs is sufficiently well represented by *Suete Iesu King of Blysse* (15), which is joined to it in some manuscripts.

It is very unlikely that all the lyrics in the manuscript are the work of a single poet. The dialect of the manuscript corresponds fairly closely with that of the *Vespasian Psalter* in Old English and that of the *Katherine Group* in early Middle English, but rhymes show that many of the lyrics were originally written in other dialects.[1] Proper names sometimes suggest the provenance of a lyric, as in *The Fair Maid of Ribblesdale* (7). When the poet says that his mistress is the fairest maid ' from Irlond into Ynde ' (12.12) or that the Virgin is the best physician ' from Catenas into Dyuelyn ' (23.34), he gives little indication of his origin, but sometimes a poet is more cautious. For example, one says of his mistress ' ffrom Weye he is wisist into Wyrhale ' (3.27), while another says that he does not know so fair a maid as his mistress ' bituene Lyncolne ant Lyndeseye, Norhamptoun ant Lounde ' (25.17). It is reasonable to suppose that the former poet was familiar with the West Midlands and that the latter poet was more familiar with the East Midlands.

Provenance. The manuscript formed part of the library of John Batteley, Archdeacon of Canterbury from 1688 to 1708, and was sold by his nephew John Batteley, Master of the Augmentation Office, to the Earl of Oxford in 1723. It became the property of the nation, along with the other Harley manuscripts, in 1753.[2] The original home of the manuscript can be guessed at from its contents. Wright [3] quotes the line ' ffrom Weye he is wisist into

---

[1] See G. L. Brook, ' The Original Dialects of the Harley Lyrics ' in *Leeds Studies in English,* II (1933), 38–61.

[2] Publications of the New Palaeographical Society, vol. II, plate 241.

[3] Preface to *Specimens of Lyric Poetry.*

Wyrhale ' as evidence that the manuscript was written somewhere in the West Midland area, but such a line provides evidence of the provenance only of that particular lyric and it does not follow that the manuscript was written in the same region. The West Midland origin of the manuscript suggested by the dialect is supported by the occurrence in it of the Latin lives of three saints who have associations with that area. The fly-leaves of the manuscript contain part of the consuetudinary of a cathedral in which Saint Ethelbert, who was the patron saint of Hereford, was especially honoured, written on the back of household accounts. On the whole it is safe to say that the manuscript is from the West Midlands and may be from Leominster or Hereford, but the ascription to Leominster Priory, which has been accepted as a fact by most writers on the lyrics, rests on no certain evidence.

Date. An earlier limit is provided by the political songs which deal with particular events, e.g. the Battle of Lewes (1264), the Battle of Courtrai (1302), the execution of Sir Simon Fraser (1306), and the death of Edward I (1307). Böddeker [1] suggested 1310 as the approximate date, and this date has been widely accepted, but the manuscript contains a version of the prophecies of Thomas of Erceldoune which refers to the Battle of Bannockburn (1314). The handwriting probably belongs to the early part of the fourteenth century, and the date c. 1314–25 suggested by the editors of the New Palaeographical Society's volume is probably the nearest that can be given.

Orthography. 1. Initially *c* is used before back vowels and *k* before front vowels, except that before front *u* (from OE. *y*) both *c* and *k* are used ; the only other exception is *kare*. Finally *c* and *k* are interchangeable, e.g. *boc, bok* ; *clerc, clerk* ; *toc, tok*. Back *cc* is represented by *ck* or *kk*, e.g. *lockes, lokkes* ; front *cc* by *(c)ch*, e.g. *dreccheþ, vachen*.

2. OE. *sc* initially is *sh* ; the only exception is *schule*. Medially and finally it is *(s)sh, shsh*, e.g. *fleish, fleishshes, wosshe*.

3. Inorganic initial *h* has been added before a vowel in *hapel, hawe, heʒe, heyse,* and *her*.

4. OE. *þ* or *ð* is usually *þ*, occasionally *th* or *ht*, never *ð*, e.g. *luthere, cloht, teht, wroht* beside *þou, wepeþ, wroþe*.

5. No distinction in spelling is made between *u* as a vowel and *v* as a consonant ; *v* is used initially and *u* medially for both vowel and consonant, e.g. *vnbold, leuedy*.

6. After initial consonants *w* is often represented by *u*, e.g. *duelle, suyre* beside *swyre*.

<hr>

[1] *Altenglische Dichtungen*, p. iii.

7. *w* is occasionally used as a spelling for *wo* or *wu*, e.g. *byswngen, vnwrþ, wrst.*

8. The letter ȝ is used to represent two quite distinct sounds : in native words it represents front fricative *g*, e.g. *dreȝe, ȝeue* ; in French loan-words it represents *s* or *z*, e.g. *encenȝ, romaunȝ.*

Two features of the spelling of the manuscript have been removed to footnotes in this edition in accordance with the usual practice, though it is not certain that they are scribal errors :

1. Confusion between *h* and *þ*. There are ten examples in the poems in this volume, five of them in No. 30. The forms may be due to the difficulty experienced by French scribes in distinguishing between two unfamiliar fricatives, cf. *darþ* for *darf*, 2.29.

2. Confusion between *w* and *wh* initially ; there are eleven examples. Such confusion is common in southerly texts in Middle English and suggests that in those dialects *w-* and *wh-* were pronounced alike in the fourteenth century, as they are by many speakers at the present day.

SECULAR LYRICS

Although MS. Harley 2253 is the earliest manuscript to contain a group of English secular lyrics, there are indications that secular songs were known several centuries earlier than the date of this manuscript. The earliest of these to survive is the song which, according to the twelfth-century chronicler Thomas of Ely, was composed by King Canute as he listened from his boat on the Ouse to the singing of the monks :

> Merie sungen ðe muneches binnen Ely
> ða Cnut cning reu ðer by ;
> Roweþ, cnites, noer the land,
> And here wve þes muneches saeng.[1]

This is only a part of the song, possibly the refrain, since the chronicler adds, ' et caetera, quae sequuntur, quae usque hodie in choris publice cantantur et in proverbis memorantur '.

By the end of the twelfth century singing and dancing in church-yards had become a common practice. In his *Gemma Ecclesiastica* Giraldus Cambrensis tells the story of a parish priest in Worcester-shire who had been kept awake all night by such singing and dancing, with the result that next day, when he began the early morning service, instead of singing the usual ' Dominus vobiscum ', he startled his congregation by substituting the refrain which had been ringing in his ears, ' Swete lamman dhin are '. So great was

[1] Trinity College, Cambridge, MS. O. 2.1, ff. 87 v., 88 r. Quoted from R. L. Greene, *The Early English Carols* (Oxford, 1935), p. xxxiv.

the scandal caused by this incident that Bishop Northall pronounced an anathema upon any person who should ever again sing that song within the limits of his diocese.[1] Giraldus, who is writing in Latin, quotes the phrase in English, and the story shows that vernacular love lyrics were known in England more than a century before the date of MS. Harley 2253.

A sermon preserved in an early thirteenth-century manuscript [2] takes a couplet from a love lyric as its text. The sermon begins :

> ' Atte wrastlinge my lemman i ches,
> and atte ston-kasting i him for-les.

. . . Mi leue frend, wilde wimmen & golme i mi contreie, wan he gon o þe ring, among manie oþere songis þat litil ben wort þat tei singin, so sein þei þus.' This passage tells us a good deal about the position of the secular lyric at the time : it tells us that the song quoted is one of many, that churchmen disparaged the secular songs, and that the song was accompanied by dancing, since that is probably the meaning of ' wan he gon o þe ring '. A full account of singing and dancing of the kind referred to here is given at the beginning of the fourteenth century by Robert Mannyng of Bourne in Lincolnshire in *Handlyng Synne*. The events which led to the growth of the legend narrated by Mannyng took place early in the eleventh century at Kölbigk in Saxony. The legend was that a priest, celebrating Mass on Christmas night, was disturbed by a party of twelve men and women singing and dancing in the churchyard. He cursed them, with the result that they had to go on singing and dancing for a year. Mannyng tells this story in order to discourage what had clearly become a common practice.

A characteristic of all the earliest English secular lyrics that have survived is that they are very short. The examples already mentioned are short because they are incomplete, but some of the lyrics which seem to be complete are almost as short ; for example, the poem ' Foweles in þe frith ', which occurs with musical notes in MS. Douce 139, f. 5 r., consists of only five lines. Another lyric belonging to the early thirteenth century is ' Mirie it is while sumer ilast ' in MS. Rawlinson G 22, f. 1 v.[3] These two lyrics, like the more famous Cuckoo Song, show the interest in nature and the association between nature and human moods which we meet with again and again in the *Harley Lyrics*. The frequent use of alliteration and alliterative phrases is another point of resemblance between these very early lyrics and the *Harley Lyrics*.

---

[1] Giraldus Cambrensis, *Opera*, ii. 120 (Rolls Series).
[2] Trinity College, Cambridge, MS. B. 1. 45, f. 41 v. Printed by Max Förster, *Anglia*, xlii, pp. 152–4.
[3] Both these lyrics are printed by Brown, XIII, p. 14.

The Cuckoo Song, ' Sumer is i-cumen in ', is notable because, beside the English words, we have the music, Latin words to fit the tune, and instructions in Latin for singing the lyric as a part-song. The date of the transcription of the lyric into the manuscript where it is preserved [1] has generally been said to be 1230 to 1240, but a later date, 1310, has recently been put forward,[2] and the later date accords better with the very highly-developed nature of the music. The relationship between English words, Latin words, and music has been much discussed, but it seems probable that the lyric as we have it is a learned composer's adaptation of a popular English *reverdie*, or lyric on spring, of the type represented by *Spring* (11). The Latin text, beginning ' Perspice christicola ', does not fit the tune very well and overlooks the ' Pes ' or burden altogether ; it is probably the result of an unskilful attempt to convert the lyric to religious uses. The careful instructions in the manuscript for the rendering of the song suggest that it was of a type unusual at the time.

The secular lyrics of MS. Harley 2253 include representatives of several different types of lyric : carol, *pastourelle*, *reverdie*, and comic poem are all represented. Most of the secular lyrics were written under the influence of the conventions of courtly love ; these lyrics (Nos. 3, 4, 5, 7, 9, 12, 14, 25 and 32) form a more or less homogeneous group and can best be considered later.

The term ' carol ' has come to be associated with Christmas, because Christmas was a festival when carols were often sung, but there is no necessary connection between the two. A carol was a dancing-song, and hence its essential characteristics are that it must be composed of uniform stanzas and that it must have a refrain. The only lyrics in this manuscript with refrains are Nos. 4, 14, 31, and 32. The metre of the last two of these poems is too irregular to allow them to be considered as carols. The other two poems are too literary to be very suitable as dancing-songs, but their refrains are very similar to those found in genuine carols.[3] The refrain of *Blow, Northerne Wynd* (14), with its simplicity and repetition, is probably popular in origin, and is quite different in style from the rest of the lyric. It seems likely that the refrain has been borrowed from a folk-song and attached to a *trouvère*-lyric. The refrain of *Alysoun* (4) is linked with each stanza of the lyric

---

[1] MS. Harley 978, a monks' commonplace-book written at Reading Abbey. See *Oxford History of Music*, 2nd ed., 1929, I. 179. A gramophone record of the part-song is available in the *Columbia History of Music*, vol. I, part 12.

[2] By Manfred F. Bukofzer, ' *Sumer is icumen in* ' *a revision*, University of California Press, 1944.

[3] See R. L. Greene, *The Early English Carols*.

by rhyme, but its tone is more cheerful than that of the rest of the poem, and in its regular alternation of short stressed with unstressed syllables it is very suitable for a dancing-chorus. It is not always practicable for the modern reader to deal with the poem in that way, but the effectiveness of the refrain is increased if the poem is read aloud.

The essential feature of the *pastourelle* is a dialogue between a man and a woman. Sometimes the poem has a narrative setting and opens as a monologue ; sometimes it begins more suddenly. Both types are represented in the Harley manuscript. *The Meeting in the Wood* (8) is an example of the first type and *De Clerico et Puella* (24) is an example of the second.

The Meeting in the Wood is written in the native alliterative metre and, like most of the lyrics in that metre, it is rather obscure. It is not possible to be quite certain about the attribution of some of the lines to their speakers, but it seems probable that, as is usual in this type of lyric, the girl first repels the man and then yields suddenly. In this lyric both the opening and the poem as a whole conform to the type of the *pastourelle*, but the *pastourelle* opening, like the Spring opening, was sometimes attached to lyrics of other kinds, and is found, for example, in *The Fair Maid of Ribblesdale* (7). *De Clerico et Puella* (24) resembles a *pastourelle* in that it consists of a dialogue between a man and a girl, each speech normally occupying a stanza ; it differs from the usual type of *pastourelle* in that this is clearly not the first meeting of the two lovers and in that the meeting apparently takes place in the lady's room, not out of doors. The poem describes a lovers' quarrel. The girl resists the man's advances at first, but gives way when he reminds her that they have kissed each other at a window fifty times. The dialogue form is later used with good effect in *The Nut-Brown Maid*, a fifteenth-century lyric in which a squire and a girl take parts to tell a story to disprove the view that women are fickle. *The Nut-Brown Maid* shows a further development in the direction of drama, since in it the two speakers are consciously taking parts, whereas in *De Clerico et Puella* they are speaking in their own characters.

These lyrics are more popular in origin than the lyrics written under the influence of the courtly love convention. Signs of their popular origin are the prominence which they give to the woman's point of view and their preoccupation with the possibility of infidelity. *The Meeting in the Wood* is free from any influence of the conventions of courtly love, though the clerk in *De Clerico et Puella* makes use of its language. The language used, especially by the women, has a more homely flavour than that found in the

other lyrics of the manuscript. There are colloquial idioms such
as ' go my gates ' and ' whet bote is hit to leʒe ? ' and some of the
phrases are of the kind that we get in proverbs : ' wiþinne nyʒe
naht ' and ' þe is bettere on fote gon þen wycked hors to ryde '.
The versification of these two lyrics is of an older kind than that
of the lyrics as a whole : native alliterative lines are used in *The
Meeting in the Wood*, and septenaries are used in *De Clerico et Puella*.

A *reverdie* is a song of greeting to Spring. Such songs were
popular in Medieval Latin, and the tune of one of them, *Tempus
adest floridum*, is well known to-day, though its real nature has
been disguised by the substitution of the regrettable words of *Good
King Wenceslas* in the nineteenth century.[1] *Spring* (11) is an
excellent example of this literary form. The description of spring
occupies most of the lyric, but towards the end the mention of the
mating of the birds reminds the poet of his own unrequited love.
The first two lines of the lyric are conventional and occur as the
opening of the *estrif, The Thrush and the Nightingale*.[2] Similar
references to spring became conventional as openings of lyrics such
as *Alysoun* (4) and later spread to other kinds of poetry. The
best-known example is the opening of the Prologue to the *Canterbury
Tales*.

One of the lyrics, *The Man in the Moon* (30), is a humorous poem
containing no mention of love, and free from French influence.
The atmosphere of the poem is that of an English village. The poet
imagines that the man in the moon has been cutting a bundle of
briar-wood and therefore a hayward has taken a pledge from him.
Experience has shown the poet how to handle the situation. All
that is necessary is to invite the hayward home, to make him
thoroughly comfortable, and, when he is as drunk as a drowned
mouse, there will be no difficulty about recovering the pledge from
him. The poet's impatience with the man in the moon for moving
so slowly and for taking no notice when he shouts to him is well
portrayed.

COURTLY LOVE

The conventions of courtly love grew up in Provence in the early
twelfth century. They first found expression in the songs of
the Provençal troubadours and quickly spread to northern France
and England. It is important to remember that, like all aspects
of human belief and behaviour, the conception of courtly love was
constantly changing. The poets of northern France introduced

---

[1] See the *Oxford Book of Carols*, p. 271.
[2] Printed by Brown, XIII, p. 101.

their own modifications of the conventions which they borrowed, and English poets introduced still further changes to make the conventions accord with the national temperament. Moreover, no set of conventions is ever uniformly observed by all the poets writing at one time. There will be individual differences of outlook, which will cause exceptions to any generalizations about the work of the troubadours or their northern French counterparts, the *trouvères*. At the same time certain trends can be noticed.

In course of time a multitude of minor conventions came to be associated with courtly love, but the central idea was that love was to be prized above all other things. It was to be valued so highly because it was thought to have an ennobling influence on the character of the lover. This is the most important of the courtly love conventions, and is to be found explicitly or implicitly wherever the influence of courtly love makes itself felt. This view stands in strong contrast to the teaching of the medieval Church, which held that chastity was the highest state and that passionate love was to be deplored.

Another important characteristic of courtly love wherever it was found was that it was aristocratic. It grew up in a feudal society, and the love of a troubadour was thought of in terms of feudal relations. The lover devoted himself to the service of his mistress, who became his liege lady. He was in her *baillie*, and had to render her the submission of a vassal. The submission which a lover owed to his lady did not conflict with his feudal obligations as a knight; in fact, it was thought that a noble could not be a true knight unless he loved a lady, to please whom he performed his warlike deeds. Jeanroy points out that such a conception of the relations between a lady and her lover would be likely to grow up in a typical Provençal castle in which there were very few women of rank but many landless knights, squires, and pages, who were feudally inferior to the lady of the castle. This relationship helps to explain the extreme humility which is one of the characteristics of courtly love. Another result of the association between courtly love and feudalism was that knightly qualities, especially courtesy and loyalty, which would in any case be desirable in a lover, came to be especially valued.

A third characteristic of courtly love was that it had little to do with marriage. This attitude is understandable when we remember the kind of environment in which the conventions of courtly love grew up. For a feudal noble, marriage was a thing with which personal preferences could not be allowed to interfere. A noble chose a wife, or had a wife chosen for him, because of her family connections, her marriage portion, and her ability to bear sons.

The troubadours thought that true love should be given freely with no sort of compulsion, whereas husband and wife were bound to each other by their marriage vows. It is sometimes said that the object of a troubadour's worship was often the wife of his patron, but, as Sir Edmund Chambers observes in this connection,[1] it is obvious that patronage has its limits, and it is necessary to remember that in Provence sexual intercourse was not a necessary part of the conception of courtly love. It is dangerous to assume that any particular poem represents actual personal relations.

A further feature of troubadour love which tended to lessen any mischief that might have been caused by the antipathy to marriage was that it was not necessarily mutual. It was essential that the lady's love should not be granted too freely, and if she chose never to grant it the lover was still expected to be faithful; love was its own reward. The poet was not entitled to say :

> If she think not well of me
> What care I how fair she be ?

Such a sentiment was the product of a later age, when reaction against the too exacting demands of the courtly love convention had had time to set in. The chief drawback to these excessive demands was that they introduced an element of unreality into troubadour poetry. The poet who took the demands of courtly love seriously was generally in love with the idea of love rather than with any human being, and his poetry in consequence tended to be self-conscious and artificial.

Another convention of courtly love was that of secrecy. This convention may have arisen in part from the conflict between love and marriage, but that was not the only cause. Desire to protect the lady's good name would cause a lover to be discreet in boasting of his success, even if she were not married. Another contributory cause of the convention was the belief that love was too sacred to be profaned by disclosure.

It may seem inconsistent that, in a society in which extra-marital love was common, chastity should have been so highly prized as to make the convention of secrecy necessary. But there were strong practical reasons why a husband, anxious for undoubted heirs, should insist upon his wife's fidelity, and both romances and chronicles show that a husband was entitled to take summary and drastic vengeance on an unfaithful wife.

When we seek to discover how far the conception of courtly love in northern France differed from that current in Provence, we are fortunate in having a contemporary treatise on the subject in the

---

[1] Chambers and Sidgwick, *Early English Lyrics*, p. 263.

De Arte Honeste Amandi of Andreas Capellanus.[1] This book, written in Latin prose, consists of an exposition of the art of love-making in a series of dialogues, which throw a good deal of light on the ideas of courtly love current at the time. The conception of love expressed by Andreas is a physical one ; sexual intercourse is for him a necessary feature of love. A second feature of Andreas's conception of love is that it must be mutual, whereas Provençal poets were content to adore without their love being returned. A consequence of this change of attitude was that more attention began to be paid to the necessity of the lover's possessing qualities which would make him attractive to ladies. There was no harm in his being handsome, but it was more important that he should be virtuous, brave, generous and courteous. The lady, for her part, must not abuse her power over her lover to gratify her own fancies. The love-poets of northern France were generally more earnest than the troubadours, and they complained more bitterly of the lady's cruelty.

Most of these characteristics find expression in the *Harley Lyrics*. The idea that love is greatly to be prized is frequently expressed. The author of *Alysoun* thinks that his good fortune is sent from heaven (4.10), and lovers' meetings are twice compared with heaven (5.39, 7.84). The author of *The Fair Maid of Ribblesdale* would rather wait for his lady's coming than be pope (7.47). The ennobling influence of love is not explicitly mentioned, but this does not mean that the poets disbelieved in it. Two centuries had elapsed since the rise of the conventions of courtly love and the idea had lost its novelty. It is so fundamental a part of courtly love that anyone who was familiar with the minor conventions, as the poets of the Harley Lyrics were, would probably take it for granted.

The aristocratic nature of courtly love is well illustrated in the English lyrics. The Fair Maid of Ribblesdale has a girdle of beaten gold adorned with rubies and emeralds ; moreover, she can read romances. The phrase most commonly used to describe the lady is ' a burde in a bour ', and the lady in *The Way of Woman's Love* (32) lives in a tower and has servants. The courtesy which was associated with the aristocratic way of life is emphasized by the adjectives used to praise the lady. She is beautiful, of course, but she is described even more often in words which apply especially to courtesy and good breeding. She is *gentil, hendy, graciouse, fyn, semly, menskful* and *dereworpe*. The feudal aspect of the relation is probably hinted at in the *Harley Lyrics* when the author of *Alysoun* says ' icham in hire baundoun ' (4.8), and when the author of *The Way of Woman's Love* speaks of himself as his lady's ' man '

[1] Ed. E. Trojel, Copenhagen, 1892.

(32.18). A passage of great interest in this connection is the stanza in *Blow, Northerne Wynd* in which the lady's good qualities are enumerated (14.47–54). She is described as possessing *godnesse, ryhtfulnesse, clannesse, bealte, largesse, prouesse, suetnesse* and *lealte,* i.e. goodness, virtue, purity, beauty, generosity, prowess, sweetness and loyalty. Of these qualities *clannesse, bealte,* and *suetnesse* are clearly appropriate to a lady, and *godnesse* and *ryhtfulnesse* are qualities which might be possessed by a person of either sex, but the remaining attributes, *largesse, prouesse,* and *lealte,* are qualities which, according to the chivalric ideal, a good knight ought to possess. The poet has transferred them to the lady. A similar disregard of the difference between the sexes is found in the last stanza of *Annot and John* (3) in which Annot is compared with heroes, as well as heroines, of romance.

On the question of the relationship between courtly love and marriage the English lyrics show few signs of the convention that the lady in whose honour the poem is written should be married. In *A Wayle Whyt ase Whalles Bon* (9) it seems likely that the lady is married, since the meaning of the sixth stanza is probably that the poet would like to change places with her husband. In most of the lyrics there is no indication whether the lady is married or not, and in *De Clerico et Puella* (24) it is clear that she is not, since it is her father's anger, not that of her husband, that she fears if her lover is found in her room. The attitude expressed in the *Harley Lyrics* to this aspect of courtly love is in keeping with that expressed a century earlier in *The Owl and the Nightingale.* The Nightingale presents the case for love poetry, while the Owl represents religious poetry.[1] The Nightingale sympathizes with the love-affairs of girls, but condemns those of married women.[2] The sympathy which the author of *The Owl and the Nightingale* shows for a girl who yields to a man's importunities [3] has a close parallel in one of the lyrics, *Advice to Women* (12). The resemblance between the two poems in this respect is the more remarkable in that such sympathetic understanding of a woman's point of view is rare in medieval literature, which generally knows of no middle course between extravagant praise and violent invective. A further point of interest in the lyric is that side by side with the warning against betrayers it contains allusions to the poet's own mistress, and appeals to her to be favourable to him.

There are several allusions to the convention of secrecy in the *Harley Lyrics.* The frequent use of the word *derne* to describe love shows that secrecy was thought to be necessary. The lover in

---

[1] *The Owl and the Nightingale,* ed. J. W. H. Atkins, pp. lviii–lx.
[2] vv. 1419, 1468.   [3] vv. 1433–1450.

A Wayle Whyt ase Whalles Bon laments the fate of the man who loves secretly and dare not tell anyone what is the matter with him (9.43 f.) ; in this lyric there may be a special reason for secrecy since it is suggested that the lady is married. Wells [1] suggests that the occasion of *The Way of Woman's Love* (32) is that the lady has cast off her lover for revealing their secret love, and there is a clear allusion to the convention in the second stanza of the lyric :

> Y wolde nemne hyre today
> Ant y dorste hire munne

Finally, there is the pun by which the author of *Annot and John* conceals the name of his mistress (3.29). But, in spite of the secrecy with which the poet surrounds the name, it would be unwise to assume that Annot was the girl's real name, and *Alysoun* (4.12) may well be a name conferred by the poet, like the Provençal *senhal*. The practice, which probably had its origin in the convention of secrecy, is mentioned in Matthew Prior's song, written several centuries later :

> The merchant, to secure his treasure,
> Conveys it in a borrowed name :
> Euphelia serves to grace my measure,
> But Cloe is my real flame.

Some of the minor conventions found both in the *Harley Lyrics* and the poems of the Provençal troubadours may be mentioned : the poet cannot sleep (4.22, 31) ; he sinks to an untimely death (4.19, 5.26) ; the lady is an enemy to the poet and his peace of mind (9.46) ; her eyes give wounds (9.25).[2] One idea found in the Provençal lyrics is that if the poet were a bird he could come nearer to his lady ; this theme is developed in the last stanza of *A Wayle Whyt ase Whalles Bon* (9).

Although the Provençal troubadours had several links with England,[3] the influence of northern French on English literature was much greater than the influence of Provençal literature. It is, therefore, natural that where the northern French conception of courtly love differs from the Provençal, the attitude revealed in the English lyrics agrees with the former. The attitude revealed in the English lyrics is certainly a physical one (cf. 5.40, 7.83, 9.14), and the poet is not content to worship his lady from a distance. In *Annot and John* (3) the poet's love seems to be returned, and in *The Way of Woman's Love* (32) it seems to have been returned in

---

[1] *Manual of the Writings in Middle English*, p. 496.
[2] For Provençal parallels see H. J. Chaytor, *The Troubadours and England*, chapter III.
[3] See H. J. Chaytor, *op. cit.*, chapters I and II.

the past, although the lady has been disloyal.   Elsewhere the poet
complains of the cruelty of the lady, but her aloofness is simply
the result of *daunger*, the vice of using her power over her lover to
keep him at a distance.   Even in northern French literature this
behaviour was so common that Andreas had specifically warned
his readers against it.

On the whole it is clear that this group of lyrics shows all the
main features of the courtly love convention, although some of
them appear in a modified form.

RELIGIOUS LYRICS

Whereas the Middle English secular lyric shows itself fitfully,
the religious lyric flows in a steady stream, and MS. Harley 2253 is
only one of many manuscripts which have to be taken into account
in studying its history.   The most important influences on Middle
English religious lyrics were the Bible, patristic writings, and the
liturgy.   The influence of Latin hymns seems to have been less
marked,[1] although they had an influence on the stanza-forms used,
and one of the lyrics in this volume, *Suete Iesu King of Blysse* (15),
is an imitation of the *Dulcis Jesu Memoria* attributed to Saint
Bernard of Clairvaux.   A further influence is that of the secular
lyric, and this influence is particularly noticeable in the religious
lyrics of the Harley manuscript.

These influences cannot be kept distinct from each other, and
often traces of all of them are to be found in a single lyric.   The
influence of the Bible, whether direct or exerted through homilies
and paraphrases, is clearly marked in *The Labourers in the Vine-
yard* (10), most of which is a paraphrase of the parable told in
Saint Matthew's Gospel xx. 1–16.   If it were not for the last stanza,
the poem could hardly be called a lyric at all, but in this stanza
there is a sudden transition to the style of the penitential lyric.
The connection of the last stanza with the rest of the lyric is not
made clear, but the idea that links the two parts is probably that
the poet fears that he himself, like the labourers who grumbled, has
forfeited God's love.   The same parable is paraphrased in *Pearl*,
vv. 497–576.   The version in this lyric is less picturesque and
vivid than that in *Pearl*, but it keeps more closely to the gospel
narrative.   Both versions achieve a dramatic effect by the frequent
use of direct speech.

A Prayer for Deliverance (28), written in alternate lines of English
and Anglo-Norman, is another poem which shows the influence of
the Bible.   It begins as a prayer to the Virgin, but most of the poem

---

[1] See F. A. Patterson, *The Middle English Penitential Lyric*, p. 25.

is an account of the events leading up to the Passion of Christ. The events are not described in the order in which they occurred, but probably the story of the Passion was so well known that the poet did not feel bound to preserve strict chronological order.

The influence of patristic writings is most clear in *The Three Foes of Man* (2), which deals with the same subject as *The Sayings of Saint Bernard*, a longer poem in the Harley manuscript.[1] The three foes of man are the World, the Flesh, and the Devil, and both poems consist of earnest, though rather obscure, warnings against them. Some of the obscurity of the poem may be due to the demands upon the poet's ingenuity made by such literary devices as alliteration and stanza-linking.

A theme frequently treated in patristic writings was that of the vanity of all earthly things, a theme which looks back to *Ecclesiastes*. This theme often appears in the religious lyrics. It is the central idea of the moralizing jingle *Earth Upon Earth* (1), of which expanded versions enjoyed great popularity in the later Middle Ages, and it is found again in *A Winter Song* (17). A mood of melancholy underlies most of the religious lyrics written under patristic influence, a mood which may be compared with the *desiderium*, or regret for vanished pleasures, which is found in *An Old Man's Prayer* (13). This mood, with its stress upon the transitoriness and uncertainty of human joys, has something in common with the mood of Old English elegiac poems, such as *The Wanderer*. There is no evidence of direct influence of Old English poetry on the Middle English religious lyric, but it is likely that the same traditional melancholy inspired the choice of theme in both kinds of poetry.

The influence of the liturgy on the religious lyric was encouraged by the existence of a large number of metrical paraphrases into English of portions of the church service. Religious lyrics were written to amplify single lines from the liturgy, and the Latin line which suggested the lyric was often incorporated into the poem either as a refrain or as an integral part of each stanza. Thus, a line from the response after the eighth lesson in the *Office of the Dead* furnished the theme of several Middle English lyrics with the refrain *Timor mortis conturbat me*.[2] In the *Harley Lyrics* the influence of the liturgy is to be seen chiefly in points of detail. Words, phrases, and ideas were borrowed from the liturgy and passed into the common idiom which any writer of religious lyrics might use. Such expressions and ideas become so common in religious lyrics that we tend to lose sight of their origin, but the idea that sin is a disease and Christ or the Virgin the physician

---

[1] Printed by Böddeker, *Altenglische Dichtungen*, p. 225.
[2] F. A. Patterson, *The Middle English Penitential Lyric*, p. 23.

(23.35), and the idea that Christ bought the world with his blood shed on the Cross (22.58), may have been borrowed through the liturgy.[1]

The most interesting feature of the religious lyrics is the way in which they have been influenced by the phraseology of love lyrics. The resemblance between *The Way of Christ's Love* (31) and *The Way of Woman's Love* (32) is so close that it is clear that one is an imitation of the other, and the secular lyric is probably the earlier (see p. 88). Such formal resemblance is often a result of an attempt to make use of a popular tune, as in the case of the Cuckoo Song. We have evidence of this practice more than two centuries earlier than the date of the Harley manuscript. William of Malmesbury says of Thomas of Bayeux, Archbishop of York (d. 1100), that if anyone sang a profane song in his hearing he at once converted it into a hymn of praise.[2] Conventional openings like the Spring and *chanson d'aventure* openings, which were first used in secular lyrics, come to be used in religious lyrics, e.g. Nos. 18 and 27, and similar conventional phrases are found in the second stanzas of two religious lyrics (Nos. 16 and 23), where their original function as openings has been lost sight of.

It is natural that the language of love lyrics should be used most often in poems addressed to the Virgin, since it was the constant effort of medieval churchmen to sublimate earthly love by encouraging the cult of the Virgin. The earlier part of *The Five Joys of the Virgin* (27) consists of praise which would be more appropriate if addressed to an earthly mistress, and in another lyric the Virgin is described as ' þat leuedy gent ant smal ' (23.45). Similar language is used with reference to Christ ; for example, in *A Spring Song on the Passion* (18) the poet says that his heart is filled with ' a suete louelongynge . . . al for a loue newe ', who is Christ. Later in the same lyric the poet returns to this theme and expresses his regret that he cannot choose Christ as his ' lemmon '. It is possible that this use of the phraseology of the secular lyrics for religious purposes is referred to in the passage in *The Owl and the Nightingale* in which the Nightingale claims that she sings of church-song.[3]

The influence was not all one way. There are passages in the secular lyrics which show the influence of religious poetry. For example, in *Blow, Northerne Wynd* the poet interrupts a description of his lady with the prayer :

> He þat reste him on þe rode
> þat leflich lyf honoure ! (14.20 f.)

---

[1] Patterson, *op. cit.*, p. 24.
[2] William of Malmesbury, *Gesta Pontificum*, p. 258 (Rolls Series).
[3] Ed. Atkins. v. 1036 ; cf. Introduction, p. lviii.

There are allusions to God and Christ elsewhere in the secular lyrics. In *Advice to Women* chaste women are described as the best things created by the high King of Heaven (12.13 f.), and in *The Fair Maid of Ribblesdale* (7) the influence of the religious lyrics appears incongruous, for the poem concludes with the reflection that the man who could lie by the lady's side at night might say that Christ had favoured him. Sometimes secular lyrics contain moral reflections which seem out of keeping with their context, but which are less obviously religious than the examples cited. An example is in *Alysoun* (4) where the reflection

> Betere is þolien whyle sore
> þen mournen euermore.

is probably due to the influence of religious lyrics. A good example of this influence is provided by a secular lyric [1] not in MS. Harley 2253. It begins like a religious lyric :

> My gostly fader, I me confesse
> First to God and then to you,

but the confession is a piece of irreverent mockery, for it is that at a window (cf. 24.23) the poet has stolen a kiss ' of grete sweteness ' which he now vows to God he will restore.

Most of the religious lyrics of MS. Harley 2253 are prayers to the Virgin and Christ. The treatment is simple and earnest, and the note of passionate sincerity is especially marked in those lyrics which deal with the Passion of Christ. The chief fault of the religious lyrics is a lack of unity of theme. For example, *Iesu Crist Heouene Kyng* (16) opens with a prayer to Christ ; there are then two stanzas of praise of the Virgin and Christ ; and the poem concludes with a stanza of penitential moralizing. The lack of unity in some of the lyrics is probably due to the transference of a stanza from one lyric into another which happens to use a similar stanza-form. There is evidence of such transferences in those lyrics which have been preserved in more than one version. Stanzas are sometimes found in one version but not in others and the order of stanzas is often changed. There are, moreover, usually considerable differences in wording between the different versions. It is safe to conclude that the lyrics were often handed down by oral transmission.

---

[1] In MS. Harley 682. Printed by Chambers & Sidgwick, *Early English Lyrics*, p. 31.

METRE

The Line. The number of stresses in a line varies from two to seven, lines with three and four stresses being the most common. Two-stress lines are found only in No. 9, where they alternate with longer lines. Five-stress lines are used only in Nos. 31 and 32 ; these are the earliest recorded English examples of five-stress lines, which later became very common in non-lyrical poetry. It is not uncommon to find a line containing fewer stresses than we should expect (e.g. 17.14, 25.20). Some of these lines may be corrupt, but it is unlikely that all of them are, and it is better to regard the occasional substitution of a three-stress for a four-stress line as a form of licence to avoid monotony. Some editors split up the alexandrines and septenaries used in Nos. 24, 25, and 26 into two, but the absence of rhyme at the caesura suggests that the lines should be treated as long ones. They represent an older stage in the history of versification than three-stress and four-stress lines, which probably had their origin in the splitting up of a septenary after the fourth stress. A trace of this origin may still be seen in the *Harley Lyrics* in the preponderance of masculine endings in the four-stress lines and the even more strongly marked preponderance of feminine endings in the three-stress lines of lyrics in which both kinds of line are used.[1]

Most of the lines are iambic, but trochaic feet are sometimes substituted, and the metre of No. 13 is predominantly trochaic. Another device used to avoid monotony is the omission of an unaccented syllable, especially at the caesura, e.g. 15.48. It can be seen from those lyrics which occur in more than one version that many irregularities may be due to corruption of the text. The scansion shows that final *-e* is generally pronounced, except when the *-e* is elided before a vowel. In most of the lyrics stressed and unstressed syllables alternate fairly evenly as in Modern English versification, but three poems (Nos. 3, 8, and 30) are written in lines descended from the Old English alliterative line with two stressed syllables and a variable number of unstressed syllables in each half. This kind of line is unusual in lyrics, though it is common in political and satirical poems.

Stanza Forms. A wide variety of stanza forms has been obtained by the use of monorhymed quatrains, quatrains with alternate

---

[1] The septenary had a stressed syllable before the caesura and a feminine ending. In the lyrics in this volume in which four-stress lines alternate with three-stress lines two-thirds of the four-stress lines have masculine endings, while nine-tenths of the three-stress lines have feminine endings.

rhymes, and tail-rhyme stanzas, both alone and in various combinations with each other. An extended form of the tail-rhyme stanza (the form later used by Drayton in *Nymphidia*) is used in No. 14. The unusual eleven-line stanza found in No. 2 may be regarded as a development of that found in No. 6 in which the eighth and ninth lines of each stanza have coalesced into one.

Sometimes different stanza forms are used in the same lyric, e.g. in No. 9. Such variations are especially common in the final stanzas of lyrics (e.g. Nos. 13, 23, and 25), possibly as a result of the influence of the *envoi*. In French and Provençal lyrics the *envoi* was a short concluding stanza, generally containing an apostrophe, and its purpose was to give the poem a personal application. The influence of the *envoi* on the subject-matter of the final stanza is to be seen in the apostrophes concluding Nos. 6 and 32 and perhaps in the personal application at the end of Nos. 10, 11 and 12.

One device which is used frequently in the lyrics is *concatenatio*, or stanza-linking : two successive stanzas are linked together by the repetition of a few words or by the use of the same alliterating sound. It is an important feature of the versification of Nos. 2, 3, 6, 8, and 13, and is found to a lesser extent in other lyrics. Stanza-linking is most common in strongly alliterative lyrics, and the words repeated usually bear the alliteration.

Alliteration. Alliteration is used very freely, and two of the lyrics (Nos. 2 and 3) show it in every line. It is more common in secular than in religious lyrics, and, as is natural, it is most strongly marked in the three lyrics using the native line (Nos. 3, 8, and 30), each of which has more than four-fifths of its lines alliterating. In these lyrics alliteration may be regarded as not merely ornamental but structural, as it was in Old English, but the arrangement of alliteration within the line does not follow Old English models. Every possible type of arrangement is represented, and the most common types are those which were rare in Old English, e.g. aa-aa, aa-bb. The same alliterating sound is often used in several successive lines, e.g. 12.43–47. Sometimes medial consonants seem to alliterate, even when they do not occur at the beginning of stressed syllables, e.g. the *m* in *emeraude* 3.8, 7.66. Alliterative phrases are common.

Alliteration sometimes provides evidence of pronunciation :

(*a*) In French loan-words *c* followed by a front vowel alliterates with *s* ; when followed by a back vowel it alliterates with English *c*, e.g. *celydoyne* . . *sauge* 3.18 beside *coynte* . . . *columbine* . . . *cunde* 3.15.

(*b*) In French loan-words *g* followed by a front vowel alliterates with consonantal *i*, e.g. *iaspe* . . . *gentil* 3.3, *gentil* . . . *Ionas* . . . *ioyep* . . . *Ion* 3.50.

(*c*) In the groups *wr-* and *kn-* the *w* and *k* were still pronounced, e.g. *waxep vnwraste* 8.17, *cayser ant knyht* 3.7.

Rhyme. Unrhymed lines are so rare in Middle English lyrics that when they occur only in one stanza corruption of the text is to be suspected, thus at 18.31 and 23.58 fairly probable emendations will restore the rhyme. In No. 27, however, the fifth lines of stanzas 4, 5, and 7 have no rhyme and it is unlikely that the text is corrupt in all these lines. Such lines are called *Waisen* ' waifs '. Several varieties of rhyme are found in the lyrics : double (e.g. *bealte* : *lealte* 14.50), extended (e.g. *on syht* : *of myht* 14.6), tumbling (e.g. *fremede* : *glemede* 8.1). Identical rhyme is fairly common, especially when the rhyming words do not occur in consecutive lines (e.g. *blod* : *blod* 27.7). Modified forms of identical rhyme consist in the rhyming together of words alike in form but not in meaning (e.g. *may*, sb. : *may*, v.) or of simple words with compounds (e.g. *lees* : *wrappelees* 10.45). Impure rhyme is found (e.g. *apon* : *noon* 7.13), but most of the apparent examples are probably due to the alteration of one of the rhyming words by a scribe (e.g. *blisse* : *mildenesse* 26.1 ; the Egerton version has *milternisse*). Assonance sometimes takes the place of rhyme ; the most frequent examples are of *m* : *n* and *ng* : *nd* (e.g. _ *tyme* : *pyne* 23.23, *wepinge* : *monkynde* 20.7).

THE LYRICS AS LITERATURE

To the literary historian the chief importance of the *Harley Lyrics* is that they show the first sustained treatment in English literature of the theme of love, but they have a value for the lover of literature far in excess of their historical importance. Their excellence is largely due to the fitness of Middle English to be a lyrical language. It is more sonorous than modern English, which is clogged with unstressed words and with long words of Latin origin, valuable for the expression of abstract ideas but of little use to a lyric poet. The Middle English vocabulary is rich in words for the common things of life, and most of these words are short and expressive. For example, to describe the idea of gaiety or merriment the poet can speak of *iolyfte*, *gale*, *gomenes*, *gleowes*, or *murpe*, to mention only words found in the *Harley Lyrics*. It is hard to find good equivalents for these words in modern English, perhaps because we are less familiar with the qualities which they describe. The associations which cling round every word in the language can be very valuable to a poet, but there are times when the poet of to-day finds himself embarrassed by the richness of associations and is driven to search for what one modern poet has described as ' clean ' words free from too many associations. The Middle English poet had no lack of such words.

The closeness to common life which marks the vocabulary of the Middle English poet is found too in the imagery he uses. It is vivid and homely, and the poet often adds a detail which makes it clear that he has the object to which he refers in his mind. His simile is no mere verbal comparison ; there is a real association of ideas. A lady is not only whiter than milk ; she is whiter than the morning milk (7.77), and her red lips are not only beautiful but are very well suited to the reading of romances (7.39). Comparisons are vivid and picturesque. A lover who cannot sleep for love is as weary as water in a troubled pool (4.32) or as restless as a roe (5.17); an old man withers like a dying flower (13.90); a lover disdained by his mistress falls like mud dropping away from a lifted foot (14.77); a lady's complexion is like a lantern at night (14.24). The same lively imagination is shown in the coining of words; the old man who feels himself no longer wanted is called *fulle-flet*, ' one who fills the floor ', and *wayteglede*, ' one who gazes at the fire ' (13.16 f.), the last a wonderfully expressive word in the context.

Some of the lyrics show great descriptive power. Descriptive passages were a well-marked feature of twelfth-century Latin poetry,[1] and formed a common school exercise. In the words of Mr. F. J. E. Raby, ' every schoolboy learned how to describe a woman's beauty and how to write an invective against women '.[2]

A good example of a descriptive lyric is *Spring* (11), one of the most vivid lyrics ever written on a subject which has never lost its attraction for poets. The delight which the poet shows in the re-awakening of nature may be contrasted with the melancholy of *A Winter Song* (17). Both poems show how responsive Middle English poets could be to the seasons of the year. In *The Fair Maid of Ribblesdale* (7) great skill is shown in the detailed description of the poet's mistress and her dress. The poet prevents the lyric from becoming a mere catalogue by interrupting the description from time to time to give expression to his longing. Similar descriptive passages occur elsewhere, for example in *Blow, Northerne Wynd* (14.14 ff.).

Another method of amplification recommended by medieval

---

[1] See J. W. H. Atkins, *English Literary Criticism : The Medieval Phase*, p. 103.
[2] *A History of Secular Latin Poetry in the Middle Ages*, II. 45.

writers on the poetic art was personification.[1] This is introduced
into two of the lyrics. In *An Old Man's Prayer* (13) the Seven
Deadly Sins are personified as having waited on the poet in his
youth, and in *Blow, Northerne Wynd* (14) Love is personified so that
the poet may complain to him of the suffering caused by his lady
and her three servants, Sighing, Sorrowing, and Grief.

The use of literary devices shows the ease and sureness of touch
that come from long familiarity. Some of the ornaments of style
recommended by medieval writers on poetic are used. There is
conduplicatio, the repetition of a word to express emotion (18.18) ;
and *contentio*, the antithesis of words (9.45 f.), as well as such
metrical devices as stanza-linking by means of repetition (2.11 f.)
and *epanaphora*, the repetition of the same group of words at the
beginning of several successive lines (14.47 ff., 79 ff.). The most
marked of these literary devices is alliteration, which is found in
nearly all the lyrics. The elaborate use of alliteration in some of
the lyrics will remind a modern reader of Swinburne's use of the
same device, but alliteration is most effective when used with
restraint, and *Alysoun* (4) is a more successful poem than *Annot
and John* (3), in which alliteration is used to excess.

In spite of the lover's laments, which are frequent, there is a note
of light-heartedness in most of the secular lyrics. Both moods are
found side by side in *Alysoun*, the laments in the poem proper and
the light-heartedness in the refrain. There is humour in some of
the lyrics, a simple rustic humour in *The Man in the Moon* (30)
and a more sophisticated kind in the love lyrics, where the humour
takes the form of good-natured and cheerful cynicism. After
praising his lady, the author of *A Wayle Whyt ase Whalles Bon* (9)
says how gladly he would change places with her husband. If he
would be so generous as to agree to an exchange, the poet would
give three for one without haggling. The humour often lies in the
choice of a single word, like the word *freo*, ' generous ', in this
passage ; or the word *wilde*, ' wanton, pleasure-loving ', which the
poet of *The Fair Maid of Ribblesdale* (7) uses to describe the women
he would choose. There is irony in the words which the author of
The Way of Woman's Love (32) uses to describe his lady who has
been unfaithful :

> a fre wymmon
> þat muche of loue had fonde

The use of irony in the lyrics sometimes leaves us uncertain how
seriously a poem should be taken. *The Poet's Repentance* (6) has
been regarded as the serious recantation of a poet whose earlier

---

[1] See J. W. H. Atkins, *op. cit.*, p. 200.

writings against women have caused offence, but it is unlikely that
the poem should be treated any more seriously than Chaucer's
Envoys to Scogan and Bukton, which were written on somewhat
similar themes and which resemble it in tone. The part of the
lyric where the poet mentions the Virgin may be serious enough,
since it was a medieval commonplace that the Virgin made amends
for the harm done to the human race by Eve, but it is hard to avoid
the impression that there is irony in the last stanza, in which the
poet congratulates Richard, a rival poet who has defended women
and who is such a favourite with them.

Beside humour there is pathos and human sympathy in the
lyrics. Sympathy for the woman who has been betrayed is well
expressed in *Advice to Women* (12) and the sorrows of old age are
feelingly described in *An Old Man's Prayer* (13) ; there is much
pathos in the *desiderium* with which the old man looks back on his
former strength and happiness. But it is natural that the poems
on the Passion should show pathos most clearly. In these poems
strong feeling is shown, although the language used is restrained.
The restraint of the language adds to its effectiveness, and the
startling under-statement that when Christ died on the Cross he
did not thereby incur guilt (31.12) is comparable with the deliberate
use of restraint for the sake of emphasis which is a feature of Old
English poetry.

The faults of the lyrics are those of most Middle English literature :
the excessive use of conventional phrases and the lack of a sense of
balance and proportion. The conventional phrases are usually
alliterative, and they probably owed their popularity to the ease
with which they could be used to satisfy the demands of strongly
alliterative metres. Other conventions, such as the Spring opening,
are used too freely, though so few secular lyrics have survived that
we are not unduly troubled by their use.

The lack of a sense of proportion is seen in the excessive use of
comparisons in *Annot and John* (3). In successive stanzas of this
poem Annot is compared to precious stones, flowers, birds, herbs,
and heroes and heroines of romance. The poem is a literary *tour
de force* which, with its strong alliteration, is unfortunately reminis-
cent of ' I love my love with an " A ". In *The Fair Maid of
Ribblesdale* (7) the medieval fondness for exaggeration makes itself
felt with an effect that seems ludicrous to a modern reader. A long
neck was thought to be beautiful, therefore the poet thinks that
a very long neck must be more beautiful still, and he describes the
lady's neck as a span longer than he has seen elsewhere (7.44).

Although the literary worth of the Harley Lyrics arises in the
main from qualities which are independent of the time when they

were written, the poems tell us a good deal about medieval life and thought. The aspect of medieval thought about which they tell us most is the theory of courtly love, but the variety of sources from which the lyrics have been drawn provides useful evidence that courtly love was only one of the contemporary ways of regarding the relations between men and women. Side by side with the veneration for women which was part of the courtly love convention we find a more realistic point of view revealed in *Advice to Women* (12) and *The Meeting in the Wood* (8), and we find evidence, too, of bitter hostility towards women. It is natural that such hostility should not often find expression in lyrics, since the hostility proceeded in the main from ecclesiastics, many of whom disapproved of the writing of lyrics as strongly as they disapproved of women. *The Three Foes of Man* (2) represents the point of view of a poet completely uninfluenced by the ideals of courtly love. To him woman is merely the most dangerous of the obstacles in the way of living the good life, and love is a thing wholly evil. The comparison of sexual intercourse to heaven, which occurs at the end of *The Fair Maid of Ribblesdale* (7) and *The Lover's Complaint* (5), would have seemed to such a poet to be the height of blasphemy. In *The Fair Maid of Ribblesdale* costly dress and jewels are described as enhancing the beauty of the wearer, but the manuscript contains a poem [1] satirizing the extravagant dress of women in which the poet consoles himself that

> In helle
> wiþ deueles he shulle duelle
> for þe clogges þat cleueþ by here chelle.

The two attitudes, of veneration and hostility, towards women continued to exist side by side, and each was to some extent a reaction against the other. It is clear that the position of women was not so happy as might be supposed from the courtly love lyrics. The woman who had been betrayed was hated and despised and forced to leave her home (8.34 f.). The lot of an unhappily married woman was little better: even if her husband beat her she could not escape from him (8.40).

Love is shown in the lyrics as triumphing over difficulties. The most formidable difficulty that the lover has to overcome is his lady's disdain, but it is not the only one. The author of *The Lover's Complaint* has aroused the ill-will of other men by his love but does not allow that to worry him (5.17 ff.). The clerk in *De Clerico et Puella* is watched day and night by the girl's kinsfolk (24.20). The lover in *The Way of Woman's Love* not only has to

---

[1] Printed by Brown, XIII, p. 133.

reproach his mistress for her inconstancy but has to contend with the evil wrought by backbiters who set her against him (32.19). Backbiters play a large part in French lyrics, where they are always on the watch to make mischief between lovers.

The social background of many of the lyrics is a pleasant one. The word *glad* and its derivatives are freely used to describe the lady and her behaviour. In *The Way of Woman's Love* (32) there is a description of the sort of cheerful scene that we have come to associate with the Middle Ages :

> Mury hit ys in hyre tour
> wyþ haþeles ant wyþ heowes.
> So hit is in hyre bour
> wiþ gomenes ant wiþ gleowes.

The Man in the Moon (30) describes rustic merry-making of a less aristocratic kind :

> drynke to hym deorly of fol god bous
> ant oure dame douse shal sitten hym by.

But some of the lyrics show a less happy state of things. There is no respect for age (13.16 f.), and there is much mention of violence in *The Meeting in the Wood* (8) and *De Clerico et Puella* (24), of a world in which a girl's parents will not hesitate to kill her lover if they find him in her room (24.19), and there are two allusions (11.36, 24.31) to the unsuccessful lover's living as a fugitive in the woods, a course that could be adopted more easily then than it can to-day. The responsiveness which the poets show to the seasons of the year no doubt resulted in part from the lack of many of the devices by which we have lessened the hardships of winter.

We learn something of the medieval interest in the properties of herbs and precious stones from *Annot and John* (3) and *The Fair Maid of Ribblesdale* (7). The information given is vague, but it is clear that the author of the latter poem shared the belief in the magical properties of precious stones to which the lapidaries bear witness.[1] One of the stones mentioned is a protection against misfortune and another has the useful property of turning water into wine. There is probably no intentional irony in the poet's comment : 'Those who saw it said so.' The author of *Annot and John* (3) had a knowledge of medieval romances which we unfortunately do not share, with the result that several of the heroes and heroines whom he mentions cannot be satisfactorily identified.

The learning shown in several of the poems is probably the result

---

[1] See Joan Evans, *Magical Jewels of the Middle Ages and the Renaissance*, Oxford, 1922.

of their having been written by *clerici vagantes*. It is noteworthy that the lover in *De Clerico et Puella* (24) is a clerk, and the macaronic poem *Dum Ludis Floribus* (19) was almost certainly written by a clerk. The irregular mixture of the three languages, Latin, Anglo-Norman, and English, reflects the unsettled state of the languages used in England at the time : the three languages were competing with each other in literary use, and English had not yet gained the mastery. Such a poem would be appreciated only by readers familiar with all three languages. There seems every reason to believe that the last stanza is genuinely autobiographical. The poem was probably written by an English clerk living in Paris who reverted to his native language in the last couplet of the lyric. Sir Edmund Chambers suggests [1] that touches of rather pedantic symbolism which are present in some of the lyrics (e.g. 14.47–54) may be a result of the ecclesiastical training of the authors.

It is necessary to remember that the lyrics of this manuscript have come from a variety of sources. Attempts to assign certain groups of lyrics to the same author have often been made, usually on very insufficient evidence, such as resemblances of stanza-forms and the use of the same alliterative phrases. Such attempts do not take sufficiently into account the existence of a common stock of conventional themes and modes of expression upon which any poet could draw. There are no two lyrics in the manuscript that we can with certainty assign to the same poet. Like most Middle English literature, they are anonymous, and they owe their inclusion in the manuscript to their having caught the fancy of a fourteenth-century anthologist. It is very fortunate for us that his taste was so good, so catholic, and so unconventional, for he has left us a representative selection of a wide variety of different types of lyric, of whose existence we should, but for him, have been ignorant.

[1] Chambers & Sidgwick, *Early English Lyrics*, p. 277.

THE TEXT

THE TEXT

The lyrics are printed in the order in which they occur in the manuscript. The spelling of the manuscript is reproduced except for the emendations indicated in footnotes. The acute accents which occur in the manuscript above certain vowels are reproduced in the text but not in the glossary. Two features of the handwriting of the manuscript which have not been reproduced, since at the date of this manuscript they seem to have no significance, are a horizontal stroke through final *h* and a hook after final *k* (ƥ). Contractions have been expanded without notice. The ampersand has been expanded to *ant* and *iħu* to *Iesu*, since these are the forms used in the manuscript when these words are written in full. No attempt has been made to follow the manuscript in word-division, punctuation, and the use of capitals. The letters *n* and *u* are almost indistinguishable from each other ; *e* resembles *o* and *c* resembles *t*.

1 EARTH UPON EARTH

Erþe toc of erþe erþe wyþ woh ;   *f.* 59 *v.*
erþe oþer erþe to þe erþe droh ;
erþe leyde erþe in erþene þroh.
Þo heuede erþe of erþe erþe ynoh.

2 THE THREE FOES OF MAN

Middelerd for mon wes mad,   *f.* 62 *v.*
 vnmihti aren is meste mede.
þis hedy haþ on honde yhad
 þat heuene hem is hest to hede.
Icherde a blisse budel vs bad   5
 þe dreri domesdai to drede,
of sunful sauhting sone be sad
 þat derne doþ þis derne dede.
  Þah he ben derne done,
 þis wrakeful werkes vnder wede,   10
  in soule soteleþ sone.

Sone is sotel, as ich ou sai,
 þis sake, alþah hit seme suete.
Þat i telle a poure play
 þat furst is feir ant seþþe vnsete.   15
þis wilde wille went awai
 wiþ mone ant mournyng muchel vnmete.
      29

þat liueþ on likyng out of lay
  his hap he deþ ful harde on hete
aȝeynȝ he howeþ henne ;   20
  alle is þriuene þewes þrete
    þat þenkeþ nout on þenne.

Aȝeynes þenne vs þreteþ þre ;
  ȝef he beþ þryuen ant þowen in þeode,
vr soule bone so broþerli be   25
  as berne best þat bale forbeode.
þat wole wihtstonden streynþe of þeo
  is rest is reued wiþ þe reode.
Fyht of oþer ne darf he floe
  þat fleishshes faunyng furst foreode,   30
    þat falsist is of fyue.
  Ȝef we leueþ eny leode,
    werryng is worst of wyue.

Wyues wille were ded wo,
  ȝef he is wicked forte welde ;   35
þat burst shal bete for hem bo,
  he shal him burewen þah he hire belde.
By body ant soule y sugge al so,
  þat some beoþ founden vnder felde
þat haþ to fere is meste fo.   40
  Of gomenes he mai gon al gelde
    ant sore ben fered on folde,
  lest he to harmes helde
    ant happes hente vnholde.

Hom vnholdest her is on   45
  wiþouten helle, ase ich hit holde,
so fele bueþ founden monnes fon ;
  þe furst of hem biforen y tolde ;
þer afterward þis worldes won
  wiþ muchel vnwynne vs woren wolde.   50
Sone beþ þis gomenes gon
  þat makeþ vs so brag ant bolde
    ant biddeþ vs ben blyþe ;
  an ende he casteþ ous fol colde
    in sunne ant serewe syþe.   55

25 MS. broerli   29 MS. fyth, darþ

In sunne ant sorewe y am seint,
   þat siweþ me so sully sore ;
my murþe is al wiþ mournyng meind,
   ne may ich myþen hit namore.
When we beþ wiþ þis world forwleynt,   60
   þat we ne lustneþ lyues lore,
þe fend in fyht vs fynt so feynt
   we falleþ so flour when hit is frore,
      for folkes fader al fleme ;
     wo him wes ywarpe ȝore   65
     þat Crist nul nowyht queme.

To queme Crist we weren ycore
   ant kend ys craftes forte knowe.
Leue we nout we buen forlore,
   in lustes þah we lyggen lowe ;   70
we shule aryse vr fader byfore,
   þah fon vs fallen vmbe þrowe ;
to borewen vs alle he wes ybore.
     Þis bonnyng when him bemes blowe,
      he byt vs buen of hyṡe   75
     ant on ys ryht hond hente rowe
      wyþ ryhtwyse men to aryse.

3 ANNOT AND JOHN

Ichot a burde in a bour ase beryl so bryht,   *f.* 63 *r.*
ase saphyr in seluer semly on syht,
ase iaspe þe gentil þat lemeþ wiþ lyht,
ase gernet in golde ant ruby wel ryht ;
ase onycle he ys on yholden on hyht,   5
ase diamaund þe dere in day when he is dyht ;
he is coral ycud wiþ cayser ant knyht ;
ase emeraude amorewen þis may haueþ myht.
   þe myht of þe margarite haueþ þis mai mere.
   ffor charbocle ich hire ches bi chyn ant by chere.   10

Hire rode is ase rose þat red is on rys ;
wiþ lilye-white leres lossum he is ;
þe primerole he passeþ, þe peruenke of pris,
wiþ alisaundre þareto, ache ant anys.
Coynte ase columbine such hire cunde ys,   15
glad vnder gore in gro ant in grys ;

he is blosme opon bleo, brihtest vnder bis,
wiþ celydoyne ant sauge, ase þou þiself sys.
   þat syht vpon þat semly to blis he is broht ;
   he is solsecle, to sauue ys forsoht.   20

He is papeiai in pyn þat beteþ me my bale ;
to trewe tortle in a tour y telle þe mi tale ;
he is þrustle þryuen in þro þat singeþ in sale,
þe wilde laueroc ant wolc ant þe wodewale ;
he is faucoun in friht, dernest in dale,   25
ant wiþ eueruch a gome gladest in gale.
ffrom Weye he is wisist into Wyrhale ;
hire nome is in a note of þe nyhtegale.
   In Annote is hire nome ; nempneþ hit non ?
   Whose ryht redeþ roune to Iohon.   30

Muge he is ant mondrake þourh miht of þe mone,
trewe triacle ytold wiþ tonges in trone ;
such licoris mai leche from Lyne to Lone ;
such sucre mon secheþ þat saneþ men sone ;
bliþe yblessed of Crist, þat bayþeþ me mi bone   35
when derne dedis in day derne are done.
Ase gromyl in greue grene is þe grone,
ase quibibe ant comyn cud is in crone,
   cud comyn in court, canel in cofre,
   wiþ gyngyure ant sedewale ant þe gylofre.   40

He is medicine of miht, mercie of mede,
rekene ase Regnas resoun to rede,
trewe ase Tegeu in tour, ase Wyrwein in wede,
baldore þen Byrne þat oft þe bor bede ;
ase Wylcadoun he is wys, dohty of dede,   *f.* 63 *v.*
ffeyrore þen Floyres folkes to fede,
cud ase Cradoc in court carf þe brede,
hendore þen Hilde, þat haueþ me to hede.
   He haueþ me to hede, þis hendy anon,
   gentil ase Ionas, heo ioyeþ wiþ Ion.   50

31 MS. þouh   35 MS. bayeþ   36 MS. dede is in dayne
41 MS. medierne   44 MS. of þe

4 ALYSOUN

Bytuene Mersh ant Aueril   *f.* 63 *v.*
  when spray biginneþ to springe,
þe lutel foul haþ hire wyl
  on hyre lud to synge.
Ich libbe in loue-longinge   5
  for semlokest of alle þynge ;
he may me blisse bringe ;
  icham in hire baundoun.

    An hendy hap ichabbe yhent,
      ichot from heuene it is me sent ;   10
    from alle wymmen mi loue is lent,
      ant lyht on Alysoun.

On heu hire her is fayr ynoh,
  hire browe broune, hire eȝe blake ;
wiþ lossum chere he on me loh,   15
  wiþ middel smal ant wel ymake.
Bote he me wolle to hire take
  forte buen hire owen make
longe to lyuen ichulle forsake
  ant feye fallen adoun.   20
    An hendy hap, &c.

Nihtes when y wende ant wake,
  forþi myn wonges waxeþ won ;
leuedi, al for þine sake
  longinge is ylent me on.   25
In world nis non so wyter mon
  þat al hire bounte telle con ;
hire swyre is whittore þen þe swon,
  ant feyrest may in toune.
    An hendi, &c.   30

Icham for wowyng al forwake,
  wery so water in wore,
lest eny reue me my make
  ychabbe yȝyrned ȝore.
Betere is þolien whyle sore   35
þen mournen euermore.
Geynest vnder gore,
  herkne to my roun.
    An hendi, &c.
        30 MS. hend

5 THE LOVER'S COMPLAINT

Wiþ longyng y am lad,   *f.* 63 *v.*
on molde y waxe mad,
  a maide marreþ me ;
y grede, y grone, vnglad,
for selden y am sad   5
  þat semly forte se.
  Leuedi, þou rewe me !
To rouþe þou hauest me rad.
Be bote of þat y bad ;
  my lyf is long on þe.   10

Leuedy of alle londe,
les me out of bonde ;
  broht icham in wo.
Haue resting on honde,
ant sent þou me þi sonde   15
  sone, er þou me slo ;
  my reste is wiþ þe ro.
Þah men to me han onde,
to loue nuly noht wonde,
  ne lete for non of þo.   20

Leuedi, wiþ al my miht
my loue is on þe liht,
  to menske when y may ;
þou rew ant red me ryht,
to deþe þou hauest me diht,   25
  y deȝe longe er my day ;
  þou leue vpon mi lay ;
treuþe ichaue þe plyht
to don þat ich haue hyht
  whil mi lif leste may.   30

Lylie-whyt hue is,
hire rode so rose on rys,
  þat reueþ me mi rest ;
wymmon war ant wys,
of prude hue bereþ þe pris,   35
  burde on of þe best.
  Þis wommon woneþ by west,
brihtest vnder bys ;
heuene y tolde al his
  þat o nyht were hire gest.   40

6 THE POET'S REPENTANCE

Weping haueþ myn wonges wet   66 *r*.
  for wikked werk ant wone of wyt ;
vnbliþe y be til y ha bet
  bruches broken, ase bok byt,
of leuedis loue, þat y ha let,   5
  þat lemeþ al wiþ luefly lyt ;
ofte in song y haue hem set,
  þat is vnsemly þer hit syt.
    Hit syt ant semeþ noht
      þer hit ys seid in song ;   10
    þat y haue of hem wroht,
      ywis hit is al wrong.

Al wrong y wrohte for a wyf
  þat made vs wo in world ful wyde ;
heo rafte vs alle richesse ryf,   15
  þat durfte vs nout in reynes ryde.
A styþye stunte hire sturne stryf,
  þat ys in heouene hert in hyde.
In hire lyht on ledeþ lyf,
  ant shon þourh hire semly syde.   20
    Þourh hyre side he shon
      ase sonne doþ þourh þe glas ;
    wommon nes wicked non
      seþþe he ybore was.

Wycked nis non þat y wot   25
  þat durste for werk hire wonges wete ;
alle heo lyuen from last of lot
  ant are al hende ase hauk in chete.
Forþi on molde y waxe mot
  þat y sawes haue seid vnsete,   30
my fykel fleish, mi falsly blod ;
  on feld hem feole y falle to fete.
    To fet y falle hem feole
      for falslek fifti-folde,
    of alle vntrewe on tele   35
      wiþ tonge ase y her tolde.

4 *The word* dunprest *or* dimprest *is written in the margin after this line.*
16 MS. durþe   28 MS. hak

þah told beon tales vntoun in toune,
  such tiding mei tide, y nul nout teme
of brudes bryht wiþ browes broune ;
  or blisse heo beyen, þis briddes breme.   40
In rude were roo wiþ hem roune
  þat hem mihte henten ase him were heme.
Nys kyng, cayser, ne clerk wiþ croune
  þis semly seruen þat mene may seme.
    Semen him may on sonde   45
    þis semly seruen so,
    boþe wiþ fet ant honde,
    for on þat vs warp from wo.

Nou wo in world ys went away,
  ant weole is come ase we wolde,   50
þourh a mihti, methful mai,
  þat ous haþ cast from cares colde.
Euer wymmen ich herie ay,
  ant euer in hyrd wiþ hem ich holde,
ant euer at neode y nyckenay   55
  þat y ner nemnede þat heo nolde.
    Y nolde ant nullyt noht,
    for noþyng nou a nede
    soþ is þat y of hem ha wroht,
    as Richard erst con rede.   60

Richard, rote of resoun ryht,
  rykening of rym ant ron,
of maidnes meke þou hast myht ;
  on molde y holde þe murgest mon.
Cunde comely ase a knyht,   65
  clerk ycud þat craftes con,
in vch an hyrd þyn aþel ys hyht,
  ant vch an aþel þin hap is on.
    Hap þat haþel haþ hent
    wiþ hendelec in halle ;   70
    selþe be him sent
    in londe of leuedis alle !

40 *There is a stroke above* r *in* or *which may represent a slip of the scribe's pen.*
44 MS. me ne   71 MS. hem

7 THE FAIR MAID OF RIBBLESDALE

Mosti ryden by Rybbesdale,   *f. 66 v.*
wilde wymmen forte wale,
   ant welde whuch ich wolde,
founde were þe feyrest on
þat euer wes mad of blod ant bon,   5
   in boure best wiþ bolde.
Ase sonnebem hire bleo ys briht ;
in vche londe heo leomeþ liht,
   þourh tale as mon me tolde.
Þe lylie lossum is ant long,   10
wiþ riche rose ant rode among,
   a fyldor fax to folde.

Hire hed when ich biholde apon,
þe sonnebéém aboute nóón
   me þohte þat y seȝe ;   15
hyre eyȝen aren grete ant gray ynoh ;
þat lussom, when heo on me loh,
   ybend wax eyþer breȝe.
Þe mone wiþ hire muchele maht
ne leneþ non such lyht anaht   20
   (þat is in heouene heȝe)
ase hire forhed doþ in day,
for wham þus muchel y mourne may,
   for duel to deþ y dreyȝe.

Heo haþ browes bend an heh,   25
whyt bytuene ant nout to neh ;
   lussum lyf heo ledes ;
hire neose ys set as hit wel semeþ ;
y deȝe, for deþ þat me demeþ ;
   hire speche as spices spredes ;   30
hire lockes lefly aren ant longe,
for sone he mihte hire murþes monge
   wiþ blisse when hit bredes ;
hire chyn ys chosen ant eyþer cheke
whit ynoh ant rode on eke,   35
   ase roser when hit redes.

    3 MS. wuch   17 MS. þ
        30 MS. spredeþ

Heo haþ a mury mouht to mele,
wiþ lefly rede lippes lele,
 romaunӡ forte rede ;
hire teht aren white ase bon of whal,   40
euene set ant atled al,
 ase hende mowe taken hede ;
swannes swyre swyþe wel ysette,
a sponne lengore þen y mette,
 þat freoly ys to fede.   45
Me were leuere kepe hire come
þen beon pope ant ryde in Rome,
 styþest vpon stede.

When y byholde vpon hire hond,
þe lylie-white, lef in lond,   50
 best heo mihte beo ;
eyþer arm an elne long,
baloygne mengeþ al bymong ;
 ase baum ys hire bleo ;
fyngres heo haþ feir to folde ;   55
myhte ich hire haue ant holde,
 in world wel were me.
Hyre tyttes aren anvnder bis
as apples tuo of Parays,
 ouself ӡe mowen seo.   60

Hire gurdel of bete gold is al,
vmben hire middel smal,
 þat trikeþ to þe to,
al wiþ rubies on a rowe,
wiþinne coruen, craft to knowe,   65
 ant emeraudes mo ;
þe bocle is al of whalles bon ;
þer wiþinne stont a ston
 þat warneþ men from wo ;
þe water þat hit wetes yn   70
ywis hit worþeþ al to wyn ;
 þat seӡen, seyden so.

Heo haþ a mete myddel smal,
body ant brest wel mad al,
 ase feynes wiþoute fere ;   75

eyþer side soft ase sylk,
whittore þen þe moren-mylk,
  wiþ leofly lit on lere.
Al þat ich ou nempne noht
hit is wonder wel ywroht,   80
  ant elles wonder were.
He myhte sayen þat Crist hym seȝe
þat myhte nyhtes neh hyre leȝe,
  heuene he heuede here.

8 THE MEETING IN THE WOOD

In a fryht as y con fare fremede   *f. 66 v.*
  y founde a wel feyr fenge to fere ;
heo glystnede ase gold when hit glemede ;
  nes ner gome so gladly on gere.
Y wolde wyte in world who hire kenede,   5
  þis burde bryht, ȝef hire wil were.
Heo me bed go my gates lest hire gremede ;
  ne kepte heo non henyng here.

' Yhere þou me nou, hendest in helde,
  nauy þe none harmes to heþe.   10
Casten y wol þe from cares ant kelde,
  comeliche y wol þe nou cleþe.'

' Cloþes y haue on forte caste,
  such as y may weore wiþ wynne ;
betere is were þunne boute laste   15
  þen syde robes ant synke into synne.
Haue ȝe or wyl, ȝe waxeþ vnwraste ;
  afterward or þonk be þynne ;
betre is make forewardes faste
  þen afterward to mene ant mynne.'   20

' Of munnyng ne munte þou namore ;   *f. 67 r.*
  of menske þou were wurþe, by my myht ;
y take an hond to holde þat y hore
  of al þat y þe haue byhyht.
Why ys þe loþ to leuen on my lore   25
  lengore þen my loue were on þe lyht ?
Anoþer myhte ȝerne þe so ȝore
  þat nolde þe noht rede so ryht.'

'Such reed me myhte spaclyche reowe
  when al my ro were me atraht ;   30
sone þou woldest vachen an newe,
  ant take anoþer wiþinne nyȝe naht.
þenne mihti hongren on heowe,
  in vch an hyrd ben hated ant forhaht,
ant ben ycayred from alle þat y kneowe,   35
  ant bede cleuyen þer y hade claht.

Betere is taken a comeliche y cloþe
  in armes to cusse ant to cluppe
þen a wrecche ywedded so wroþe
  þah he me slowe ne myhti him asluppe.   40
þe beste red þat y con to vs boþe
  þat þou me take ant y þe toward huppe ;
þah y swore by treuþe ant oþe,
  þat God haþ shaped mey non atluppe.

Mid shupping ne mey hit me ashunche ;   45
  nes y neuer wycche ne wyle ;
ych am a maide, þat me ofþuncheþ ;
  luef me were gome boute gyle.'

9 A WAYLE WHYT ASE WHALLES BON

A wayle whyt ase whalles bon,   *f. 67 r.*
a grein in golde þat godly shon,
a tortle þat min herte is on,
  in tounes trewe ;
hire gladshipe nes neuer gon,   5
  whil y may glewe.

When heo is glad,
of al þis world namore y bad
þen beo wiþ hire myn one bistad,
  wiþoute strif ;   10
þe care þat icham yn ybrad
  y wyte a wyf.

A wyf nis non so worly wroht ;
when heo ys blyþe to bedde ybroht,
wel were him þat wiste hire þoht,   15
  þat þryuen ant þro.
Wel y wot heo nul me noht ;
  myn herte is wo.

31 MS. þo   33 MS. hengren   47 MS. ofþunche

Hou shal þat lefly syng
þat þus is marred in mournyng ?   20
Heo me wol to deþe bryng
  longe er my day.
Gret hire wel, þat swete þing
  wiþ eзen gray.

Hyre heзe haueþ wounded me ywisse,   25
hire bende browen, þat bringeþ blisse ;
hire comely mouth þat mihte cusse
  in muche murþe he were ;
y wolde chaunge myn for his
  þat is here fere.   30

Wolde hyre fere beo so freo
ant wurþes were þat so myhte beo,
al for on y wolde зeue þreo,
  wiþoute chep.
From helle to heuene ant sonne to séé   35
  nys non se зééþ
ne half so freo.
Whose wole of loue be trewe, do lystne me.

Herkneþ me, y ou telle,
in such wondryng for wo y welle,   40
nys no fur so hot in helle
  al to mon
þat loueþ derne ant dar nout telle
  whet him ys on.

Ich vnne hire wel ant heo me wo ;   45
ycham hire frend ant heo my fo ;
me þuncheþ min herte wol breke atwo
  for sorewe ant syke.
In Godes greting mote heo go,
  þat wayle whyte.   50

Ich wolde ich were a þrestelcok,
a bountyng oþer a lauercok,
  swete bryd !
Bituene hire curtel ant hire smok
  y wolde ben hyd.   55

24 MS. eзenen   38 MS. wose

10 THE LABOURERS IN THE VINEYARD

Of a mon Matheu þohte,   *f.* 70 *v., col.* 2
þo he þe wynȝord wrohte,
  ant wrot hit on ys boc.
In marewe men he sohte,
at vnder mo he brohte,   5
  ant nom, ant non forsoc.
At mydday ant at non
he sende hem þider fol son
  to helpen hem wiþ hoc;
huere foreward wes to fon   10
so þe furmest heuede ydon,
  ase þe erst vndertoc.

At euesong euen neh
ydel men ȝet he seh
  lomen habbe an honde.   15
To hem he sayde an heh
þat suyþe he wes vndreh
  so ydel forte stonde.
So hit wes bistad
þat no mon hem ne bad   20
  huere lomes to fonde.
Anon he was byrad
to werk þat he hem lad;
  for nyht nolde he nout wonde.

Huere hure anyht hue nome,   25
he þat furst ant last come,
  a peny brod ant bryht.
Þis oþer swore alle ant some,
þat er were come wiþ lome,
  þat so nes hit nout ryht,   30
ant swore somme vnsaht
þat hem wes werk bytaht
  longe er hit were lyht;
for ryht were þat me raht
þe mon þat al day wraht   35
  þe more mede anyht.

2 MS. whrohte

þenne seiþ he ywis :
' Why, naþ nout vch mon his ?
   Holdeþ nou or pees.
Away, þou art vnwis !   *f. 71 r., col.* 2
Tak al þat þin ys,
   ant fare ase foreward wees.
Ʒef y may betere beode
to mi latere leode,
   to leue nam y nout lees ;   45
to alle þat euer hider eode
to do to-day my neode
   ichulle be wraþþelees.'

Þis world me wurcheþ wo ;
rooles ase þe roo,   50
   y sike for vnsete,
ant mourne ase men doþ mo
for doute of foule fo,
   hou y my sunne may bete.
Þis mon þat Matheu ʒef   55
a peny þat wes so bref,
   þis frely folk vnfete,
ʒet he ʒyrnden more,
ant saide he come wel ʒore,
   ant gonne is loue forlete.   60

11 SPRING

Lenten ys come wiþ loue to toune, *f. 71 v., col.* 1
wiþ blosmen ant wiþ briddes roune,
   þat al þis blisse bryngeþ.
Dayeseʒes in þis dales,
notes suete of nyhtegales,   5
   vch foul song singeþ.
Þe þrestelcoc him þreteþ oo ;
away is huere wynter wo
   when woderoue springeþ.
Þis foules singeþ ferly fele,   10
ant wlyteþ on huere wynne wele,
   þat al þe wode ryngeþ.

þe rose rayleþ hire rode,
þe leues on þe lyhte wode
  waxen al wiþ wille.   15
þe mone mandeþ hire bleo,
þe lilie is lossom to seo,
  þe fenyl ant þe fille.
Wowes þis wilde drakes ;
miles murgeþ huere makes,   20
  ase strem þat strikeþ stille.
Mody meneþ, so doþ mo ;
ichot ycham on of þo,
  for loue þat likes ille.

þe mone mandeþ hire lyht ;   25
so doþ þe semly sonne bryht,
  when briddes singeþ breme.
Deawes donkeþ þe dounes ;
deores wiþ huere derne rounes,
  domes forte deme ;   30
wormes woweþ vnder cloude,
wymmen waxeþ wounder proude,
  so wel hit wol hem seme.
ʒef me shal wonte wille of on
þis wunne weole y wole forgon   35
  ant wyht in wode be fleme.

12 ADVICE TO WOMEN

In May hit murgeþ when hit dawes *f. 71 v., col.* 2
in dounes wiþ þis dueres plawes,
  ant lef is lyht on lynde ;
blosmes bredeþ on þe bowes,
al þis wylde wyhtes wowes,   5
  so wel ych vnderfynde.
Y not non so freoli flour
ase ledies þat beþ bryht in bour,
  wiþ loue who mihte hem bynde ;
so worly wymmen are by west ;   10
one of hem ich herie best
  from Irlond into Ynde.

22 MS. doh   28 deawes : a *written over* o

Wymmen were þe beste þing
þat shup oure heȝe heuene kyng,
  ȝef feole false nere ; 15
heo beoþ to rad vpon huere red
to loue þer me hem lastes bed
  when heo shule fenge fere.
Lut in londe are to leue,
þah me hem trewe trouþe ȝeue, 20
  for tricherie to ȝere ;
when trichour haþ is trouþe yplyht,
byswyken he haþ þat suete wyht,
  þah he hire oþes swere.

Wymmon, war þe wiþ þe swyke, 25
þat feir ant freoly ys to fyke ;
  ys fare is o to founde ;
so wyde in world ys huere won
in vch a toune vntrewe is on
  from Leycestre to Lounde. 30
Of treuþe nis þe trichour noht,
bote he habbe is wille ywroht
  at steuenyng vmbe stounde ;
ah, feyre leuedis, be on war,
to late comeþ þe ȝeynchar 35
  when loue ou haþ ybounde.

Wymmen bueþ so feyr on hewe   *f. 72 r., col.* I
ne trowy none þat nere trewe,
  ȝef trichour hem ne tahte ;
ah, feyre þinges, freoly bore, 40
when me ou woweþ, beþ war bifore
  whuch is worldes ahte.
Al to late is send aȝeyn
when þe ledy liht byleyn
  ant lyueþ by þat he lahte ; 45
ah wolde lylie-leor in lyn
yhere leuely lores myn,
  wiþ selþe we weren sahte.

13 AN OLD MAN'S PRAYER

Heʒe Louerd, þou here my bone, *f. 72 r., col.* 1
þat madest middelert ant mone,
  ant mon of murþes munne.
Trusti kyng ant trewe in trone,
þat þou be wiþ me sahte sone,   5
  asoyle me of sunne.
ffol ich wes in folies fayn,
in luthere lastes y am layn,
  þat makeþ myn þryftes þunne,
þat semly sawes wes woned to seyn.   10
Nou is marred al my meyn,
  away is al my wunne.

Vnwunne haueþ myn wonges wet,
  þat makeþ me rouþes rede.
Ne semy nout þer y am set,   15
þer me calleþ me fulle-flet
  ant waynoun wayteglede.

Whil ich wes in wille wolde,
in vch a bour among þe bolde
  yholde wiþ þe heste ;   20
nou y may no fynger folde,
lutel loued ant lasse ytolde,
  yleued wiþ þe leste.
A goute me haþ ygreyþed so
ant oþer eueles monye mo ;   25
  y not whet bote is beste.
Þar er wes wilde ase þe ro
nou y swyke, y mei nout so,
  hit siweþ me so faste.

ffaste y wes on horse heh   30
  ant werede worly wede ;
nou is faren al my feh,
wiþ serewe þat ich hit euer seh,
  a staf ys nou my stede.

When y se steden styþe in stalle   *col.* 2
ant y go haltinde in þe halle,
  myn huerte gynneþ to helde.
Þat er wes wildest inwiþ walle
nou is vnder fote yfalle
  ant mey no fynger felde.   40

Þer ich wes luef icham ful loht,
ant alle myn godes me atgoht,
   myn gomenes waxeþ gelde.
Þat feyre founden me mete ant cloht,
hue wrieþ awey as hue were wroht ;   45
   such is euel ant elde.

Euel ant elde ant oþer wo
   foleweþ me so faste
me þunkeþ myn herte brekeþ atuo.
Suete God, whi shal hit swo ?   50
   Hou mai hit lengore laste ?

Whil mi lif wes luþer ant lees ;
Glotonie mi glemon wes,
   wiþ me he wonede a while ;
Prude wes my plowe-fere,   55
Lecherie my lauendere ;
   wiþ hem is Gabbe ant Gyle.
Coueytise myn keyes bere,
Niþe ant Onde were mi fere,
   þat bueþ folkes fyle ;   60
Lyare wes mi latymer,
Sleuthe ant Slep mi bedyuer,
   þat weneþ me vmbe while.

Vmbe while y am to wene,
   when y shal murþes meten.   65
Monne mest y am to mene ;
Lord, þat hast me lyf to lene,
   such lotes lef me leten.

Such lyf ich haue lad fol ȝore.
Merci, Louerd, y nul namore ;   70
   bowen ichulle to bete.
Syker hit siweþ me ful sore,
gabbes les ant luþere lore ;
   sunnes bueþ vnsete.
Godes heste ne huld y noht,   75
bote euer aȝeyn is wille y wroht ;
   mon lereþ me to lete.
Such serewe haþ myn sides þurhsoht
þat al y weolewe away to noht
   when y shal murþes mete.   80

63 MS. vnbe   64 MS. whene

To mete murþes ich wes wel fous   *f. 72 v., col.* I
  ant comely mon ta calle
(y sugge by oþer ase bi ous)
alse ys hirmon halt in hous,
  ase heued-hount in halle.   85

Dredful deþ, why wolt þou dare?
Bryng þis body þat is so bare
  ant yn bale ybounde.
Careful mon ycast in care,
y falewe as flour ylet forþfare,   90
  ychabbe myn deþes wounde.
Murþes helpeþ me no more;
help me, Lord, er þen ich hore,
  ant stunt my lyf a stounde.
þat ȝokkyn haþ yȝyrned ȝore,   95
nou hit sereweþ him ful sore,
  ant bringeþ him to grounde.

To grounde hit haueþ him ybroht;
  whet ys þe beste bote
bote heryen him þat haht vs boht,   100
vre Lord þat al þis world haþ wroht,
  ant fallen him to fote?

Nou icham to deþe ydyht,
  ydon is al my dede.
God vs lene of ys lyht   105
þat we of sontes habben syht
  ant heuene to mede! Amen.

14 BLOW, NORTHERNE WYND

Blow, northerne wynd,   *f. 72 v., col.* I
sent þou me my suetyng!
Blow, norþerne wynd,
blou! blou! blou!

Ichot a burde in boure bryht   5
þat sully semly is on syht,
menskful maiden of myht,
  feir ant fre to fonde.

In al þis wurhliche won
a burde of blod ant of bon 10
neuerȝete y nuste non
   lussomore in londe.
      Blow, &c.

Wiþ lokkes lefliche ant longe,
wiþ frount ant face feir to fonde, 15
wiþ murþes monie mote heo monge,
   þat brid so breme in boure,
wiþ lossom eye grete ant gode, *col. 2*
wiþ browen blysfol vnder hode.
He þat reste him on þe rode 20
   þat leflich lyf honoure !
      Blou, &c.

Hire lure lumes liht
ase a launterne anyht,
hire bleo blykyeþ so bryht, 25
   so feyr heo is ant fyn.
A suetly suyre heo haþ to holde,
wiþ armes, shuldre ase mon wolde
ant fyngres feyre forte folde.
   God wolde hue were myn ! 30

Middel heo haþ menskful smal ;
hire loueliche chere as cristal,
þeȝes, legges, fet, ant al
   ywraht wes of þe beste.
A lussum ledy lasteles 35
þat sweting is ant euer wes ;
a betere burde neuer nes
   yheryed wiþ þe heste.

Heo is dereworþe in day,
graciouse, stout, ant gay, 40
gentil, iolyf so þe iay,
   worhliche when heo wakeþ.
Maiden murgest of mouþ ;
bi est, bi west, by norþ ant souþ,
þer nis fiele ne crouþ 45
   þat such murþes makeþ.

Heo is coral of godnesse,
heo is rubie of ryhtfulnesse,
heo is cristal of clannesse,
  ant baner of bealte ;   50
heo is lilie of largesse,
heo is paruenke of prouesse,
heo is solsecle of suetnesse,
  ant ledy of lealte.

To Loue, þat leflich is in londe,   55
y tolde him, as ych vnderstonde,
hou þis hende haþ hent in honde
  on huerte þat myn wes,
ant hire knyhtes me han so soht,
Sykyng, Sorewyng, ant þoht,   60
þo þre me han in bale broht
  aʒeyn þe poer of Péés.

To Loue y putte pleyntes mo,   *f. 73 r., col.* 1
hou Sykyng me haþ siwed so,
ant eke þoht me þrat to slo   65
  wiþ maistry, ʒef he myhte,
ant Serewe sore in balful bende
þat he wolde for þis hende
me lede to my lyues ende
  vnlahfulliche in lyhte.   70

Hire loue me lustnede vch word
ant beh him to me ouer bord,
ant bed me hente þat hord
  of myne huerte hele,
'ant bischeþ þat swete ant swote,   *col.* 2
er þen þou falle ase fen of fote,
þat heo wiþ þe wolle of bote
  dereworþliche dele.'

For hire loue y carke ant care,
for hire loue y droupne ant dare,   80
for hire loue my blisse is bare,
  ant al ich waxe won ;
for hire loue in slep y slake,
for hire loue al nyht ich wake,
for hire loue mournyng y make   85
  more þen eny mon.

15 SUETE IESU, KING OF BLYSSE

Suete Iesu, king of blysse,   *f. 75 r., col.* 2
myn huerte loue, min huerte lisse,
þou art suete myd ywisse.
Wo is him þat þe shal misse!

Suete Iesu, min huerte lyht,   5
þou art day wiþoute nyht,
þou ӡeue me streinþe ant eke myht
forte louien þe aryht.

Suete Iesu, min huerte bote,
in myn huerte þou sete a rote   10
of þi loue, þat is so swote,
ant leue þat hit springe mote.

Suete Iesu, myn huerte gléém,
bryhtore þen þe sonnebéém,
ybore þou were in Bedlehéém,   15
þou make me here þi suete dréém.

Suete Iesu, þi loue is suete,
wo is him þat þe shal lete!
Þarefore me shulden ofte þe grete
wiþ salte teres ant eӡe wete.   20

Suete Iesu, kyng of londe,
þou make me fer vnderstonde
þat min herte mote fonde
hou suete bueþ þi loue-bonde.

Swete Iesu, Louerd myn,   *f. 75 v., col.* 1
my lyf, myn huerte, al is þin ;
vndo myn herte ant liht þeryn,
ant wite me from fendes engyn.

Suete Iesu, my soule fode,
þin werkes bueþ bo suete ant gode ;   30
þou bohtest me vpon þe rode,
for me þou sheddest þi blode.

20 MS. wepe

Suete Iesu, me reoweþ sore
gultes þat y ha wroht ȝore;
þarefore y bidde þin mylse ant ore;   35
Merci, Lord, y nul namore.

Suete Iesu, Louerd god,
þou me bohtest wiþ þi blod;
out of þin huerte orn þe flod;
þi moder hit seh þat þe by stod.   40

Suete Iesu, bryht ant shene,
y preye þe þou here my bene,
þourh erndyng of þe heuene quene,
þat my bone be nou sene.

Suete Iesu, berne best,   45
wiþ þe ich hope habbe rest;
wheþer y be souþ oþer west,
þe help of þe be me nest.

Suete Iesu, wel may him be
þat þe may in blisse se.   50
After mi soule let aungles te;
for me ne gladieþ gome ne gle.

Suete Iesu, heuene kyng,
feir ant best of alle þyng,
þou bring me of þis longing   55
ant come to þe at myn endyng.

Suete Iesu, al folkes rééd,
graunte ous er we buen ded
þe vnderfonge in fourme of bred,
ant seþþe to heouene þou vs led.   60

16   IESU CRIST, HEOUENE KYNG

Iesu Crist, heouene kyng,   *f.* 75 *v., col.* 1
ȝef vs alle god endyng
   þat bone biddeþ þe.
At þe biginnyng of mi song,
Iesu, y þe preye among   5
   in stude al wher y be.

34 MS. wroþt   46 þe *not in MS.*

ffor þou art kyng of alle, *col.* 2
to þe y clepie ant calle,
þou haue merci of me !

þis ender day in o morewenyng, 10
wiþ dreri herte ant gret mournyng
on mi folie y þohte ;
one þat is so suete a þing,
þat ber Iesse, þe heuene kyng,
merci y besohte. 15

Iesu, for þi muchele myht,
þou graunte vs alle heuene lyht
þat vs so duere bohtes.
For þi merci, Iesu suete,
þin hondywerk nult þou lete, 20
þat þou wel ȝerne sohtes.

Wel ichot ant soþ hit ys
þat in þis world nys no blys,
bote care, serewe, ant pyne ;
þarefore ich rede we wurchen so 25
þat we mowe come to
þe ioye wiþoute fyne.

17   A WINTER SONG

Wynter wakeneþ al my care, *f.* 75 *v.,* col. 2
nou þis leues waxeþ bare ;
ofte y sike ant mourne sare
when hit comeþ in my þoht
of þis worldes ioie hou hit geþ al to noht. 5

Nou hit is ant nou hit nys,
also hit ner nere ywys.
Þat moni mon seiþ soþ hit ys :
al goþ bote Godes wille,
alle we shule deye þah vs like ylle. 10

Al þat grein me graueþ grene,
nou hit faleweþ al bydene ;
Iesu, help þat hit be sene,
ant shild vs from helle,
for y not whider y shal ne hou longe her duelle. 15

21 MS. sohtest   10 MS. þaþ   11 MS. gren

18 A SPRING SONG ON THE PASSION

When y se blosmes springe   *f.* 76 *r.*
  ant here foules song,
a suete loue-longynge
  myn herte þourhout stong,
al for a loue newe,   5
þat is so suete ant trewe,
  þat gladieþ al my song;
ich wot al myd iwisse
my ioie ant eke my blisse
  on him is al ylong.   10

When y miselue stonde
  ant wiþ myn eჳen seo
þurled fot ant honde
  wiþ grete nayles þreo—
blody wes ys heued,   15
on him nes nout bileued
  þat wes of peynes freo—
wel wel ohte myn herte
for his loue to smerte
  ant sike ant sory beo.   20

Iesu, milde ant softe,
  ჳef me streynþe ant myht
longen sore ant ofte
  to louye þe aryht,
pyne to þolie ant dreჳe   25
for þe, swete Marye;
  þou art so fre ant bryht,
mayden ant moder mylde,
for loue of þine childe,
  ernde vs heuene lyht.   30

Alas, þat y ne con
  turne to him my þoht
ant cheosen him to lemmon;
  so duere he vs haþ yboht,
wiþ woundes deope ant stronge,   35
wiþ peynes sore ant longe;
  of loue ne conne we noht.
His blod þat feol to grounde
of hise suete wounde
  of peyne vs haþ yboht.   40

26 swete, MS. sone   31 MS. couþe

Iesu, milde ant suete,
  y synge þe mi song;
ofte y þe grete
  ant preye þe among;
let me sunnes lete,   45
ant in þis lyue bete
  þat ich haue do wrong;
at oure lyues ende,
when we shule wende,
  Iesu, vs vndefong!   50
    Amen.

19 DUM LUDIS FLORIBUS

Dum ludis floribus velud lacinia   *f. 76 r.*
le dieu d'amour moi tient en tiel angustia,
merour me tient de duel e de miseria
si ie ne la ay quam amo super omnia.

Eius amor tantum me facit feruere   5
qe ie ne soi quid possum inde facere;
pur ly couent hoc seculum relinquere
si ie ne pus l'amour de li perquirere.

Ele est si bele e gente dame egregia
cum ele fust imperatoris filia,   10
de beal semblant e pulcra continencia,
ele est la flur in omni regis curia.

Quant ie la vey ie su in tali gloria
come est la lune celi inter sidera;
Dieu la moi doint sua misericordia   15
beyser e fere que secuntur alia.

Scripsi hec carmina in tabulis;
mon ostel est en mi la vile de Paris;
may y sugge namore, so wel me is;
ʒef hi deʒe for loue of hire, duel hit ys. 20

49 MS. whe   17 MS. scripsit

20 DIALOGUE BETWEEN THE VIRGIN AND CHRIST ON THE CROSS

'Stond wel, moder, vnder rode,   *f. 79 r., col.* 2
byholt þy sone wiþ glade mode,
 blyþe, moder, myht þou be!'
'Sone, hou shulde y bliþe stonde?
Y se þin fet, y se þin honde   5
 nayled to þe harde tre.'

'Moder, do wey þy wepinge.
Y þole deþ for monkynde,
 for my gult þole y non.'
'Sone, y fele þe dedestounde,   10
þe suert is at myn herte grounde
 þat me byhet Symeon.'

'Moder, merci! Let me deye,   *f. 79 v., col.* 1
for Adam out of helle beye
 ant his kun þat is forlore.'   15
'Sone, what shal me to rede?
My peyne pyneþ me to dede.
 Lat me deȝe þe byfore.'

'Moder, þou rewe al of þi bern,
þou wosshe awai þe blody tern;   20
 hit doþ me worse þen my ded.'
'Sone, hou may y teres werne?
Y se þe blody stremes erne
 from þin herte to my fet.'

'Moder, nou y may þe seye,   25
betere is þat ich one deye
 þen al monkunde to helle go.'
'Sone, y se þi bodi byswngen,
fet ant honden þourhout stongen;
 no wonder þah me be wo!'   30

'Moder, now y shal þe telle,
ȝef y ne deȝe, þou gost to helle;
 y þole ded for þine sake.'
'Sone, þou art so meke ant mynde,
ne wyt me naht, hit is my kynde   35
 þat y for þe þis sorewe make.'

' Moder, nou þou miht wel leren
whet sorewe haueþ þat children beren,
   whet sorewe hit is wiþ childe gon.'
' Sorewe ywis y con þe telle ;   40
bote hit be þe pyne of helle,
   more serewe wot y non.'

' Moder, rew of moder kare,
for nou þou wost of moder fare,
   þou þou be clene mayden-mon.'   45
' Sone, help at alle nede
alle þo þat to me grede,
   maiden, wif, ant fol wymmon.'

' Moder, may y no lengore duelle,
þe time is come y shal to helle ;   50
   þe þridde day y ryse vpon.'
' Sone, y wil wiþ þe founden,
y deye ywis for þine wounden,
   so soreweful ded nes neuer non.'

When he ros, þo fel hire sorewe,   55
hire blisse sprong þe þridde morewe.
   Blyþe, moder, were þou þo !
Leuedy, for þat ilke blisse,   *col.* 2
bysech þi sone of sunnes lisse ;
   þou be oure sheld aȝeyn oure fo !   60

Blessed be þou, ful of blysse.
Let vs neuer heuene misse,
   þourh þi suete sones myht !
Louerd, for þat ilke blod
þat þou sheddest on þe rod,   65
   þou bryng vs into heuene lyht.
      Amen.

21 IESU, FOR ÞI MUCHELE MIHT

Iesu, for þi muchele miht,   *f. 79 v., col.* 2
   þou ȝef vs of þi grace,
þat we mowe dai ant nyht
   þenken o þi face.
In myn herte hit doþ me god   5
when y þenke on Iesu blod,
   þat ran doun bi ys syde,

from is herte doun to is fot ;
for ous he spradde is herte blod,
   his wondes were so wyde.   10

When y þenke on Iesu ded,
   min herte ouerwerpes ;
mi soule is won so is þe led
   for mi fole werkes.
Ful wo is þat ilke mon   15
þat Iesu ded ne þenkes on,
   what he soffrede so sore.
For my synnes y wil wete,
ant alle y wyle hem forlete,
   nou ant euermore.   20

Mon þat is in ioie ant blis
   ant liþ in shame ant synne,
he is more þen vnwis
   þat þerof nul nout blynne.
Al þis world hit geþ away,   25
me þynkeþ hit neȝyþ domesday,
   nou man gos to grounde.
Iesu Crist, þat þolede ded,
he may oure soules to heuene led
   wiþinne a lutel stounde.   30

Þah þou haue al þi wille,
   þenk on Godes wondes ;
for þat we ne shulde spille,
   he þolede harde stoundes.
Al for mon he þolede ded ;   35
ȝyf he wyle leue on is red
   ant leue his folie,
we shule haue ioie ant blis,
more þen we conne seien ywys,
   in Iesu compagnie.   40

Iesu, þat wes milde ant fre,
   wes wiþ spere ystongen ;
he was nailed to þe tre,
   wiþ scourges yswongen ;
al for mon he þolede shame,   45
wiþouten gult, wiþouten blame,
   boþe day ant oþer.

42 MS. ystonge

Mon, ful muchel he louede þe,
when he wolde make þe fre
   ant bicome þi broþer.   50

22 I SYKE WHEN Y SINGE

I syke when y singe   *f. 80 r., col.* I
   for sorewe þat y se
when y wiþ wypinge
   biholde vpon þe tre
ant se Iesu þe suete   5
is herte blod forlete
   for þe loue of me ;
ys woundes waxen wete,
þei wepen stille ant mete.
   Marie, reweþ þe.   10

Heȝe vpon a doune,
   þer al folk hit se may,
a mile from vch toune,
   aboute þe midday,
þe rode is vp arered,   15
his frendes aren afered,
   ant clyngeþ so þe clay.
Þe rode stond in stone ;
Marie stont hire one,
   ant seiþ ' Weylaway ! '   20

When y þe biholde
   wiþ eyȝen bryhte bo
ant þi bodi colde—
   þi ble waxeþ blo,
þou hengest al of blode   25
so heȝe vpon þe rode,
   bituene þeues tuo—
who may syke more ?
Marie wepeþ sore
   ant siht al þis wo.   30

Þe naylles beþ to stronge,
   þe smyþes are to sleye,
þou bledest al to longe,
   þe tre is al to heyȝe,
þe stones beoþ al wete.   35

Alas ! Iesu, þe suete,
   for nou frend hast þou non
bote seint Iohan mournynde
ant Marie wepynde
   for pyne þat þe ys on.   40

Ofte when y sike
   ant makie my mon,
wel ille þah me like
   wonder is hit non,
when y se honge heȝe   45
ant bittre pynes dreȝe
   Iesu, my lemmon,
his wondes sore smerte,
þe spere al to is herte
   ant þourh is sydes gon.   50

Ofte when y syke,
   wiþ care y am þourhsoht ;
when y wake, y wyke,
   of serewe is al mi þoht.
Alas ! Men beþ wode   55
þat suereþ by þe rode
   ant selleþ him for noht
þat bohte vs out of synne.
He bring vs to wynne
   þat haþ vs duere boht.   60

23 AN AUTUMN SONG

Nou skrinkeþ rose ant lylie-flour   *f.* 80 *r., col.* 2
þat whilen ber þat suete sauour
   in somer, þat suete tyde ;
ne is no quene so stark ne stour
ne no leuedy so bryht in bour   5
   þat ded ne shal by glyde.
Whose wol fleysh lust forgon
   ant heuene blis abyde,
on Iesu be is þoht anon,
   þat þerled was ys side.   10

1 MS. skrnkeþ
7 *The* h *of* fleysh *has a horizontal stroke through it which may represent final* -e

From Petresbourh in o morewenyng,
as y me wende o my pleyȝyng,
   on mi folie y þohte ;
menen y gon my mournyng
to hire þat ber þe heuene kyng,   15
   of merci hire bysohte.
Ledy, preye þi sone for ous,
   þat vs duere bohte,
ant shild vs from þe loþe hous
   þat to þe fend is wrohte.   20

Myn herte of dedes wes fordred
of synne þat y haue my fleish fed
   ant folewed al my tyme,
þat y not whider i shal be led
when y lygge on deþes bed,   25
   in ioie ore into pyne.
On o ledy myn hope is,
   moder ant virgyne,
we shulen into heuene blis
   þurh hire medicine.   30

Betere is hire medycyn
þen eny mede or eny wyn ;
   hire erbes smulleþ suete ;
from Catenas into Dyuelyn
nis þer no leche so fyn   35
   oure serewes to bete.
Mon þat feleþ eni sor
   ant his folie wol lete,
wiþoute gold oþer eny tresor
   he mai be sound ant sete.   40

Of penaunce is his plastre al,
ant euer seruen hire y shal
   nou ant al my lyue ;
nou is fre þat er wes þral,
al þourh þat leuedy gent ant smal ;   45
   heried be hyr ioies fyue !
Wherso eny sek ys,
   þider hye blyue ;
þurh hire beoþ ybroht to blis
   bo mayden ant wyue.   50

29 MS. whe

For he þat dude is body on tre
    of oure sunnes haue piete
      þat weldes heouene boures!
Wymmon, wiþ þi iolyfte,
      þou þench on Godes shoures.   55
Þah þou be whyt ant bryht on ble,
      falewen shule þy floures.
Iesu, haue merci of me,
      þat al þis world honoures.
         Amen.   60

24   DE CLERICO ET PUELLA

'My deþ y loue, my lyf ich hate, for a leuedy shene,   *f.* 80 *v.*
heo is briht so daies liht, þat is on me wel sene;
al y falewe so doþ þe lef in somer when hit is grene.
Ʒef mi þoht helpeþ me noht, to wham shal y me mene?

Sorewe ant syke ant drery mod byndeþ me so faste   5
þat y wene to walke wod ʒef hit me lengore laste;
my serewe, my care, al wiþ a word he myhte awey caste.
Whet helpeþ þe, my suete lemmon, my lyf þus forte gaste?'

'Do wey, þou clerc, þou art a fol, wiþ þe bydde y noht chyde;
shalt þou neuer lyue þat day mi loue þat þou shalt byde.   10
Ʒef þou in my boure art take, shame þe may bityde;
þe is bettere on fote gon þen wycked hors to ryde.'

'Weylawei! Whi seist þou so? Þou rewe on me, þy man!
Þou art euer in my þoht in londe wher ich am.
Ʒef y deʒe for þi loue, hit is þe mykel sham;   15
þou lete me lyue ant be þi luef ant þou my suete lemman.'

'Be stille, þou fol, y calle þe riht; cost þou neuer blynne?
Þou art wayted day ant nyht wiþ fader ant al my kynne.
Be þou in mi bour ytake, lete þey for no synne
me to holde ant þe to slon, þe deþ so þou maht wynne!'   20

'Suete ledy, þou wend þi mod, sorewe þou wolt me kyþe.
Ich am al so sory mon so ich was whylen blyþe.
In a wyndou þer we stod we custe vs fyfty syþe;
feir biheste makeþ mony mon al is serewes mythe.'

56 MS. bryth   58 MS. vs
2 MS. brith   17 MS. riþt

'Weylawey! Whi seist þou so? Mi serewe þou makest newe. 25
Y louede a clerk al par amours, of loue he wes ful trewe;
he nes nout blyþe neuer a day bote he me sone seзe;
ich louede him betere þen my lyf, whet bote is hit to leзe?'

'Whil y wes a clerc in scole, wel muchel y couþe of lore;
ych haue þoled for þy loue woundes fele sore,   30
fer from hom ant eke from men vnder þe wode-gore.
Suete ledy, þou rewe of me; nou may y no more!'

'Þou semest wel to ben a clerc, for þou spekest so stille;
shalt þou neuer for mi loue woundes þole grylle;
fader, moder, ant al my kun ne shal me holde so stille   35
þat y nam þyn ant þou art myn, to don al þi wille.'

25 WHEN ÞE NYHTEGALE SINGES

When þe nyhtegale singes þe wodes waxen grene;   *f. 80 v.*
lef ant gras ant blosme springes in Aueryl, y wene,
ant loue is to myn herte gon wiþ one spere so kene,
nyht ant day my blod hit drynkes; myn herte deþ me tene.

Ich haue loued al þis зer, þat y may loue namore;   *f. 81 r.*
ich haue siked moni syk, lemmon, for þin ore.
Me nis loue neuer þe ner, ant þat me reweþ sore.
Suete lemmon, þench on me, ich haue loued þe зore.

Suete lemmon, y preye þe of loue one speche;
whil y lyue in world so wyde oþer nulle y seche.   10
Wiþ þy loue, my suete leof, mi blis þou mihtes eche;
a suete cos of þy mouþ mihte be my leche.

Suete lemmon, y preзe þe of a loue-bene;
зef þou me louest ase men says, lemmon, as y wene,
ant зef hit þi wille be, þou loke þat hit be sene.   15
So muchel y þenke vpon þe þat al y waxe grene.

Bituene Lyncolne ant Lyndeseye, Norhamptoun ant Lounde,
ne wot y non so fayr a may as y go fore ybounde.
Suete lemmon, y preзe þe þou louie me a stounde.
        Y wole mone my song   20
        on wham þat hit ys on ylong.

31 hom *not in MS.*   32 me *altered from* my
                13 MS. preeзe

26 BLESSED BE þOU, LEUEDY

Blessed be þou, leuedy, ful of heouene blisse, *f. 81 r.*
suete flur of Parays, moder of mildenesse,
preyӡe Iesu þy sone þat he me rede ant wysse
so my wey forte gon þat he me neuer misse.

Of þe, suete leuedy, my song y wile byginne, 5
þy deore suete sones loue þou lere me to wynne ;
ofte y syke ant serewe among, may y neuer blynne ;
leuedi, for þi milde mod, þou shilde me from synne.

Myne þohtes, leuedy, makeþ me ful wan,
to þe y crie ant calle, þou here me for þi man ; 10
help me, heuene quene, for þyn euer ycham,
wisse me to þi deore sone ; þe weies y ne can.

Leuedy, seinte Marie, for þi milde mod
soffre neuer þat y be so wilde ne so wod
þat ich her forleose þe þat art so god, 15
þat Iesu me to bohte wiþ is suete blod.

Bryhte ant shene sterre cler, lyht þou me ant lere
in þis false fykel world myselue so to bere
þat y ner at myn endyng haue þe feond to fere ;
Iesu, mid þi suete blod þou bohtest me so dere. 20

Leuedi, seinte Marie, so fair ant so briht, *f. 81 v.*
al myn help is on þe bi day ant by nyht ;
leuedi fre, þou shilde me so wel as þou myht,
þat y neuer forleose heueriche lyht.

Leuedy, seinte Marie, so fayr ant so hende, 25
preye Iesu Crist, þi sone, þat he me grace sende
so to queme him ant þe er ich henne wende
þat he me bringe to þe blis þat is wiþouten ende.

Ofte y crie ' Merci ' ; of mylse þou art welle ;
alle buen false þat bueþ mad boþe of fleysh ant felle ; 30
leuedi suete, þou vs shild from þe pine of helle,
bring vs to þe ioie þat no tonge hit may of telle.

3 MS. preͬreyӡe
29 *Second half of line written over erasure, of which the first letter,* a, *is legible*

Iesu Crist, Godes sone, Fader ant Holy Gost,
help vs at oure nede as þou hit al wel wost ;
bring vs to þin riche, þer is ioie most ;   35
let vs neuer hit misse for non worldes bost !

27 THE FIVE JOYS OF THE VIRGIN

Ase y me rod þis ender day   *f. 81 v., col.* I
by grene wode to seche play,
mid herte y þohte al on a may,
    suetest of alle þinge.
Lyþe, ant ich ou telle may   5
    al of þat suete þinge.

Þis maiden is suete ant fre of blod,
briht ant feyr, of milde mod,
alle heo mai don vs god
    þurh hire bysechynge ;   10
of hire he tok fleysh ant blod,
    Iesus heuene kynge.

Wiþ al mi lif y loue þat may,
he is mi solas nyht ant day,
my ioie ant eke my beste play,   15
    ant eke my louelongynge ;
al þe betere me is þat day
    þat ich of hire synge.

Of alle þinge y loue hire mest,
my dayes blis, my nyhtes rest,   20
heo counseileþ ant helpeþ best
    boþe elde ant ȝynge ;
nou y may ȝef y wole
    þe fif ioyes mynge.

Þe furst ioie of þat wymman   25
when Gabriel from heuene cam
ant seide God shulde bicome man
    ant of hire be bore,
ant bringe vp of helle pyn
    monkyn þat wes forlore.   30

---

36 w *of* worldes *written over* oþ   7 suete ant fre *written over erasure*
12 MS. ihc *with stroke through* h   25 MS. wynman

þat oþer ioie of þat may
wes o Cristesmasse day,
when God wes bore on þoro lay,
    ant brohte vs lyhtnesse ;
þe ster wes seie byfore day,   35
    þis hirdes bereþ wytnesse.

þe þridde ioie of þat leuedy,   *col. 2*
þat men clepeþ þe Epyphany,
when þe kynges come wery
    to presente hyre sone   40
wiþ myrre, gold, ant encenȝ,
    þat wes mon bicome.

þe furþe ioie we telle mawen
on Estermorewe when hit gon dawen,
hyre sone, þat wes slawen,   45
    aros in fleysh ant bon ;
more ioie ne mai me hauen,
    wyf ne mayden non.

þe fifte ioie of þat wymman
when hire body to heuene cam,   50
þe soule to þe body nam,
    ase hit wes woned to bene.
Crist, leue vs alle wiþ þat wymman
    þat ioie al forte sene.

Preye we alle to oure leuedy,   55
ant to þe sontes þat woneþ hire by,
þat heo of vs hauen merci,
    ant þat we ne misse
in þis world to ben holy
    ant wynne heuene blysse.   60
        Amen.

28   A PRAYER FOR DELIVERANCE

Mayden moder milde,   *f. 83 r.*
    oieȝ cel oreysoun ;
from shome þou me shilde
    e de ly mal feloun ;

35 MS. þest *followed by* i *above the line as if to represent* ri   44 MS. wen

for loue of þine childe   5
    me meneȝ de tresoun.
Ich wes wod ant wilde,
    ore su en prisoun.

Þou art feyr ant fre
    e plein de doucour ;   10
of þe sprong þe ble,
    ly souerein creatour ;
mayde, byseche y þe
    vostre seint socour ;
meoke ant mylde be wiþ me   15
    pur la sue amour.

Þo Iudas Iesum founde,
    donque ly beysa ;
he wes bete ant bounde
    que nus tous fourma.   20
Wyde were is wounde
    qe le Gyw ly dona ;
he þolede harde stounde,
    me poi le greua.

On stou ase þou stode,   25
    pucele, tot pensaunt,
þou restest þe vnder rode,
    ton fitȝ veites pendant ;
þou seȝe is sides of blode,
    l'alme de ly partaunt ;   30
he ferede vch an fode
    en mound que fust viuaunt.

Ys siden were sore,
    le sang de ly cora ;
þat lond wes forlore,   35
    mes il le rechata.
Vch bern þat wes ybore
    en enfern descenda.
He þolede deþ þerfore,
    en ciel puis mounta.   40

Þo Pilat herde þe tydynge,
    molt fu ioyous baroun ;
he lette byfore him brynge
    Iesu Naȝaroun.

He was ycrouned kynge
  pur nostre redempcioun.
Whose wol me synge
  auera grant pardoun.

45

29 GOD, ÞAT AL ÞIS MYHTES MAY

God, þat al þis myhtes may,   *f.* 106 *r.*
  in heuene ant erþe þy wille ys oo ;
ichabbe be losed mony a day,
  er ant late ybe þy foo ;
ich wes to wyte ant wiste my lay,   5
  longe habbe holde me þerfro ;
vol of merci þou art ay,
  al vngreyþe icham to þe to go.

To go to him þat haþ ous boht,
  my gode deden bueþ fol smalle ;   10
of þe werkes þat ich ha wroht
  þe beste is bittrore þen þe galle.
My god ich wiste, y nolde hit noht,
  in folie me wes luef to falle ;
when y myself haue þourhsoht,   15
  y knowe me for þe wrst of alle.

God, þat deȝedest on þe rod,
  al þis world to forþren ant fylle,
for ous þou sheddest þi suete blod ;
  þat y ha don me lykeþ ylle ;   20
bote er aȝeyn þe stiþ y stod,
  er ant late, loude ant stille,
of myne deden fynde y non god ;
  Lord, of me þou do þy wille.

In herte ne myhte y neuer bowe,   25
  ne to my kunde Louerd drawe ;
my meste vo ys my loues trowe,
  Crist ne stod me neuer hawe.
Ich holde me vilore þen a Gyw,
  ant y myself wolde bue knowe.   30
Lord, merci, rewe me now ;
  reyse vp þat ys falle lowe !

God, þat al þis world shal hede,
   þy gode myht þou hast in wolde ;
on erþe þou come for oure nede,   35
   for ous sunful were boht ant solde.
When we bueþ dempned after vr dede
   a domesday, when ryhtes bueþ tolde,
when we shule suen þy wounde blede,
   to speke þenne we bueþ vnbolde.   40

Vnbold icham to bidde þe bote,
   swyþe vnreken ys my réés ;
þy wille ne welk y ner afote,
   to wickede werkes y me chéés ;
fals y wes in crop ant rote   45
   when y seyde þy lore wes léés.
Iesu Crist, þou be mi bote,
   so boun icham to make my péés.

Al vnreken ys my ro,
   Louerd Crist, whet shal y say ?   50
Of myne deden fynde y non fro,
   ne noþyng þat y þenke may.
Vnwrþ icham to come þe to,
   y serue þe nouþer nyht ne day.
In þy merci y me do,   55
   God, þat al þis myhtes may.

30 THE MAN IN THE MOON

Mon in þe mone stond ant strit,   *f.* 114 *v.*
   on is bot-forke is burþen he bereþ ;
hit is muche wonder þat he nadoun slyt,
   for doute leste he valle he shoddreþ ant shereþ.
When þe forst freseþ muche chele he byd ;   5
   þe þornes beþ kene, is hattren to-tereþ.
Nis no wyht in þe world þat wot when he syt,
   ne, bote hit bue þe hegge, whet wedes he wereþ.

Whider trowe þis mon ha þe wey take ?   *f.* 115 *r.*
   He haþ set is o fot is oþer toforen.   10
ffor non hihte þat he haþ ne syht me hym ner shake,
   he is þe sloweste mon þat euer wes yboren.

7 MS. wyþt, wen   11 MS. hiþte, syþt

Wher he were o þe feld pycchynde stake,
   for hope of ys þornes to dutten is doren,
he mot myd is twybyl oþer trous make   15
   oþer al is dayes werk þer were yloren.

Þis ilke mon vpon heh whener he were,
   wher he were y þe mone boren ant yfed,
he leneþ on is forke ase a grey frere ;
   þis crokede caynard sore he is adred.   20
Hit is mony day go þat he was here ;
   ichot of is ernde he naþ nout ysped.
He haþ hewe sumwher a burþen of brere,
   þarefore sum hayward haþ taken ys wed.

Ʒef þy wed ys ytake, bring hom þe trous,   25
   sete forþ þyn oþer fot, stryd ouer sty.
We shule preye þe haywart hom to vr hous
   ant maken hym at heyse for þe maystry,
drynke to hym deorly of fol god bous,
   ant oure dame douse shal sitten hym by.   30
When þat he is dronke ase a dreynt mous,
   þenne we schule borewe þe wed ate bayly.

Þis mon hereþ me nout þah ich to hym crye ;
   ichot þe cherl is def, þe Del hym to-drawe !
Þah ich ʒeʒe vpon heh nulle nout hye,   35
   þe lostlase ladde con nout o lawe.
Hupe forþ, Hubert, hosede pye !
   Ichot þart amarscled into þe mawe.
Þah me teone wiþ hym þat myn teþ mye,
   þe cherl nul nout adoun er þe day dawe.   40

31 THE WAY OF CHRIST'S LOVE

Lvtel wot hit any mon   *f.* 128 *r.*
   hou loue hym haueþ ybounde
þat for vs o þe rode ron
   ant bohte vs wiþ is wounde.
   Þe loue of him vs haueþ ymaked sounde,   5
   ant ycast þe grimly gost to grounde.
Euer ant oo, nyht ant day, he haueþ vs in is þohte ;
he nul nout leose þat he so deore bohte.

35 MS. heþ   39 MS. teh   40 MS. cherld

He bohte vs wiþ is holy blod;
  what shulde he don vs more?   10
He is so meoke, milde, ant good,
  he nagulte nout þerfore.
    þat we han ydon, y rede we reowen sore
    ant crien euer to Iesu, 'Crist, þyn ore!'
Euer ant oo, niht ant day, &c.   15

He seh his fader so wonder wroht
  wiþ mon þat wes yfalle,
wiþ herte sor he seide is oht
  we shulde abuggen alle.
    His suete sone to hym gon clepe ant calle,   20
    ant preiede he moste deye for vs alle.
Euer ant oo, &c.

He brohte vs alle from þe deþ
  ant dude vs frendes dede.
Suete Iesu of Naȝareth,   25
  þou do vs heuene mede.
    Vpon þe rode why nulle we taken hede?
    His grene wounde so grimly conne blede.
Euer ant oo, &c.

His deope wounden bledeþ fast;   30
  of hem we ohte munne.
He haþ ous out of helle ycast,
  ybroht vs out of sunne.
    ffor loue of vs his wonges waxeþ þunne;
    his herte blod he ȝef for al monkunne.   35
Euer ant oo, &c.

32 THE WAY OF WOMAN'S LOVE

Lutel wot hit any mon   *f.* 128 *r.*
  hou derne loue may stonde,
bote hit were a fre wymmon
  þat muche of loue had fonde.
    þe loue of hire ne lesteþ nowyht longe;   5
    heo haueþ me plyht ant wyteþ me wyþ wronge.
Euer ant oo for my leof icham in grete þohte;
y þenche on hire þat y ne seo nout ofte.

19 MS. whe

Y wolde nemne hyre to-day
   ant y dorste hire munne ;   10
heo is þat feireste may
   of vch ende of hire kunne ;
    bote heo me loue, of me heo haues sunne.
Wo is him þat loueþ þe loue þat he ne may ner ywynne.
Euer ant oo, &c.   15

Adoun y fel to hire anon
   ant crie, ' Ledy, þyn ore !
Ledy, ha mercy of þy mon !
   Lef þou no false lore !
    ʒef þou dost, hit wol me reowe sore.   20
    Loue dreccheþ me þat y ne may lyue namore.'
Euer ant oo, &c.

Mury hit ys in hyre tour
   wyþ haþeles ant wyþ heowes.
So hit is in hyre bour,   25
   wiþ gomenes ant wiþ gleowes.
    Bote heo me louye, sore hit wol me rewe. *f.* 128 *v.*
    Wo is him þat loueþ þe loue þat ner nul be trewe.
Euer ant oo, &c.

ffayrest fode vpo loft,   30
   my gode luef, y þe grééte
ase fele syþe ant oft
   as dewes dropes beþ wééte,
    ase sterres beþ in welkne ant grases sour ant suete.
    Whose loueþ vntrewe, his herte is selde sééte.   35
Euer ant oo, &c.

14 MS. who

NOTES

1. EARTH UPON EARTH

This lyric is the earliest recorded form of a moralizing poem of which expanded versions later became very popular. All the known texts are edited with an introduction by Miss Hilda Murray, *Earth upon Earth*, EETS., 1911.

2. THE THREE FOES OF MAN

3. *hedy* is probably for *edy*, from OE. *ēadig* adj. used here as a noun to refer to either God or Christ. For the addition of initial *h* cf. *heȝe* 9.25, *heyse* 30.28. The expression ' to have on hand ', here and at 5.14, means ' to have care or responsibility for ' (NED. s.v. Hand, sb. sense 32a). The meaning of the line is thus : ' This Blessed One has brought it about '.

4. *hem* refers to *mon* in v. 1 ; the change of number is paralleled in vv. 39 *f*. *hest* is the superlative of *heh*, and may be used adverbially in the sense ' supremely ', as Brown takes it, or it may be used adjectivally in the sense ' most important '.

5. *blisse* is gen.sg. ; *a blisse budel* is a messenger or preacher who tells of the joys of heaven.

7. Professor Kemp Malone takes *sunful sauhting* to mean ' vengeance ', but this translation does not agree with the etymology of *sauhting*, which normally means ' agreement '. Probably *sunful sauhting* means ' having anything to do with sin ' and *sad of* means ' satisfied or surfeited with '.

8. This line is an adjectival clause qualifying *vs* in v. 5 : ' a messenger of joy bade us, who secretly commit these secret deeds, that we should soon be sated with sin '.

16. ' Unrestrained carnal pleasure passes away.'

18. *likyng out of lay* ' unlawful pleasure '.

19. Böddeker misreads *hete* as *hede*. Gibson derives *hete* from OE. *hete*, sb. and takes it to mean ' abhorrence '. Brown takes *on-hete* to be a compound verb which he glosses ' strike, knock against ', referring to *Anhit*, v. in NED. But *hete* cannot very well be derived from ON. *hitta*, which must be the etymology if Brown's suggestion is correct, and the form is fixed by the rhyme. It is probably best to take *on* as a preposition governing *his hap* and to derive *hete* from OE. *hātan* ' to call ', since in Midland dialects from the beginning of the fourteenth century the infinitive of this verb often took the vowel *ē* of the preterite (see NED., s.v. Hight, *v.*[1]). The meaning of v. 19 is thus ' He calls full hard on his fortune ', i.e. ' He bitterly laments his lot.'

20. Brown takes *howeþ* to be a form of the verb *hove* and translates it ' move, pass (on) '. This does not seem very likely, as the use of *w* for *v* is not a feature of the spelling of this manuscript, and Böddeker is probably right in deriving the verb from OE. *hogian* ' to think '. A verb of motion has to be understood after *howeþ* and the line means ' when he thinks of going hence ', i.e. ' of dying '.

21 f. Gibson takes *is* to be the 3rd singular present indicative of the verb ' to be ', *þewes* as the genitive singular of the noun meaning ' slave ' (OE. *þēow*), and *þrete* as a noun ' punishment '. He translates the lines ' All ready is the punishment of the wretch (slave) who thinks not upon that time.' Böddeker inserts *vn* before *þriuene*. Gibson's version is forced and does not account

73

for the final -e of *priuene*, and Böddeker's emendation does not improve the sense. Professor Menner translates *is priuene pewes* ' his ingrained habits ', but *pewes* in Middle English generally refers to good qualities and *priuene* often means ' honourable ' or ' noble ' and these meanings fit the context here. Probably we should take *prete* to be the 3rd plural present indicative of a verb ' accuse, reproach ' and *pat* to be a pronoun ' the man who '. The meaning of the two lines is thus ' All the better parts of his nature accuse him who does not think about that time.' This use of *penne* in the sense ' that time ' survives in Modern English with other prepositions, e.g. *by then, till then* (see NED., s.v. Then, sense 7).

23. *pre* sc. ' foes '. The allusion is to the World, the Flesh, and the Devil, the three foes of man who form the subject of the poem.

24–6. *vr soule bone* certainly does not mean ' unser Gebein allein ', as Böddeker takes it, and probably does not mean ' our soul's good ', which is Brown's gloss. Professor Menner points out that the expression occurs in *Ancren Riwle* (ed. J. Morton, p. 222), and he takes *bone* to mean ' destroyer '. Since the verb *bep* is plural, *bone* should probably be regarded as plural (OE. *banan*, pl.), and *vr soule bone* means ' the destroyers of our soul ', i.e. the three foes of man referred to in v. 23. If we accept Brown's emendation of *broerli* to *broperli*, vv. 24–6 may contain a warning that the three foes of man may present themselves in an attractive form : ' if they are thriving and prosperous among men, the enemies of our soul are as affectionate as the best of men who prevent harm '.

28. i.e. he is as restless as a reed swaying in the wind.

29 f. ' He who has first withstood the temptation of the flesh need not flee from combat with any other (enemy).'

30. Brown reads *fannyng*, which he glosses as a form of *fandinge* ' temptation ', but there are no parallels in the manuscript to the assimilation of *nd* to *nn*, and it is better to read *faunyng* ' caressing, fondling ' (from OE. *fagnian* ' to fawn or flatter ').

31. *fyue* i.e. the five senses.

33. ' The fight (against temptation) is worst where women are concerned.'

34. Professor Kemp Malone takes *wille* to mean ' will ', but in the context it probably means ' lust, pleasure ' ; *wyues* means ' of woman '.

35. ' if she is hard to control '

74. *bonnyng*. Brown follows Böddeker in reading *bounyng*, which he derives from the verb (NED. Boun, *v.* sense 3) and translates ' setting-out ', treating it as an accusative of time, but this form is apparently not recorded elsewhere in Middle English and the meaning is not very appropriate in the context. The word should probably be read as *bonnyng* (*n* and *u* are almost identical in this manuscript). Although the usual meanings of this word are ' cursing ' and ' prohibition ', it is derived from OE. *bannan* ' to summon by proclamation ', and the sense ' summons ' fits in well with the context. The line means : ' when trumpets blow this summons for him.'

3. ANNOT AND JOHN

1–10. Comparisons of a lady to precious stones are common in Middle English literature, cf. Brown XIII, 43.171 ff., and *Emare*, vv. 90 ff.

5. Böddeker removes the first *on*, but both metre and alliteration show that it should be kept. The first *on* is a pronoun, the second a preposition. Professor Malone takes *on hyht* to mean ' in relief ' and thinks that there is a reference to a cameo made of onyx, but it seems more likely that *yholden on hyht* means ' highly esteemed '.

6. Böddeker takes *he* to refer to *diamaund*, which he thinks is here regarded as masculine, but *he* is the usual form of the feminine 3rd personal pronoun in this poem and it is more natural to take it to mean ' she ' here, referring to *burde* in v. 1.

20. *sauue.* Böddeker and Brown read *sanne*, which they derive from ON. *sanna*, but Brown's translation of this word as ' to maintain, defend ' and his gloss of *forsoht* as ' afflicted ' do not make sense of the line. Professor Menner suggests that *sanne* is the same word as *saneþ* in v. 34 ' to heal ' (Lat. *sānāre*), but this explanation leaves the *nn* unaccounted for. Since *u* is used medially in this manuscript to represent both *u* and *v*, it is better to read *sauue*, i.e. ' save ' (OF. *sauver*), since this verb has the sense ' to heal ' in fourteenth-century English. The meaning of *forsoht* is ' sought out ', and the meaning of the line is ' she is the marigold which is sought after for healing.' Chaytor (*The Troubadours and England*, p. 109) quotes the line as a parallel to the Provençal image of the sunflower always turning to the sun, but *sanne* cannot without emendation mean ' sun ' and *forsoht* does not elsewhere mean ' turned '.

21. *in pyn* refers to *me* : ' who cures my pain for me when I am in torment.'

22. Böddeker's emendation of *to* to *þou* is unnecessary. The syntax of the manuscript reading is paralleled at 14.55 f.

23. Although *þryuen ant þro* is a common alliterative phrase, it is not necessary to follow Böddeker in emending *in* to *ant*. *Þro* is here a noun meaning ' dispute, contention ', and *þryuen* means ' doughty, successful '. Brown points out that the thrush had a reputation for contentiousness and refers to the *estrif The Thrush and the Nightingale* (Brown XIII, p. 101).

25. Böddeker's emendation of *dernest* to *derrest* is quite unjustified, since it spoils the sense of the passage and leaves *rr*, which is hard to account for if we follow him in deriving the word from OE. *dēor*. The meaning of *dernest* is ' most discreet ', and the word is an allusion to the convention of secrecy to which there are several references in the lyrics of this manuscript ; cf. vv. 29 f. of this lyric.

26. Gibson points out that *gome* may be either from OE. *gamen* ' amusement, game ' or from OE. *guma* ' man '. What seems to be the same alliterative phrase occurs in *William and the Werwolf*, ' to glad wiþ uch gome þat here gle herde ' (v. 824), and the context there shows that *gome* is from OE. *guma*.

28. *nyhtegale.* The form shows that the insertion of medial *n* was not yet general, although forms with medial *n* occur frequently in the Cotton MS. of *The Owl and the Nightingale*, which is about a century earlier than MS. Harley 2253.

29. The convention of secrecy discouraged the poet from revealing the name of his mistress. It is in keeping with the ingenuity shown by the author of this lyric that he conceals the lady's name, Annot, a diminutive of Ann, by means of a pun. The poet makes the pun easier to detect by the spelling with *nn*, which would be irregular if the meaning were simply ' a note '. The poet's own name is apparently John, and v. 30 means ' Whoever guesses correctly, let him whisper to John.'

33. *from Lyne to Lone.* These are river-names : the Lyn in Devonshire and the Lune in Lancashire.

34. *saneþ.* It is possible that the manuscript reading is *saueþ* ; a similar doubt exists whenever the verb *sane* is found in Middle English. Whichever reading we adopt the meaning is ' heals ' (cf. note on v. 20).

35. *bayþeþ.* Böddeker and Brown keep MS. *bayeþ* and derive it from OF. *baillier*, but this derivation is not phonologically probable. Professor Malone

derives *bayeþ* from OE. *bycgan*. But *bayþen a bone* is an alliterative phrase (cf. *Sir Gawain and the Green Knight*, v. 327), and we should probably follow NED. (s.v. Baithe, *v*.) in emending.

36. Brown keeps the manuscript reading and derives *indayne* from OF. *indigne* ' unworthy ', but the phonology of this development is irregular and the line as interpreted by Brown does not fit very well into the context. The emendation of *dede is* to *dedis* was proposed by Böddeker. Since *dayne* is not a likely form of the accusative or dative of *day*, we should probably emend it to *day*, on the assumption that the scribe's eye has been caught by the final *ne* of the next word. The first *derne* is an adjective and the second *derne* is an adverb ; cf. 2.8.

38. *cud is in crone*. Böddeker suggests that the subject ' she ' is to be understood, but Gibson is probably right in suggesting that a relative *þat* has been omitted and that the subject is *comyn* ' which is known (or remarkable) by reason of its head '. The cummin is an umbelliferous plant and so has a conspicuous flower.

39. *canel*, i.e. cinnamon. Some of these comparisons seem far-fetched but most of them can be paralleled in Middle English. For example, cinnamon is used as a term of endearment in Chaucer's *Miller's Tale*, v. 513.

41–50. It is not possible to identify with certainty all the heroes and heroines of romance mentioned in this stanza. Floyres is a common spelling of the name of Blancheflur's lover, and Cradoc can be identified with confidence as one of Arthur's knights (see note to v. 47), so it is clear that men as well as women are included. For suggested identifications of these and the other proper names in this stanza see Brown XIII, pp. 226–8.

41. *medicine*. Böddeker and Brown keep the manuscript reading *medierne*. Böddeker does not gloss the word, probably assuming it to be a proper name. Brown takes the word to mean ' covetous ' and compares ME. *med-ȝeorne*, but in this manuscript *i* is not used to represent the development of OE. front *g*. It is probably best to emend *medierne* to *medicine*. This emendation involves very little alteration of the manuscript reading and gives a word which is very appropriate in the context, since *mezina* is used as a term of praise in Provençal lyrics (see H. J. Chaytor, *The Troubadours and England*, pp. 121 f.), and *medicine* is used in a somewhat similar sense in one of the religious lyrics of the Harley manuscript (23.30 f.). Brown suggests that *mercie* is used as an adjective ' generous ', but it is more straightforward to regard it as a noun, parallel with *medicine*.

47. The relative pronoun ' who ' is to be understood after *Cradoc*. The allusion is to Craddock who, alone of Arthur's knights, succeeded in carving a boar's head and thereby proved that his wife was faithful. See the ballad *The Boy and the Mantle* (*English and Scottish Popular Ballads*, ed. Sargent and Kittredge, p. 46).

4. ALYSOUN

29. ' She is the ' is to be understood before *feyrest*.

5. THE LOVER'S COMPLAINT

9. Brown's translation of *bad* as ' asked, prayed ' gives better sense in the context than Professor Kemp Malone's ' declared, proclaimed ' and is the usual meaning of the word (OE. *bæd*, preterite of *biddan*).

17. i.e. I am as restless as a roe. *Rooles ase þe roo* is a common alliterative phrase, cf. 10.50.

23. Böddeker inserts *þe* after *menske*, but this emendation is not necessary.

Although no instance of an intransitive use of *menske* is recorded in NED., such a use could easily develop from the noun (ON. *mennska*), or the object here may be understood. Gibson defends Böddeker's emendation, saying that it improves the rhythm, but the final -*e* of *menske* was probably pronounced and the insertion of *þe* introduces an extra unaccented syllable which does not improve the metre.

6. THE POET'S REPENTANCE

4 f. *bruches broken*. The two words are etymologically related, and *bruches* is a semi-cognate accusative. The same idiom is found in *The Thrush and the Nightingale*, vv. 28–30. Böddeker takes *bok of leuedis loue* to refer to a treatise of the type found in the Provençal *Leys d'amor*, but probably *of leuedis loue* modifies *bruches* and, if *bok* refers to any particular book, the Bible is perhaps intended. The sense of vv. 3–5 is thus : ' I shall be unhappy until I have made atonement, as the Bible commands, for the offences that I have committed in connexion with ladies' love, which I have forfeited.'

13. The woman referred to here is Eve, who was regarded by medieval satirists as a symbol of the mischief caused by women.

16. ' who had no need to ride us on reins (to show her mastery over us).' The allusion is to a legend which was very popular in the Middle Ages and the subject of many carvings and engravings : Aristotle rebuked his pupil Alexander for wasting time with an Indian girl, who, in revenge, caused the philosopher to fall in love with her. She demanded that he should prove his love by allowing her to ride on his back while he was saddled and bridled like a horse. He consented, and Alexander saw the incident from a window, whereupon Aristotle, with great presence of mind, said that it proved his point. If an old man like himself was liable to be led into folly by love, a young man like Alexander was in even greater danger. (J. Bédier, *Les Fabliaux*, cinquième édition, 1925, pp. 204–12, 446 f.)

If the emendation of *durþe* to *durfte* is correct, the manuscript reading may be explained by assuming an intermediate form *durhte*, since *ht* is sometimes found as a variant of *þ* in this manuscript (cf. *wihtstonden* 2.27), and confusion between *f* and *h* is found in the forms of this verb in Middle English (see NED. s.v. Tharf, *v.*).

17. *styþye*. Brown thinks that the reference is to Christ, but it is more likely that the Virgin is intended, since otherwise there would be no one for the pronoun *hire* in v. 19 to refer to.

19. *In hire lyht* ' alighted in her ', i.e. ' born of her ' ; *on* is a pronoun referring to Christ, and *ledeþ lyf* is a common periphrasis for ' lives ', cf. 7.27.

21 f. The comparison of Christ entering the Virgin's womb to the sun shining through glass is common in medieval literature.

25 f. ' I know of no one so wicked that he dared cause them to weep for grief.'

27. *from last of lot* ' free from every fault of behaviour '.

31. This line is to be regarded as an amplification of *y* in the preceding line.

32. Brown treats *feole* in v. 32 as an adverb ' much ', puts a comma after it, and takes *on-feld* to be the preterite singular of a verb meaning ' defiled, slandered ' and compares OE. *afȳlan* v. and *unfǣle* adj. But *on feld* cannot be very closely connected with either of these forms, and the absence of final -*e* makes it unlikely that it is the preterite of a verb. A further objection to this interpretation is that, by separating *feole* and *fete*, it interferes with the stanza-linking which is a well-marked feature of the versification of this poem. The repetition of *feole* linked with *to fet y falle* in v. 33 suggests that

feole, falle, and *fete* go together in v. 32 also. It is better to take *on feld* as a phrase made up of a preposition and a noun, but it is not necessary to follow Böddeker in emending *feld* to *fold*. It is probable that *on feld(e)* (OE. *feld*) and *on folde* (OE. *folde*) were both used with the sense ' on the ground '.

41. Böddeker emends *In* to *A* and *roo* to *who*, but the heavy alliteration of the lyric as a whole suggests that *roo* should be kept. Brown keeps the manuscript reading and takes *rude* to mean ' complexion, face ' (OE. *rudu*), but the development of OE. *rudu* in this manuscript is elsewhere always *rode*. Professor Malone suggests that *in rude* means ' tête à tête ' without suggesting any etymology. It is possible that the line means ' Among the violent it would be peace to speak with them '.

42. *hem.* Böddeker and Brown read *he*, but the *e* has above it a horizontal stroke which represents a following *m* or *n*. The reading is therefore *hem*, referring to *þis briddes breme* of v. 40.

43 f. ' There is no king, emperor, or tonsured clerk who would seem to be humiliated by serving these seemly ones (i.e. women).'

55 f. 'and, when necessary, I deny having said anything that they did not wish me to say '.

7. THE FAIR MAID OF RIBBLESDALE

10. Bennett and Smithers take *þe* as a relative referring back to *heo* 8 or *bleo* 7, and *lylie-lossum* as a compound adjective. *Heo* is a better antecedent than *bleo*, since *long* is not an appropriate adjective to describe *bleo*, but it seems less strained to regard *þe* as the definite article and *lylie* as a noun used metaphorically to refer to the poet's mistress.

20. The manuscript reading may be *leneþ* (OE. *lǣnan*) or *leueþ* (OE. *lǣfan*). The meaning is ' gives, grants' in either case.

24. A relative pronoun is to be understood after *duel* : ' on account of grief which I endure until death.'

33. Bennett and Smithers are probably right in taking *hit* to refer to *blisse* and in translating the line ' in the midst of any social gaiety that may be afoot '.

48. *styþest.* This emendation is to be preferred to Böddeker's emendation to *styþe* since it avoids the hiatus of *styþe vpon*.

50. Bennett and Smithers are probably right in regarding *lylie-white* as a sb. ' the lily-white (one) ' and in deriving *lef* from OE *lēof*, but it is less certain that they are right in thinking that *lef* is used substantivally. It may be an adjective.

63. *trikeþ.* This is the only recorded occurrence of this word in English. NED. suggests that it may be connected with *trickle* or that it may be an error for *strikeþ*, of which the original sense was ' goes '. Possibly it is from OE. *strīcan* with initial *s* lost after words ending in *s*.

70. ' in which it is dipped '.

75. *wiþoute fere* ' without companion ' is appropriate since the phoenix was unique.

8. THE MEETING IN THE WOOD

5. *y wolde wyte.* ' I wished to know ', i.e. ' I asked '.

8. *henyng.* Böddeker reads the manuscript as *heuyng* and emends to *heþyng* (cf. ON. *hæða*), but the emendation is unnecessary. The manuscript reading

is *henyng*, a derivative of OE.Ang. *hēnan* ' to insult, humiliate '. NED. (s.v. Hean, *v.*) quotes an example of the verbal noun : ' Heo heveden him in henyng ' (Ritson's *Metrical Romances*, II. 313). The meaning of v. 8 is : ' She did not wish to hear any insulting suggestions.'

11. The older form of this alliterative phrase occurs at 6.52 and suggests that *cares ant kelde* is a hendiadys for *cares colde* ' bitter sorrow '.

29. Up to this point the speeches of the man and the woman have occupied alternate stanzas, but from this line until the end of the poem the woman seems to be speaking.

32. Böddeker takes *nyʒe* to be a form of *neh* ' near ', but this interpretation does not suit either the form or the sense of the word. The meaning of *nyʒe* is ' nine ' (OE. *nigon*), and the word is used in the sense which it has in the proverbial expression ' a nine days' wonder '. The earliest quotation given in *The Oxford Dictionary of Proverbs* for this expression is about fifty years later than the date of this manuscript, and there too *night* is used instead of *day* : ' For wonder last but nine night nevere in toune ' (Chaucer's *Troylus*, IV. 588).

36. ' and bid cling where I had embraced,' i.e. ' and beg the man whom I had embraced to remain faithful to me.'

40. *asluppe* may be from an OE. verb **aslyppan*, from Gmc. **aslupjan*, with *u* in ablaut relationship to the *ū* in OE. *slūpan*.

41 f. The sudden yielding of the woman is a characteristic of the pastourelle.

43 f. ' Though I swore by truth and oath (that I would not consent), none may escape what God has decreed.' NED. gives both *luppe* and *lippe* as fourteenth-century forms of the verb *leap*, but it is not easy to see how these forms can be derived from OE. *hlēapan*. Possibly *luppe* and *atluppe* are from OE. **(æt)-hlyppan*, a weak verb cognate with *hlēapan*. The stem-vowels are in ablaut relation, and go back to IE. *u* and *ou* respectively.

45. *ashunche*. This is the only recorded occurrence of this verb. The verb without prefix is found only in texts of the Katherine Group, where it has the sense ' scare away, cause to start aside '. Miss S. T. R. O. d'Ardenne (*An Edition of þe Liflade ant te Passiun of Seinte Iuliene*, p. 164) suggests that it is a blend-word composed of the material provided by such words as *schunien*, *blenchen*, and *schrenchen*, all words whose meaning resembles that which the context shows *ashunche* to have here.

47. Bennett and Smithers quote examples of rhymes of *-e* with *-eþ* which justify the emendation of MS. *ofþunche*.

9. A WAYLE WHYT ASE WHALLES BON

11 f. Böddeker takes *y wyte* to be the 3rd singular present subjunctive of (*ge*)-*witan* and translates v. 12 ' möge ein Weib kennen lernen,' but it is more natural to regard *y* as a pronoun and *wyte* as the 1st singular present indicative of the verb meaning ' to blame ' (OE. *wītan*). The two lines mean ' I blame a woman for the sorrow which I suffer.'

19. Since *þat* is used elsewhere in the sense ' he who ' (cf. 13.95), it is probable that *þat* is here a pronoun and *lefly* an adverb : ' How can the man who is thus afflicted with sorrow sing well ? ' An alternative interpretation is to regard *þat* as an adjective and *lefly* as a noun (cf. *þat semly* 3.19).

29. *myn*. Gibson takes this to mean ' my mirth ', but it is more likely that it means ' my lot ' or that, like the next four lines, it is a cynical reference to the poet's wife or former mistress of whom he has tired. Such cynicism is common in medieval French lyrics and is occasionally found in English lyrics.

31–4. ' If her mate would be so generous and if there were worthy equivalents, I would give three (women) for one without bargaining.'

35. Böddeker takes *séé* to be the verb ' to see ', but it is probably better to regard the second half of the line as parallel with the first half and to take *séé* as a noun ' sea '. The rhyme with *eo* is no obstacle to taking *séé* as a noun, since OE. *ēo* had probably become an unrounded vowel in the dialect of this lyric.

52. *lauercok* is recorded by NED. from the fifteenth century and probably represents a blend of OE. *lāferce* and *cocc*. The confusion would be assisted here by the occurrence of *prestelcok* in the preceding line.

10. THE LABOURERS IN THE VINEYARD

1. It is very unlikely that Professor Kemp Malone is right in regarding *pohte* as meaning ' taught '. He quotes the form *thech* as a parallel but leaves the development of *o* from OE. *ǣ* unexplained. It gives quite satisfactory sense to give to *pohte* its normal meaning ' thought '.

2. *he* refers to *mon* of v. 1, but the subject of *wrot* in v. 3 is *Matheu*.

7. The context suggests that *non* here has its old sense of ' ninth hour (from sunrise) '.

17 f. An example of ellipsis : ' he was very unwilling (to see them) stand so idle.'

24. Böddeker emends *nyht* to *noht* but the emendation weakens the sense and misses the point of the line, which means ' He was not deterred (sc. from employing the labourers) by the fact that night was approaching.'

45. *to leue* is passive infinitive : ' I am not to be believed to be unjust.'

46. As the line stands *euer* and *hider* have to be pronounced as monosyllables, as often in Middle English before vowels, but it is possible that one of the two adverbs is a later addition.

49. There is an abrupt change here from narrative to the style of the penitential lyric, but there is no need to assume corruption of the text. The poet remembers that he, as well as the labourers in the vineyard, is in danger of losing God's love.

11. SPRING

11. *wynne wele*. The emendation of *wynter* to *wynne* is suggested in NED. (s.v. Wlite, *v.*). The scribe's mistake can be explained by the presence of *wynter* followed by a word beginning with *w* in v. 8. With the expression *wynne wele* ' wealth of joys ' cf. v. 35.

20. Professor Tolkien, in the Glossary to Sisam's *Fourteenth Century Verse and Prose*, suggests the emendation of *miles murgeþ* to *meles murge wiþ*. If we keep the manuscript reading, the most likely etymon of *miles* is Welsh *mil* ' animal '. Although Welsh loan-words are not common in Middle English, their presence in a West Midland text is understandable, and it is probable that some of these lyrics, like the manuscript, come from that region. Other possible examples of Welsh loan-words are *wolc* 3.24 and *crouþ* 14.45.

29. Böddeker regards *deores* as a second object of *donkeþ*, but it is perhaps better to regard it as the subject of some verb which is to be understood.

12. ADVICE TO WOMEN

15. The theme of the poem as a whole shows that *feole* means ' many men ', not ' many (of them) '.

19. Böddeker takes *lut* as an adverb and understands ' men ' as the subject

of *are*, but more probably *lut* is a pronoun ' few ' and is the subject of *are*.
to leue is a passive infinitive, like *to founde* v. 27.

21. Brown regards *to ȝere* ' this year ' as unsatisfactory and proposes to
emend *ȝere* to *were* (from OE. *werian* ' to protect, defend '). But this inter-
pretation forces the meaning of *for*, and emendation is unnecessary ; *to ȝere*
is simply a tag, of the kind common in Middle English poetry, and has been
weakened to an expletive.

30. *Lounde.* This place-name occurs again in a similar phrase at 25.17.
It probably refers to one of the three places now called Lound in Lincs.,
Notts., and Suffolk respectively, all of them derived from ON. *lundr* ' grove '.
Lounde is a possible fourteenth-century spelling of London (cf. *Lounde* : *stounde*
Beues v. 3490), but London is rather a long way from the other places
mentioned.

45. Perhaps the line means ' fares according to what she got '.

13. AN OLD MAN'S PRAYER

18. *wille wolde.* *wille* is gen.sg. and *wolde* is a noun. ' I was enslaved to
the pursuit of pleasure.'

21. Brown takes *folde* here and *felde* in v. 40 to mean ' bend ', but the
occurrence of the same alliterative phrase at 7.55 suggests that the meaning
is ' clasp '. The line probably means that the poet is too old for love.

27. *þar.* Böddeker's emenation to *þat* receives support from such lines
as vv. 44 and 95 (occurring in corresponding positions in the stanza), but the
manuscript reading gives satisfactory sense, cf. v. 41.

28. *so*, i.e. ' behave as I did when I was as wild as a roe '.

29. *hit*, i.e. the gout referred to in v. 24, or possibly old age in general is
intended.

56. *lauendere* may be used here, as elsewhere in Middle English, as a
euphemism for ' harlot '. See G. P. Krapp, *Modern Language Notes*, 17.204.

58. Brown takes *keyes-bere* to be a compound noun ' key-bearer ', but it
is unusual for the first element of a compound to be in the plural and the
Old English noun for ' bearer ' had the stem-vowel *o* (cf. OE. *cǣg-bora*). It
is more likely that *bere* is the past tense of the verb : ' Covetousness carried
my keys '.

59. *Niþe ant Onde* occur in a similar list of the Seven Deadly Sins in *The
Owl and the Nightingale*, v. 1401, where they probably mean Wrath. Envy
and Wrath are the two sins missing from the list here, and it is possible that
Niþe refers to Envy and *Onde* to Anger. *Lyare* has been added to the list
of sins.

60. Brown quotes parallels in support of his view that *fyle* here is a noun
' file ', and that the line means that Malice and Envy serve a disciplinary
purpose, but it seems more straightforward to take *fyle* as an adjective ' vile,
unpleasant '. The form with initial *f* occurs elsewhere in this manuscript
(*fyl dungheep*, Böddeker, G.L. XVII. 59).

70. This line was conventional in penitential lyrics, cf. 15.36.

79. *weolewe* is probably an ablaut variant of OE. *wealwian* ' to wither, fade '
(NED. Wallow, *v.²*). The form *wellow* is still common in dialects (E. M.
Wright, *Rustic Speech and Folk-Lore*, p. 52).

85. Brown takes *heued-hount* to mean ' chief hound '. It seems slightly
better to take it to mean ' chief huntsman ' (OE. *hunta*). The loss of final
vowel may have been due to elision before the initial vowel of the next word.
It is possible that the lengthening of the stem-vowel was due to association
with *hound*.

14. BLOW, NORTHERNE WYND

26. *fyn.* *fin* is a common epithet in the lyrics of the troubadours (Chaytor, *The Troubadours and England*, p. 147).

45. Böddeł r's emendation of *fiele* to *fiþele* has been accepted by later editors, but it is not certain that it is necessary. Although the noun *vielle* is not recorded in English by NED. before the eighteenth century, the form *viele* occurred in Old French as the name of a stringed musical instrument, and *fiele* may be derived from this word. The development of the initial consonant may have been influenced by confusion with OE. *fiþele*. A parallel to the representation of initial *v* by *f* in a French loan-word is to be found in the adjective *fyl* (Böddeker, *Altenglische Dichtungen*, G.L. XVII. 59), which is probably from OF. *vil*, perhaps confused with OE. *fūl*. Apart from the possibility of confusion with native words, the forms with initial *f* may be explained as inverse spellings made possible by the voicing of initial *f* in Southern dialects. (See R. Jordan, *Handbuch der mittelenglischen Grammatik*, paragraph 215 Anm.).

55–78. These lines contain an allegory. The poet complains to Love that his lady has taken possession of his heart.

71. *Hire* should perhaps be removed. Kölbing suggested that the scribe's eye may have been caught by *hire loue* which occurs repeatedly in the next stanza.

15. SUETE IESU, KING OF BLYSSE

This lyric occurs in several manuscripts, usually in combination with a longer poem, ' Iesu, suete is þe loue of þe ', of which a version occurs in MS. Harley 2253, though it is not included in this edition. For a list of manuscripts in which the poem occurs, see Carleton Brown, *Register of Middle English Religious Verse*, II. 310. The versions referred to here are R (BM. Royal 17 B xvii, f. 13b, ed. Horstmann, *Yorkshire Writers*, II. 9) and V (Bodley 3938, f. 298a, ed. Horstmann, *Minor Poems of the Vernon MS.*, EETS., 1892–1901, p. 449). Each stanza is a self-contained prayer and stanzas could very easily be added, lost, or displaced.

19 f. The reading of R is better :

> Gyf me grace for to grete
> For my synnes teres wete.

Emendation of *wepe* to *wete* is necessary to make sense of the Harley reading. *me* in v. 19 may possibly be regarded as a reduced form of the pronoun *man* ' one ' (cf. 10.34), though this elsewhere takes a singular verb, and it is possible that *me* is a survival of the original reading, which has been preserved in R. Another possibility is that *me* should be emended to *we*.

32. The line is too short, possibly as a result of the loss of *and*, which is found in the other versions.

44. The use of *sene* in the sense ' granted ' is unusual, and the reading of VR is to be preferred :

> þat þi loue on me be sene.

51 f. The sequence of thought is confused. Better sense is given by the other manuscripts which agree with V :

> Wiþ loue-cordes drauȝ þou me
> þat I may comen and wone wiþ þe.

55 f. R is better :

> Brynge in-to me þat luf-longynge
> To come to þe at myn endynge.

57–60. This stanza is not recorded in any other version.

16. IESU CRIST, HEOUENE KYNG

10–15. This stanza is not very appropriate to the context since it refers to the Virgin, whereas the rest of the lyric refers to Christ. The stanza resembles 23.11–16 and it was probably a conventional *chanson d'aventure* opening, like that of No. 27, which could easily be transferred from one lyric to another and which has been unskilfully incorporated into this lyric. This poem shows an excessive use of conventional tags and lines to which parallels may be quoted from other lyrics. For example, cf. v. 5 with 18.44 and v. 16 with 21.1.

21. Since -*est* is the usual ending of the 2 sg.pa.t.ind. in this manuscript, whereas -*es* is the ending in more northerly dialects, it is probable that the original had the rhyme *bohtes : sohtes* and that the northern form has been replaced in one line but not in the other. Brown emends *bohtes* to *bohtest*, but this emendation suggests no reason for the error.

17. A WINTER SONG

15. The line is elliptic : a verb of motion is to be understood after *shal*, and *y shal* is to be understood before *her*.

18. A SPRING SONG ON THE PASSION

Another version occurs in MS. BM. Royal 2 F viii, f. 1b, printed by Brown, XIII, p. 120 (R). The order of the third and fourth stanzas of H is reversed in R and R contains a stanza (the second) not found in H. R consistently uses the singular pronoun, whereas H sometimes substitutes the plural.

4. Böddeker takes *stong* as present indicative and derives it from ON. *stanga*. He suggests that the inflexional ending may have been dropped for the sake of the rhyme or that the present of ON. *stanga* may have been confused with the preterite of OE. *stingan*. But Böddeker's explanation of the lack of an inflexional ending in *stong* is unconvincing and the word should be regarded as the preterite of OE. *stingan*. Sudden transitions from present to preterite or vice versa are a feature of the language of the *Harley Lyrics* (cf. 32.16 f.), and a similar change of tense is found in R : Nv yh she . . . hic herde. The adverb *þourh-out* is used with the past participle of the same verb at 20.29, ‘ fet & honden þourh-out stongen ’.

12. ‘ Him ’ (i.e. Christ) is to be understood as the object of *seo*.

17. ‘ who was noble (or generous) where suffering was concerned ’.

24. *longen*. R has *longinge*, which is parallel to the other nouns *streynþe* and *myht*.

25. The rhyme is disguised by the archaic spelling *dreȝe*, although *eȝ* had probably become *ī* in pronunciation at the time when the poem was written. R has the newer and more phonetic spelling *drye*.

26. The emendation of *sone* to *swete* has the support of R and is to be preferred to Böddeker's emendation of *þe* to *þi*.

31. The emendation of *couþe* to *con* is necessary for the sake of the rhyme and has the support of R.

34. The reading of R is better : þat þvs me haued hy-bovt.

19. DUM LUDIS FLORIBUS

This poem shows the use of the macaronic style in a secular lyric, whereas No. 28 shows its use in a religious lyric. One difference between the two poems is that in No. 28 the alternation of the two languages used is quite regular, whereas in this lyric three languages are used in a much less orderly way.

1. *velud* for *velut* is an inverse spelling made possible by the unvoicing of final *d*, of which there are examples in the spelling of this manuscript (cf. note on 20.21).

20. DIALOGUE BETWEEN THE VIRGIN AND CHRIST ON THE CROSS

Other texts of this English version of the Sequence *Stabat iuxta Christi crucem* occur in MS. Bodley 1687 (Digby 86), f. 127a, printed by Brown, XIII, p. 87 (D), and MS. BM. Royal 12 E i, f. 193a, printed by Brown, XIII, p. 89 (R). An incomplete version occurs in St. John's College Cambridge MS. 111, f. 106b, printed by Brown, XIII, p. 203 (C). The first stanza is quoted in a Latin sermon preserved on the fly-leaves of MS. BM. Royal 8 F ii (printed by Brown, XIII, p. 204). R and C are accompanied by musical notation.

8. The reading of R, ' for mannes thinge ', gives a rhyme instead of the assonance of H.

12. *Symeon*. See St. Luke ii. 25–35. He is often referred to in religious lyrics.

21. *ded* is a form of *deþ* especially common in Northern dialects, cf. *dedestounde* v. 10. The rhyme illustrates the tendency to unvoice final *d*, of which there are occasional examples in this manuscript, e.g. *mot* 6.29.

40. *Sorewe*. Although the manuscript reading gives good sense, Wülcker's emendation to *Sone* is reasonable, since this is the reading of RD and the second half of most of the other stanzas begins with *Sone*.

45. The first *þou* is a conjunction ' though ', the second a pronoun ' thou '.

21. IESU FOR þI MUCHELE MIHT

12. *ouerwerpes*. Although no intransitive use of the verb *Overwarp* is recorded by NED., the verb is here clearly intransitive and provides a parallel for the interpretation of *Beowulf*, vv. 1543 ff. (*Modern Language Review*, XXV. 78).

15. In the original form of this construction *wo* would be a noun and *þat ilke mon* would be regarded as dative (cf. ' Woe is me ! '), but the use of the adverb *ful* here shows that the construction has already been misunderstood and that *wo* was regarded as an adjective qualified by *ful* (cf. the Shakespearean ' I am woe for't ' as in *The Tempest*, V. i. 139).

22. I SYKE WHEN Y SINGE

Another version occurs in the Bodleian MS. Digby 2, f. 6a, printed by Brown, XIII, p. 122 (D). The Digby version transposes stanzas 4 and 5.

10. *reweþ* is impersonal : ' Mary, it grieves thee.'

31 f. Brown refers to the legend of the smith who forged the nails for the Crucifixion (*The Northern Passion*, ed. F. A. Foster, EETS., 1912, vv. 1339–1502).

37, 40. D preserves the rhyme-scheme found in the other stanzas :

> feu frendis hafdis ney [e] . . .
> þat al þi sorue seye.

38 f. See St. John xix. 26 f.

48, 50. *smerte* and *gon* are infinitives depending on *y se* of v. 45.

23. AN AUTUMN SONG

10. Böddeker takes *ys* to be a contraction of *yn is* ' in his '. It is better to regard *þat . . . ys* as meaning ' whose ', a survival of the Old English method of expressing inflexion in the relative pronoun by adding the appropriate case of the personal pronoun.

13. *folie* in Old French often meant ' illicit love ', and this may be the meaning here, cf. *Handlyng Synne*, vv. 12393 ff.

29. A verb of motion is understood after *shulen*.

34. *from Catenas to Dyuelyn* ' from Caithness to Dublin '. This phrase is probably of Scandinavian origin, since Caithness and Dublin were the limits of the coasts occupied by the Western vikings.

48. *hye* is jussive subjunctive : ' let him hasten thither '.

51. *he* has been used for *him* because a subject of the relative clause is looked for.

55. f. The rhyme-scheme of this stanza differs from that of the other stanzas of the lyric. For this reason Brown transposes vv. 55 and 56 and assumes the loss of a line after v. 56. But .there are other examples of differences of structure between the last stanza of a lyric and the other stanzas (cf. No. 9), and it is not necessary to assume that a line has been lost. As it stands in the manuscript v. 58 does not rhyme with any other line in the stanza, but the emendation of *vs* to *me* restores the rhyme.

24. DE CLERICO ET PUELLA

12. Apparently a proverb.

19. *lete þey for no synne*, i.e. they will not allow the fear of committing a sin to prevent them.

31. Some word has clearly been omitted by a scribe. Böddeker supplies *hom* and Brown supplies *bour*.

33. *stille*. Brown reads *scille*, which he takes to mean ' cleverly, plausibly ', and which Professor Malone translates ' eloquently '. But OE. *sc* is represented by *sh* in this manuscript, and the manuscript reading is probably *stille* ' softly '. Cf. *Sir Gawain and the Green Knight*, v. 1117.

25. WHEN ÞE NYHTEGALE SINGES

4. Böddeker misreads the *me* of the manuscript as *to* and his mistake has been copied by most anthologists. Brown has the correct reading, but it seems best to regard OE. *tēaman*, which he gives as the etymon of *tene*, as a misprint. It is possible to regard *tene* as a noun ' grief ' (OE. *tēona*) or as a verb ' to grieve, cause to suffer ' (OE. *tēonian*). If *tene* is a noun, *deþ* has the meaning ' causes ' ; if *tene* is a verb, *deþ* is an auxiliary. There is a similar ambiguity when the expression is used elsewhere in Middle English, e.g. ' þat shent þe fende and doþe hym tene ', *Handlyng Synne*, v. 12040.

13. Böddeker says that *of* goes with the preceding pronoun *þe* and not with *loue bene*, but the verb ' to pray ' was formerly constructed with ' of ' followed by the thing desired where to-day we should use ' for ' (cf. NED. s.v. Pray, *v.*, sense 1c). In ' y preye þe of loue one speche ' in v. 9 the force of *of* is not the same : there *preye* takes the direct object of the thing prayed for : ' a speech of love '.

20 f. The substitution of a short couplet for the last line of the lyric is probably the result of the influence of the *envoi* ; cf. note to 23.55 f.

26. BLESSED BE ÞOU, LEUEDY

Another version occurs in MS. BM. Egerton 613, f. 2a, printed by R. Morris, *An Old English Miscellany*, EETS., 1872, p. 195. Each version has two stanzas not found in the other and the order of the stanzas is not the same.

10. Böddeker takes *for þi man* to mean ' for the sake of Christ '. But probably *man* is used in the sense of ' servant ' in the conventions of courtly love. Cf. ' ic am þi mon ' (Brown, XIII, 60.22) ; there too the words are addressed to the Virgin.

17. The Virgin was often addressed as a star ; cf. the two lyrics with the title *Ave Maris Stella* in Brown, XIV, pp. 20 and 58.

27. THE FIVE JOYS OF THE VIRGIN

12. The manuscript has *ihc* with a stroke through the *h*. Böddeker expands this to *iesu crist*, but it should probably be expanded to *iesus*. Apart from palaeographical considerations, Böddeker's reading causes the line to have four stresses, whereas the corresponding lines in all the other stanzas have only three stresses.

14. Brown's emendation of *he* to *heo* is unjustified, since *he* is a common form of the 3rd person singular feminine of the personal pronoun in this manuscript. In No. 3, for example, *he* occurs thirteen times as the feminine pronoun, whereas *heo* occurs only once.

33. *on þoro lay.* Böddeker reads the manuscript as *þore*, which he emends to *þorwe*, taking it to mean ' crib ' (OE. *þrūh*), but this development is phono-logically unlikely and OE. *þrūh* means ' coffin ' rather than ' crib '. Brown reads *on þoro lay*, which he translates ' according to due law ' or ' in due form '. Sister Mary Immaculate (*A Note on ' A Song of the Five Joys '*, *Modern Language Notes*, LV (1940), pp. 249–54) argues that this description is theologically inappropriate to the Virgin Birth of Christ, and suggests that *lay* means ' light ' from OMerc. *lēg* (NED. s.v. Leye). This explanation seems the most satisfactory in view of v. 35 and the passages quoted by Sister Mary Immaculate from sermons on the Nativity which stress the miraculous brilliance of the star ; for example, St. Bernard says ' Nox enim ut dies illuminata est ' (Migne, P.L. vol. 183, col. 126).

35. Brown's reading *þe ster* fits the sense much better than Böddeker's reading *þestri*, but the latter is probably the reading of the manuscript, since the hook used to represent *er* in this manuscript is much rounder than the short vertical stroke used here. It is therefore necessary to regard the reading *þe ster* as an emendation.

28. A PRAYER FOR DELIVERANCE

The English lines of the first stanza of this lyric served as the basis of the short prayer at the end of the *Aʒenbite of Inwit*. The prayer is there written as prose, the order of the lines has been changed, and two three-stress lines (common tags) have been added. Dan Michel's version (MS. BM. Arundel 57,

f. 96b) is : ' Mayde and moder mylde, uor loue of þine childe, þet is god an man, Me þet am zuo wylde uram zenne þou me ssylde ase ich þe bydde can. Amen.'

25. *stou* ' place '. Alternatively the manuscript may be read as *ston*, which in Old and Middle English can mean ' stony ground '.

31. Brown glosses *ferede* under *feren* ' to feel fear ', but the syntax of the line demands the transitive sense ' to cause fear to ' : ' He caused fear in every living creature.'

29. GOD ÞAT AL ÞIS MYHTES MAY

Another version occurs in the Pratt MS., written at the end of the fourteenth century and sold at Sotheby's 27 July 1925 to Quaritch (printed by Brown, XIII, p. 158). An eighteenth-century transcript is contained in BM. Additional 5901.

5. ' I was to blame and knew my duty ', i.e. ' I sinned knowingly ' ; cf. v. 13.

6. The subject is to be understood from the preceding line.

8. The metre would be improved by the omission of *al*.

22. Tags of this kind are common in Middle English poetry and mean ' in all circumstances '.

27. *my loues trowe* ' my trust in praise '.

28. This is the earlier form of the idiom ' to stand in awe of '. For the construction, cf. NED. s.v. Stand, *v.*, senses 45a and b.

31. *Lord*. The metre suggests that the original had the disyllabic form *Louerd*, which occurs elsewhere in this poem (v. 50).

51 f. ' I find no consolation from my (former) deeds nor from anything that I can think of.'

30. THE MAN IN THE MOON

6. *þornes*, like *hegge*, v. 8, refers to the bundle of thorns which the man in the moon was supposed to carry. Cf. ' One must come in with a bush of thorns and a lanthorn and say he comes to present the person of Moonshine ' (*A Midsummer Night's Dream*, III, i).

9. Professor Malone takes *ha* to mean ' hath ' and thinks that final þ may have been lost because the next word begins with þ, but this interpretation leaves *trowe* unexplained. It is possible that *ha* is infinitive and that *trowe* is for *troweþ*, since *trowe* too is followed by a word with initial þ.

27. A verb of motion is to be understood. The same idiom is found in *Handlyng Synne*, v. 5876 ' And preyde hem home to hys halle.'

31. A proverbial expression, cf. ' dronken as a mous ', *Canterbury Tales*, D 246.

35. *nulle*. Böddeker says that ' he ' is to be understood as the subject, but *nulle* is probably a contraction of *nul* (or *nulle*) *he*, cf. *nullyt* 6.57.

38. *amarscled*. Brown takes this to be the past participle of a verb ' to marshal ', but the spelling with *sc* is unusual and the sense in the context is not clear. In view of the mention of *mawe* it may be that *amarscled* means ' stuffed full (of drink) ', but both the meaning and the etymology of the word are obscure.

31. THE WAY OF CHRIST'S LOVE

There is clearly some connexion between this lyric and the next. Light is thrown on the relation between the two poems by two fragments of lyrics transcribed by Brown, III, p. 235 f. Texts of the two fragments, based on Brown's transcripts, are given in (*a*) and (*b*).

H.L.—G

(*a*) Caius College Cambridge MS. 512, f. 260b.

> Lytel wot yt ony man
> hu derne loue was fu[n]de
> But he þat was on Rode don
> and bouth vs wyth his wonde.
> ffor loue of man he made hymself vnsunde.
> He haueth ykast a griysli gast to grunde.
> He bouth vs wyth hys suete blod.
> Hu myth he don vs more?

(*b*) BM. Egerton 613, f. 2b.

> Litel uo[t] it eni man
> hu trewe loue bisto[n]det
> bute hure swete Leuedi
> þat muchel þerof haud fondet.
> þe loue of hire hit lassted swþe longe.
> he haweþ ws plist he wele hus underfonge.
>   Awre Mo is mi lif and ic in grete þovte;
>   i þencke of hire þat al hure blisse hus bro[h]te.

The first of these fragments closely resembles the opening of No. 31 except for the word *derne* in the second line. Brown is probably right in regarding the presence of this word as a sign that the religious poem was an adaptation of a secular lyric and that the two fragments represent independent attempts to convert No. 32 into a religious lyric. No. 31 may be a successful attempt to complete the version in the Caius manuscript.

13. *ydon.* The form of the past participle without prefix suits the metre better.

32. THE WAY OF WOMAN'S LOVE

24, 26. *heowes* : *gleowes.* In view of the rhyme-scheme of the other stanzas it is probable that the *s* in these two words has been added by a scribe.

GLOSSARY

In the Glossary inflected forms of nouns, adjectives, and verbs have been recorded only when they present features of special interest. No attempt has been made to record all the occurrences of any word. In alphabetical arrangement *y* is included under *i*, consonantal *i* is treated as *j*, and vocalic *u/v* is separated from consonantal *u/v*. The occasional examples of *u* as a spelling for *w* are included with vocalic *u*. The letters *ȝ* and *þ* have separate alphabetical places immediately after *g* and *t* respectively. In Old English forms the sign ⁻ is used to indicate vowels which were long in early Old English ; the sign ' is used to indicate vowels which were lengthened during the Old English period when the forms in the text suggest that such lengthening has taken place.

ABBREVIATIONS

AN.	Anglo-Norman
Ang.	The Anglian dialect of Old English
Cf.	in etymologies indicates uncertain or indirect relation
From	in etymologies means that the word illustrated has an affix not found in the etymon
infl.	influenced
LOE.	Late Old English
ME.	Middle English
Merc.	The Mercian dialect of Old English
MDu.	Middle Dutch
MLG.	Middle Low German
n.	See note
NED.	New English Dictionary
Nhb.	The Northumbrian dialect of Old English
OE.	Old English
OF.	Old French
ON.	Old Norse
ONF.	Northern dialects of Old French
prec.	Preceding word
VP.	The dialect of the Vespasian Psalter in Old English
WS.	West Saxon
*	is prefixed to forms theoretically reconstructed and not recorded in texts
+	between elements in an etymology means that a compound or derivative is first recorded in Middle English

a. See A(N), *art.* ; A(N), *prep.*

abyde, *v.* to wait for, expect 23.8. (OE. *abīdan*.)

aboute, *prep.* near (of time) 7.14, 22.14. (OE. *abūtan*.)

abuggen, *v.* to pay the penalty 31.19. (OE. *abycgan*.)

ache, *sb.* smallage, wild celery 3.14. (OF. *ache*.)

adoun, *adv.* down 4.20, 30.40. (OE. *adūne*.)

adred, *pp.* afraid 30.20. (OE. *ofdrǣd(d)*.)

afered, *pp.* afraid 22.16. (OE. *afǣred*.)

afote, *adv.* on foot 29.43. (A, *prep.* + OE. *fōtum*, dat.pl.)

after, *prep.* for 15.51, according to 29.37. (OE. *æfter.*)

afterward, *adv.* later, afterwards 8.18, 20. (OE. *æftenweard,* infl. by prec.)

aȝeyn, *adv.* back 12.43 ; *prep.* against 13.76, 20.60. (OE. *ongegn.*)

aȝeynes, aȝeynȝ, *prep.* with regard to 2.23 ; *cj.* by the time that, before 2.20. (Prec. + gen. *-es.*)

ah, *cj.* but 12.34, 40. (OE. *ah,* variant of *ac.*)

ahte, *sb.* peril, risk 12.42. (Cf. ON. *hætta.*)

ay, *adv.* always 6.53, 29.7. (ON. *ei.*)

al, *adv.* quite, wholly, completely 2.58, 7.53, (intensifying following ' to ') 9.42. (OE. *al(l).*) See AL(LE).

alas, *interj.* alas 18.31, 22.36. (OF. *alas.*)

alisaundre, *sb.* alexanders, horse-parsley 3.14. (OF. *alisaundre.*)

al(le), *adj. and sb.* all 6.6, 7.79, 10.46, 31.21 ; *alle ant some,* all, one and all 10.28. (OE. *al(l).*)

alse, *adv.* as 13.84. (Reduced from next.)

also, *cj.* as if 17.7. (OE. *al(l) swā.*) See ALSE, AS(E).

alþah, *cj.* although 2.13. (AL, *adv.* + ÞAH, *cj.*)

am, *1 sg.pres.* am 5.5, 24.22. (OE.Ang. *am, eam.*) See NAM.

amarscled, *pp.* stuffed full (?) 30.38.

amen, *interj.* amen 13.108. (Lat. *āmēn.*)

among, *prep.* among 13.19 ; *adv.* here and there 7.11, at this time, all the while 16.5. (OE. *onmang,* earlier *on gemang.*)

amorewen, *adv.* in the morning 3.8. (OE. *on morgen.*)

a(n), *art.* a, one, some 3.1, 4.9. (OE. *ān.*) See ON(E).

a(n), *prep.* on, in 2.54, 10.15, 29.38. (Weakened form of ON, *prep.*)

anaht, anyht, *adv.* at night 7.20, 10.25. (OE. *on næht, on niht.*)

anys, *sb.* anise 3.14. (OF. *anis.*)

anon, *adv.* at once, forthwith 3.49, 10.22. (OE. *on ān.*)

anoþer, *pron.* another 8.27. (OE. *ān + ōþer.*)

ant, *cj.* and 2.42, if 32.10. (OE *and.*)

anvnder, *prep.* under 7.58. (AN, *prep.* + OE. *under.*)

apon. See VPON.

apples, *sb.pl.* apples 7.59. (OE. *æppel.*)

are(n), *3 pl.pres.* are 3.36, 7.16. (OE. Nhb. *aron,* Merc. *earun.*)

arered, *pp.* raised, lifted 22.15. (OE. *arǣran.*)

aryht, *adv.* rightly 15.8, 18.24. (OE. *ariht.*)

aryse, *v.* to arise 2.71 ; *3 sg.pa.t.* **aros** 27.46. (OE. *arīsan.*)

arm, *sb.* arm 7.52. (OE. *arm.*)

art, *2 sg.pres.* art 15.6. (OE. *eart.*)

as(e), *adv.* as, like 7.76 ; *cj.* as 3.18, when 8.1, as if 13.45. (Reduced from ALSE.)

ashunche, *v.* to frighten 8.45 n. (Obscure.)

asluppe, *v.* to slip away, escape 8.40. (OE. **aslyppan,* cf. *aslūpan.*)

asoyle, *2 sg.imper.* absolve 13.6. (OF. *asoillir.*)

at, *prep.* at 6.55, (of place) 20.11, (of time) 10.5. (OE. *æt.*)

ate, from the 30.32. (Prec. + ÞE.)

atgoht, *3 pl.pres.* go away, pass away 13.42. (OE. *ætgān.*)

atled, *ppl.adj.* arranged, placed 7.41. (ON. *ætla.*)

atluppe, *v.* to escape from 8.44. (Cf. OE. *æthlēapan.*)

atraht, *pp.* taken away 8.30. (OE. *æt- + rǣcan.*)

atwo, atuo, *adv.* into two parts 9.47, 13.49. (OE. *on twā.*)

aþel, *sb.* excellence, power 6.67, man 6.68. (OE. *æþelu.*) See HAÞEL.

aungles, *sb.pl.* angels 15.51. (OF. *aungele.*)

Aueril, Aueryl, *sb.* April 4.1, 25.2. (OF. *avril.*)

awai, away, awey, *adv.* away 2.16, 6.49, 13.45. (OE. *on weg.*)

bad. See BIDDE.

bayly, *sb.* bailiff, steward 30.32. (OF. *bailli.*)

bayþeþ, *3 sg.pres.* grants 3.35. (ON. **beiðna,* later *beina.*)

baldore, *adj.comp.* bolder 3.44. (From OE.Ang. *bald.*) See BOLDE.

bale, *sb.* harm, torment 2.26, 3.21. (OE. *balu.*)

baloygne, *sb.* whalebone 7.53. (Cf. OF. *baleine.*)

balful, *adj.* pernicious, injurious 14.67. (OE. *bealofull.*)

baner, *sb.* banner 14.50. (OF. *banere.*)

bare, *adj.* bare 17.2, poor, unprotected 13.87. (OE. *bær.*)

baum, *sb.* balsam, aromatic juice 7.54. (OF. *baume.*)

baundoun, *sb.* power, control 4.8. (OF. *bandun.*)

be, *v.* to be 2.7 ; **ben** 9.55, **beo** 7.51, **beon** 7.47, **bue** 29.30, **buen** 4.18, **bene** 27.52 ; *1 sg.pres.* **be** 6.3 ; *1 pl.* **beþ** 2.60, **bueþ** 29.37, **buen** 2.69 ; *3 pl.* **beþ** 22.55, **beoþ** 2.39, **bueþ** 2.47, **buen** 26.30 ; *1, 2, 3 sg.pres.subj.* **be** 6.71, 13.5, 15.47, **bue** 30.8 ; *1, 3 pl.pres.subj.* **be** 23.46, **ben** 2.9, **beon** 6.37, **buen** 15.58 ; *2 sg.imper.* **be** 5.9 ; *2 pl.imper.* **be** 12.34 ; *pp.* **be** 29.3. (OE. *bēon.*) See AM, ARE(N), ART, IS, WES.

bealte, *sb.* beauty 14.50. (OF. *bealte.*)

bed. See BEODE.

bed(de), *sb.* bed 23.25, 9.14. (OE. *bedd.*)

bede. See BEODE.

bedyuer, *sb.pl.* bed-fellows 13.62. (OE. *bedd + gefēra.*)

beh. See BOWE(N).

beye, *v.* to buy, redeem 20.14 ; *3 sg.pa.t.* **bohte** 22.58 ; *pp.* **boht** 13.100, **yboht** 18.34. (OE. *bycgan.*)

belde, *3 sg.pres.subj.* defend, protect, shelter 2.37. (OE.Ang. *beldan.*)

bemes, *sb.pl.* trumpets 2.74. (OE. *bēme.*)

bend, ybend, *ppl.adj.* curved, arched 7.18, 25 ; *pl.* **bende** 9.26. (OE. *bendan.*)

bene, *sb.* prayer 15.42. (OE. *bēn.*)

beode, *v.* to command 8.7, bid, entreat 8.36, challenge 3.44, offer 10.43 ; *2, 3 sg.pa.t.* **bed(e)** 3.44, 8.7, 36. (OE. *bēodan.*)

bere, *v.* to bear 27.36, carry 13.58, 30.2, carry away, gain 5.35, produce, bring forth 23.2, give birth to 6.24, (reflex.) behave 26.18 ; *3 sg.pa.t.* **ber** 16.14, **bere** 13.58 ; *pp.* **bore** 12.40, **boren** 30.18, **ybore** 6.24, **yboren** 30.12. (OE. *beran.*)

beryl, *sb.* beryl 3.1. (OF. *beril.*)

bern, *sb.*[1] son 20.19. (OE. *bearn.*)

bern, *sb.*[2] man 28.37 ; *gen.pl.* **berne** 2.26, 15.45. (OE. *beorn.*)

besohte. See BYSECHE.

best(e), *adj.superl.* best 2.26, 5.36, 8.41 ; *adv.* to the fullest extent, most 7.51, 12.11. (OE. *betst.*)

bete, *pp.* beaten 7.61, 28.19. (OE. *bēatan.*)

bete, *v.* to cure, assuage 3.21, 23.36, atone for 2.36, 6.3 ; *pp.* **bet** 6.3. (OE. *bētan.*)

bet(t)ere, betre, *adj.comp.* better 4.35, 8.19, 24.12 ; *adv.* better 10.43, 24.28. (OE. *betera.*)

bi, by, *prep.* by, past 17.1, through 7.1, according to 12.45, during 26.22, concerning 2.38, judging by 3.10, (in oath) 8.22, near (following its case) 15.40, 30.30 ; *by west,* in the west 5.37. (OE. *bī.*)

bicome, *v.* to become 21.50 ; *pp.* **bicome** 27.42. (OE. *bicuman.*)

bidde, *v.* to pray 16.3, ask, beg, demand 5.9, 9.8, desire, wish 24.9, warn, advise 2.5, command (infl. by sense of BEODE) 2.75, 6.4 ; *3 sg.pres.* **byt** 2.75 ; *1, 3 sg.pa.t.* **bad** 2.5, 5.9. (OE. *biddan.*)

byde, *v.* to obtain 24.10, endure 30.5 ; *3 sg.pres.* **byd** 30.5. (OE. *bīdan.*)

bydene, *adv.* forthwith 17.12. (See NED.)

bifore(n), byfore, *prep.* before 27.35, in the presence of 2.71, 28.43 ; *adv.* before 2.48, 12.41. (OE. *biforan.*)

byginne, *v.* to begin 26.5. (OE. *biginnan.*)

biginnyng, *sb.* beginning 16.4. (From prec.)

biheste, *sb.* promise 24.24. (OE. *bihǣs.*)

byhet, *3 sg.pa.t.* promised 20.12 ; *pp.*
byhyht 8.24. (OE. *bi-, behātan.*)

biholde, byholde, *1 sg.pres.* see,
behold 7.13, 49 ; *2 sg.imper.*
byholt 20.2. (OE. *biháldan.*)

byleyn, *ppl.adj.* deflowered 12.44.
(OE. *bi-, belicgan.*)

bileued, *pp.* believed 18.16. (OE.
bi- + Ang. *lēfan.*)

bymong, *prep.* among 7.53. (OE.
gemang, with change of prefix.)

bynde, *v.* to bind, fetter 12.9 ; *pp.*
bounde 28.19, **ybounde** 12.36.
(OE. *bindan.*)

byrad, *ppl.adj.* resolved 10.22. (OE.
bi- + *rǣdan.*)

bis, bys, *sb.* fine linen 3.17, 5.38.
(OF. *bysse.*)

byseche, *1 sg.pres.* beseech, implore
(constr. w. *of* or two accusatives)
16.15, 23.16 ; *1 sg.pa.t.* **bysohte**
23.16, **besohte** 16.15. (OE. *bi-,
be-* + *sēcan.*)

bysechynge, *sb.* intercession 27.10.
(From prec.)

bistad, *pp.* placed 9.9, settled,
arranged 10.19. (OE. *bi-* + ON.
staddr, pp. of *steðja.*)

byswyken, *pp.* betrayed 12.22.
(OE. *bi-, beswīcan.*)

byswngen, *pp.* scourged 20.28.
(OE. *bi-, beswingan.*)

byt. See BIDDE.

bytaht, *pp.* allotted, assigned 10.32.
(OE. *bi-, betǣcan.*)

bityde, *v.* to befall 24.11. (OE.
bi- + *tīdan.*)

bittre, *adj.* bitter 22.46 ; *comp.*
bittrore 29.12. (OE. *bit(t)er.*)

bituene, bytuene, *prep. and adv.*
between 4.1, 7.26, 22.27. (OE.
bi-, betwēonum.)

blake, *adj.* black 4.14. (OE. *blæc.*)

blame, *sb.* blame, fault 21.46. (OF.
bla(s)me.)

blede, *v.* to bleed 29.39. (OE. *blēdan.*)

ble(o), *sb.* face 3.17, complexion 7.7,
22.24, light, radiance 11.16, noble
person 28.11. (OE. *blēo.*)

blessed, yblessed, *pp.* blessed 3.35,
20.61. (OE. *bletsian.*)

blykyeþ, *3 sg.pres.* gleams, shines
14.25. (OE. **blician,* cf. *blīcan.*)

blynne, *v.* to cease 21.24, 24.17.
(OE. *blinnan.*)

blysfol, *adj.* blessed 14.19. (From
next.)

blis(se), blys(se), *sb.* joy, happiness
3.19, 11.3, 15.1, 16.23 ; *gen.sg.*
blisse 2.5. (OE. *bliss.*)

bliþe, blyþe, *adj.* happy, cheerful
2.53 ; *adv.* happily, cheerfully 9.14,
20.4. (OE. *blīþe.*)

blyue, *adv.* quickly 23.48. (OE.
bi + *līfe.*)

blo, *adj.* livid, leaden-coloured 22.24.
(ON. *blár.*)

blod(e), *sb.* blood 6.31, 15.32.
(OE. *blōd.*)

blody, *adj.* bloody 18.15, 20.20.
(OE. *blōdig.*)

blosme, *sb.* flower 3.17 ; *pl.* blos-
men, blosmes 11.2, 12.4. (OE.
blōs(t)ma.)

blowe, *v.* to blow 14.1, to be sounded
2.74 ; *2 sg.imper.* blou 14.4. (OE.
blāwan.)

bo, *adj. and cj.* both 2.36, 15.30.
(OE. *bā.*)

boc, bok, *sb.* book 6.4, 10.3. (OE.
bōc.)

bocle, *sb.* buckle 7.67. (OF. *bucle.*)

bodi, body, *sb.* body 13.87, 20.28.
(OE. *bodig.*)

boht(e), bok. See BEYE, BOC.

bolde, *adj.* brave 2.52 ; *as sb.pl.*
powerful ones 7.6, 13.19. (OE.
báld.) See BALDORE.

bon, *sb.* bone 7.40, 9.1 ; *blod ant bon,*
flesh and blood 7.5, 14.10. (OE.
bān.)

bonde, *sb.* bonds 5.12. (ON. *band.*)

bone, *sb.*¹ prayer 3.35, 13.1. (ON.
bón.)

bone, *sb.*² *pl.* slayers 2.25. (OE.
bana.)

bonnyng, *sb.* summons 2.74. (From
OE. *bannan.*)

bor, *sb.* boar 3.44. (OE. *bār.*)

bord, *sb.* table 14.72. (OE. *bord.*)

borewe, *v.* to obtain 30.32. (OE.
borgian.)

borewen, burewen, *v.* to save
2.37, 73. (OE. *beorgan.*)

bost, *sb.* pomp, vainglory 26.36.
(Unknown.)

bote, sb. remedy 5.9, 13.26 ; *whet bote,* what is the use 24.28. (OE. *bōt.*)

bote, cj. except 17.9, 22.38, but 13.76. (OE. *būtan.*)

bot-forke, sb. forked stick 30.2. (ME. *bat* + OE. *forca.*)

boþe, adj. and adv. both 6.47, 8.41. (ON. *báðar.*)

boun, adj. ready 29.48. (ON. *búinn.*)

bounte, sb. excellence, worth 4.27. (OF. *bonte.*)

bountyng, sb. bunting 9.52. (Unknown.)

bour(e), sb. bower 3.1, house, dwelling 7.6. (OE. *būr.*)

bous, sb. strong drink 30.29. (Cf. Dutch *buise,* drinking-vessel.)

boute, prep. without 8.15, 48. (OE. *būtan.*) See BOTE, cj.

bowe(n), v. to humble oneself, yield 13.71, 29.25, reflex. to bend 14.72 ; 3 sg.pa.t. **beh** 14.72. (OE. *būgan.*)

bowes, sb.pl. boughs 12.4. (OE. *bōg.*)

brag, adj. spirited, lively 2.52. (Obscure.)

bred, sb. bread 15.59. (OE. *brēad.*)

brede, sb. roast meat 3.47. (OE.Ang. *brēde.*)

bredes, 3 sg.pres. spreads, extends 7.33 ; pp. **ybrad** 9.11. (OE. *brǣdan.*)

bredeþ, 3 pl.pres. grow 12.4. (OE. *brēdan.*)

bref, adj. little 10.56. (OF. *bref.*)

breʒe, sb. eye-brow 7.18. (OE.Ang. *brēg.*) See BROWE(N).

breke, v. to break 9.47 ; pp. **broken** 6.4. (OE. *brecan.*)

breme, adj. excellent 6.40, 14.17 ; adv. clearly, loudly 11.27. (OE. *brēme.*)

brere, sb.pl. briars 30.23. (OE.Ang. *brēr.*)

brest, sb. breast 7.74. (OE. *brēost.*)

brid, bryd, sb bird 9.53, girl, maiden 14.17 ; pl. **briddes** 6.40. (OE. *brid.*)

briht, bryht(e), adj. bright, fair 3.1, 7.7, 22.22 ; comp. **bryhtore** 15.14 ; superl. **brihtest** 3.17. (OE. *beorht, bryht.*)

bring(e), brynge, v. to bring, take 4.7, 9.21, 28.43 ; 3 sg.pa.t. **brohte** 10.5 ; pp. **broht** 3.19, **ybroht** 9.14. (OE. *bringan.*)

brod, adj. broad 10.27. (OE. *brād.*)

broht(e). See BRING(E).

broken. See BREKE.

broþer, sb. brother 21.50. (OE. *brōþor.*)

broþerli, adj. brotherly, affectionate 2.25. (OE. *brōþorlic.*)

broune, adj. brown 4.14, 6.39. (OE. *brūn.*)

browe(n), browes, sb.pl. eye-brows 4.14, 6.39, 9.26. (OE. *brū.*) See BREʒE.

bruches, sb.pl. transgressions 6.4. (OE. *bryce.*)

brudes, sb.pl. women 6.39. (OE. *brȳd.*)

budel, sb. herald, messenger 2.5. (OE. *bydel.*)

burde, sb. maiden 3.1, 5.36. (See NED.)

burewen. See BOREWEN.

burst, sb. damage, injury 2.36. (OE. *byrst.*)

burþen, sb. load, bundle 30.2, 23. (OE. *byrþen.*)

caynard, sb. idler, lazy fellow 30.20. (OF. *cagnard.*)

cayser, sb. emperor 3.7, 6.43. (MDu. *keiser,* ON. *keisari.*)

calle, v. to cry out 31.20, call, name 13.16 ; ta calle, worthy to be called 13.82. (OE. *ceallian,* ON. *kalla.*)

cam, can. See COME, v., CON, v.[1]

canel, sb. cinnamon 3.39. (OF. *canele.*)

care, kare, sb. grief, sorrow 16.24, 20.43. (OE. *caru.*)

care, 1 sg.pres. grieve 14.79. (OE. *carian.*)

careful, adj. sorrowful 13.89. (OE. *carful.*)

carf, 3 sg.pa.t. carved 3.47 ; pp. **coruen** 7.65. (OE. *ceorfan.*)

carke, 1 sg.pres. grieve, sorrow 14.79. (ONF. *carkier,* cf. OF. *chargier.*)

caste(n), v. to remove 24.7 ; pp. **cast** 6.52, **ycast** 13.89 ; awey caste, to remove, get rid of 24.7, casten from, to protect from 8.11, on caste, to wear 8.13. (ON. *kasta.*)

celydoyne, *sb.* celandine 3.18. (OF. *celidoine*.)

charbocle, *sb.* red precious stone 3.10. (OF. *charbucle*.)

chaunge, *v.* to exchange 9.29. (OF. *changer*.)

chees. See CHEOSEN.

cheke, *sb.* cheek 7.34. (OE. *cēace*.)

chele, *sb.* cold 30.5. (OE.Ang. *cele*.)

cheosen, *v.* to choose 18.33, recognize 3.10, choose a course, turn 29.44 ; *1 sg.pa.t.* **ches** 3.10, **chees** 29.44 ; *pp.* **ycore** 2.67. (OE. *cēosan*.) See CHOSEN.

chep, *sb.* bargaining 9.34. (OE. *cēap*.)

chere, *sb.* face, expression 3.10, 4.15. (OF. *chere*.)

cherl, *sb.* man 30.34. (OE. *ceorl*.)

ches. See CHEOSEN.

chete, *sb.* hall, room 6.28. (OE. *cete, cyte*, cottage, chamber.)

chyde, *v.* to wrangle, contend 24.9. (OE. *cīdan*.)

childe, *sb.* child 18.29, 20.39, *pl.* **children** 20.38. (OE. *cild*.)

chyn, *sb.* chin 3.10, 7.34. (OE. *cinn*.)

chosen, *ppl.adj.* excellent, beautiful 7.34. (OE. *cēosan*.) See CHEOSEN.

claht, *pp.* grasped, seized 8.36. (OE. **clǣcean*.)

clay, *sb.* clay 22.17. (OE. *clǣg*.)

clannesse, *sb.* purity 14.49. (OE. *clǣnness*.)

clene, *adj.* pure 20.45. (OE. *clǣne*.)

clepe, *v.* to cry, call 31.20, to name 27.38 ; *1 sg.pres.* **clepie** 16.8. (OE. *cleopian*.)

cler, *adj.* clear, bright 26.17. (OF. *cler*.)

clerc, clerk, *sb.* priest, scholar 6.43, 24.9. (OE. *clerc*.)

cleþe, *v.* to provide with clothes 8.12. (OE. *clǣþan*, ON. *klæða*.)

cleuyen, *v.* to cling, remain faithful 8.36. (OE. *cleofian*.)

clyngeþ, *3 pl.pres.* become dispirited 22.17. (OE. *clingan*, ' to shrivel up '.)

cloht, cloþe, *sb.* clothes 8.37, 13.44 ; *pl.* **cloþes** 8.13. (OE. *clāþ*.)

cloude, *sb.* earth, ground 11.31. (OE. *clūd*.)

cluppe, *v.* to embrace 8.38. (OE. *clyppan*.)

cofre, *sb.* box, chest 3.39. (OF. *cofre*.)

coynte, *adj.* pretty 3.15. (OF. *cointe*.)

colde, *adj.* cold 22.23, unpleasant, severe 6.52 ; *adv.* severely 2.54. (OE. *cáld*.)

columbine, *sb.* the plant columbine 3.15. (OF. *colombine*.)

come, *v.* to come 15.56 ; *2 sg.pa.t.* **come** 29.35 ; *3 sg.* **cam** 27.26 ; *3 pl.* **come** 10.26 ; *pp.* **come** 6.50. (OE. *cuman*.)

come, *sb.* coming, arrival 7.46. (OE. *cyme*, infl. by prec.)

comely, comeliche, *adj.* beautiful 9.27, seemly, important 6.65, 13.81; *as sb.* comely person 8.37. (OE. *cȳmlīc*, infl. by ME. *becomen*.)

comeliche, *adv.* suitably, well 8.12. (OE. *cȳmlīce*, infl. as prec.)

comyn, *sb.* cummin 3.38. (OF. *comin*.)

compagnie, *sb.* company 21.40. (OF. *compagnie*.)

con, *v.¹* know, know how to, can ; *1, 3 sg.pres.* **con** 8.41, 30.36, **can** 26.12 ; *2 sg.* **cost** 24.17 ; *1 pl.* **conne** 18.37. (OE. *cann*.)

con, *v.²* (used w. infin. as equiv. of simple pa.t.) ; *3 sg.pa.t.* **con** 6.60 ; *3 pl.* **conne** 31.28. (OE. *(on)-gann*, pret. confused with prec.) See GYNNEÞ.

coral, *sb.* red coral 3.7, 14.47. (OF. *coral*.)

coruen. See CARF.

cos, *sb.* kiss 25.12. (OE. *coss*.)

cost. See CON, *v.¹*.

counseileþ, *3 sg.pres.* advises 27.21. (OF. *conseiller*.)

court, *sb.* large house, palace 3.39, 47. (OF. *court*.)

coueytise, *sb.* Avarice (personified) 13.58. (OF. *coveitise*.)

craft, *sb.* cunning, skill 6.66, 7.65 ; *pl.* **craftes**, power 2.68. (OE. *cræft*.)

crie, *1 sg.pres.* cry, beg 26.10. (OF. *crier*.)

cristal, *sb.* crystal 14.32, 49. (OF. *cristal*.)

Cristesmasse, *sb.* Christmas 27.32. (OE. *Cristes mæsse.*)

crokede, *adj.* deformed, bowed 30.20. (From ON. *krókr.*)

crone, croune, *sb.* top, head 3.38, tonsure 6.43. (OF. *corone.*)

crop, *sb.* top, head (of a plant) 29.45. (OE. *cropp.*)

croune. See CRONE.

crouþ, *sb.* a stringed instrument 14.45. (W. *crwth.*)

cud. See KYÞE.

cunde. See KYNDE, KUNDE.

curtel, *sb.* woman's gown 9.54. (OE. *cyrtel.*)

cusse, *v.* to kiss 8.38, 9.27 ; *we custe vs,* we kissed each other 24.23. (OE. *cyssan.*)

day, dai, *sb.* day 10.35, 21.3, by day 31.7 ; *gen.sg.* **dayes** 30.16, **daies** 24.2 ; *neuer a day,* never 24.27 ; *boþe day ant oþer,* continually 21.47. (OE. *dæg.*)

dayeseȝes, *sb.pl.* daisies 11.4. (OE. *dæges ēage.*)

dale, *sb.* valley 3.25. (OE. *dæl.*)

dame, *sb.* dame, housewife 30.30. (OF. *dame.*)

dar, *3 sg.pres.* dare 9.43 ; *1 sg.pa.t.* **dorste** 32.10 ; *3 sg.* **durste** 6.26. (OE. *dearr.*)

dare, *v.* to lie motionless, lurk 13.86. (OE. **darian.*)

darf, *3 sg.pres.* need 2.29 ; *3 sg.pa.t.* **durfte** 6.16. (OE. *þearf.*)

dawen, *v.* to dawn 27.44. (OE. *dagian.*)

deawes, *sb.pl.* dew 11.28 ; *gen.sg.* **dewes** 32.33. (OE. *dēaw.*)

ded, *adj.* dead 15.58, absolute, complete 2.34. (OE. *dēad.*) See DEÞ(E).

dede, *sb.* deed 2.8 ; *pl.* **dede** 3.45, **dedes** 23.21, **deden** 29.10, **dedis,** 3.36. (OE. *dǣd.*)

dedestounde, *sb.* hour of death 20.10. (OE. *dēaþes stúnd.*)

def, *adj.* deaf 30.34. (OE. *dēaf.*)

deȝe, deye, *v.* to die 20.13, 18. (ON. *deyja* or OE. **dēgan.*)

Del, *sb.* Devil 30.34. (OE. *dēofol.*)

dele, *v.* to deal 14.78. (OE. *dǣlan.*)

deme, *v.* to speak 11.30, judge, condemn 7.29 ; *domes forte deme,* to tell their tales, 11.30. (OE. *dēman.*)

dempned, *pp.* judged 29.37. (OF. *dampner, condemner.*)

deope, *adj.* deep 18.35, 31.30. (OE. *dēop.*)

deore, duere, dere, *adj.* dear, beloved 26.6, costly 3.6 ; *adv.* at a high price 16.18. (OE. *dēore.*)

deores, *sb.pl.* animals 11.29 ; *gen.pl.* **dueres** 12.2. (OE. *dēor.*)

deorly, *adv.* affectionately 30.29. (OE. *dēorlīce.*)

dere. See DEORE, *adj.*

dereworþe, *adj.* excellent, beloved 14.39. (OE. *dēorwurþe.*)

dereworþliche, *adv.* affectionately 14.78. (From prec.)

derne, *adj.* secret, hidden 2.8, discreet 3.25 ; *adv.* secretly 2.9. (OE.Ang. *derne.*)

deþ. See DO(N).

deþ(e), ded, *sb.* death 7.24, 9.21, 20.21 ; *gen.sg.* **deþes** 23.25. (OE. *dēaþ.*)

dewes. See DEAWES.

diamaund, *sb.* diamond 3.6. (OF. *diamant.*)

diht, (y)dyht, *pp.* set, placed 3.6, condemned 5.25, prepared 13.103. (OE. *dihtan.*)

do. See DO(N).

dohty, *adj.* doughty, mighty 3.45. (OE. *dohtig.*)

domes, *sb.pl.* opinions 11.30. (OE. *dōm.*)

domesday, domesdai, *sb.* Day of Judgment 2.6, 21.26. (OE. *dōmes dæg.*)

do(n), *v.* to do 3.36, put, place 23.51, give 31.26, finish 13.104 (as auxiliary) 25.4, (intensifying a foll. infin.) 2.19, (intensifying a foll. imper.) 9.38, (replacing another verb to avoid repetition) 6.22 ; *3 sg.pres.* **doþ** 20.21, **deþ** 2.19 ; *3 sg.pa.t.* **dude** 23.51 ; *pp.* **do** 18.47, **don** 29.20, **done** 2.9, **ydon** 10.11 ; *do wey,* cease 20.7, 24.9. (OE. *dōn.*)

donkeþ, *3 pl.pres.* moisten 11.28. (Cf. ON. *dǫkk,* pool.)

doren, *sb.pl.* doors 30.14. (OE. *duru, dor.*)

dorste, doþ. See DAR, DO(N).

doun, *adv.* down 21.7, 8. (Aphetic form of ADOUN.)

doune, *sb.* down, hill 22.11. OE. *dūn.*

douse, *adj.* sweet, pleasant 30.30. (OF. *dous.*)

doute, *sb.* fear 10.53, 30.4. (OF. *doute.*)

drakes, *sb.pl.* drakes 11.19. (See NED.)

drawe, *v.* to go 29.26, add 1.2; *3 sg.pa.t.* droh 1.2. (OE. *dragan.*)

dreccheþ, 3 *sg.pres.* afflicts 32.21. (OE. *dreccan.*)

drede, *v.* to fear 2.6. (OE. *(on)-drǣdan.*)

dredful, *adj.* terrible 13.86. (From prec.)

dreem, *sb.* melody 15.16. (OE. *drēam.*)

dre(y)ʒe, *v.* to endure, suffer 7.24, 18.25, 22.46. (OE. *drēogan.*)

dreynt, *pp.* drowned 30.31. (OE. *drencan.*)

dreri, drery, *adj.* terrible 2.6, 24.5. (OE. *drēorig.*)

drynke, *v.* to drink 30.29. (OE. *drincan.*) See DRONKE.

droh. See DRAWE.

dronke, *ppl.adj.* drunk 30.31. (OE. *(ge)-druncen,* pp. of *drincan.*) See DRYNKE.

dropes, *sb.pl.* drops 32.33. (OE. *dropa.*)

droupne, *1 sg.pres.* pine away, languish 14.80. (Cf. ON. *drúpa.*)

dude. See DO(N).

duel, *sb.* grief 7.24, grievous thing 19.20. (OF. *duel.*)

duelle, *v.* to remain 17.15, 20.49. (OE. *dwellan.*)

duere(s). See DEORE, *adj.,* DEORES, *sb.pl.*

durste. See DAR.

dutten, *v.* to close, stop up 30.14. (OE. *dyttan.*)

eche, *v.* to increase 25.11. (OE.Ang. *ēcan.*)

eʒe(n), eye, eyʒen, *sb.pl.* eyes 4.14, 7.16, 9.24, 14.18, 18.12. (OE. *ēage.*)

eyþer, *adj.* each 7.18, 34. (OE. *ǣgþer.*)

eke, *adv.* also 7.35, 15.7. (OE. *ēac.*)

elde, *sb.* old age 13.46, 47. (OE.Ang. *eldo.*)

elde, *adj. as sb.pl.* old people 27.22. (OE. *éald.*)

elles, *adv.* otherwise 7.81. (OE. *elles.*)

elne, *sb.* ell 7.52. (OE. *eln.*)

emeraude, *sb.* emerald 3.7. (OF. *emeraude.*)

encenʒ, *sb.* incense 27.41. (OF. *encenz.*)

ende, *sb.* end, finish 2.54, 14.69. (OE. *ende.*)

ende. See HENDE.

ender, *adj.* recent ; *þis ender day,* a day or two ago 16.10, 27.1 (ON. *endr,* adv.)

endyng, *sb.* death 15.56, 16.2. (OE. *endung.*)

engyn, *sb.* device, trick 15.28. (OF. *engin.*)

eny, eni, any, *adj.* any 2.32, 23.37, 31.1 ; *pron.* anyone 4.33. (OE. *ænig.*)

eode, 3 *pl.pa.t.* went 18.46. (OE. *ēodon,* pret.pl.) See GO(N).

Epyphany, *sb.* Epiphany 27.38. (OF. *epiphanie.*)

er, *adv.*[1] always 29.21. (OE. *ǣfre.*)

er, her, *adv.*[2] formerly 6.36, 13.27, early 10.29 ; *prep.* before 5.26, 9.22 ; *cj.* before 10.33 ; *er þen,* before 13.93, 14.76. (OE. *ǣr.*) See ERST.

erbes, *sb.pl.* flowers 23.33. (OF. *(h)erbe.*)

ernde, *sb.* errand 30.22. (OE. *ǣrende.*)

ernde, *2 sg.imper.* obtain by intercession 18.30. (OE. *ǣrendian.*)

erndyng, *sb.* intercession 15.43. (OE. *ǣrendung.*)

erne, *v.* to run, flow 15.39, 20.23, 21.7, bleed 31.3 ; *3 sg.pa.t.* **orn** 15.39, **ron** 31.3, **ran** 21.7. (OE.Ang. *eornan,* pa.t. *ran, orn.*)

erst, *adj.superl. as sb.* first 10.12 ; *adv.* first 6.60. (OE. *ǣrest.*)

erþe, *sb.* earth 1.1, 29.2. (OE. *eorþe.*)

erþene, *adj.* earthen 1.3. (From prec.)

est, *sb.* east 14.44. (OE. *ēast,* adv.)

Estermorewe, *sb.* Easter morning 27.44. (OE. *ēastor-* + *morgen.*)

euel, *sb.* evil, hardship 13.46, 47. (OE. *yfel.*)

euen(e), *adv.* quite, just 10.13, regularly, evenly 7.41. (OE. *efen, efne.*)

euer, *adv.* always 13.76, ever 7.5, 30.12 ; *euer ant oo,* always 32.7. (OE. *æfre.*) See ER, *adv.*[1]

euermore, *adv.* always 4.36, 21.20. (OE. *æfre* + *māre,* cf. *æfre mā.*)

eueruch, *adj.* each, every 3.26. (OE. *æfre* + *ylc,* cf. *æfre ælc.*)

euesong, *sb.* time of evensong 10.13. (OE. *æfensang.*)

face, *sb.* face 14.15, 21.4. (OF. *face.*)

fader, *sb.* father 2.64, 26.33. (OE. *fæder.*)

fayn, *adj.* glad 13.7. (OE. *fægen.*)

fair, fayr. See FEYR(E).

falewen, *v.* to fade, wither 23.57. (OE. *fealewian.*)

falle(n), *v.* to fall 13.102, abate 20.55 ; *3 sg.pres.subj.* **valle** 30.4 ; *1, 3 sg.pa.t.* **fel** 20.55, 32.16, **feol** 18.38 ; *pp.* **falle** 29.32, **yfalle** 13.39 ; *fallen adoun,* die 4.20. (OE. *feallan.*)

fallen, *3 pl.pres.subj.* overthrow, defeat 2.72. (OE.Ang. *fællan,* causative of prec.)

fals(e), *adj.* false, faithless 12.15, untrue 32.19, wrong 29.45, evil 26.18 ; *superl.* **falsist** 2.31. (OE. *fals,* OF. *fals.*)

falslek, *sb.* falsehood 6.34. (Prec. + ON. *-leikr.*)

falsly, *adj.* false, deceptive 6.31. (OE. *fals* + *-lic.*)

fare, *sb.* behaviour 12.27, way, course, destiny 20.44. (OE. *faru.*)

fare, *v.* to walk 8.1, go away 13.32, act 10.42. (OE. *faran.*)

fast(e), *adv.* firmly 24.5, closely 13.29, quickly 31.30. (OE. *fæste.*)

faste, *adj.* firm, secure 8.19. (OE. *fæst.*)

faucoun, *sb.* falcon 3.25. (OF. *faucon.*)

faunyng, *sb.* caressing, fondling 2.30. (From OE. *fagnian.*)

fax, *sb.* hair 7.12. (OE. *feax.*)

fede, *v.* to feed, rear 30.18, please 3.46, give pleasure 7.45 ; *pp.* **fed** 23.22, **yfed** 30.18. (OE. *fēdan.*)

feh, *sb.* wealth 13.32. (OE. *feoh.*)

feye, *adj.* doomed, dying 4.20. (OE. *fæge.*)

feynes, *sb.* phoenix 7.75. (OE. *fēnix.*)

feynt, *adj.* feeble, cowardly 2.62. (OF. *feint.*)

feyr(e), feir, fayr, fair, *adj.* beautiful, pleasant, noble 8.2, 12.26, 34, 14.8, 25.18, 26.21 ; *comp.* **ffeyrore** 3.46. (OE. *fæger.*)

feyre, *adv.* generously, kindly 13.44. (OE. *fægre.*)

fel. See FALLE(N).

feld(e), *sb.* field 30.13, ground 6.32. (OE. *feld.*)

felde. See FOLDE, *v.*

fele, feole, *adj.* many 2.47 ; *pron.* many 12.15 ; *adv.* very 24.30, much 6.32. (OE. *feolu, fela.*)

fele, *1 sg.pres.* to feel, experience 20.10. (OE. *fēlan.*)

felle, *sb.* skin 26.30. (OE. *fell.*)

fen, *sb.* mud 14.76. (OE. *fenn.*)

fend, feond, *sb.* Devil 2.62, 26.19 ; *gen.sg.* **fendes** 15.28. (OE. *fēond.*)

fenge, *sb.* booty, prize 8.2, 12.18. (OE. *feng.*)

fenyl, *sb.* fennel 11.18. (OE. *fenol.*)

feol, feole, feond. See FALLE(N), FELE, *adj.,* FEND.

fer, *adj.* far 24.31. (OE. *feorr.*)

fer. See FOR.

fere, *sb.* wife 2.40, husband 9.30 ; *pl.* **fere** 13.59. (OE. *(ge)-fēra,* Nhb. *fēra.*)

fere, *v.*[1] to meet, encounter 8.2, 12.18. (OE. *fēran.*)

fere, *v.*[2] to frighten 2.42, to fear 26.19. (OE. *fǣran.*)

ferly, *adv.* wonderfully 11.10. (OE. *fǣrlīce.*)

fet(e). See FOT(E).

fiele, *sb.* stringed musical instrument 14.45. (OF. *viele,* OE. *fiþele.*)

fif, fyue, *adj.* five 2.31, 23.46, 27.24. (OE. *fīf.*)

fifte, *adj.* fifth 27.49. (OE. *fīfta.*)

fyfty, *adj.* fifty 24.23. (OE. *fīftig.*)

fifti-folde, *adj.* excessive 6.34. (Cf. OE. *fīftigfeald.*)

fyht, *sb.* fight, battle 2.62. (OE. *feoht.*)

fyke, *v.* to flatter, deceive 12.26. (Cf. OE. *(be)-fīcian.*)

fykel, *adj.* treacherous, unreliable 6.31, 26.18. (OE. *ficol.*)

fyldor, *sb.* gold thread 7.12. (OF. *fil d'or.*)

fyle, *adj.* vile, unpleasant 13.60. (OF. *vil,* perhaps infl. by OE. *fūl.*)

fille, *sb.* chervil, wild thyme 11.18. (OE. *fille.*)

fylle, *v.* to make perfect 29.18. (OE. *fyllan.*)

fyn, *adj.* beautiful 14.26, skilled 23.35. (OF. *fin.*)

fynde, *v.* to find, discover 12.6, 29.23, provide 13.44 ; *3 sg.pres.* **fynt** 2.62 ; *1, 3 sg.pa.t.* **founde** 8.2, 28.17 ; *3 pl.* **founden** 13.44 ; *pp.* **founde** 7.4, **founden** 2.39. (OE. *findan.*)

fyne, *sb.* end 16.27. (OF. *fin.*)

fynger, *sb.* finger 13.21 ; *pl.* **fyngres** 7.55, 14.29. (OE. *finger.*)

fynt, fyue. See FYNDE, FIF.

fleish, fleysh, *sb.* flesh 23.22, 26.30 ; *gen.sg.* **fleishshes** 2.30. (OE. *flǣsc.*)

fleme, *sb.* fugitive 11.36 ; *pl.* **fleme** 2.64. (OE.Ang. *flēma.*)

flod, *sb.* stream (of blood) 15.39. (OE. *flōd.*)

floe, *v.* to flee 2.29. (OE. *flēon.*)

flour, flur, *sb.* flower 2.63, 26.2 ; *pl.* **floures,** complexion 23.57. (OF. *flour.*)

fode, *sb.* food 15.29, creature 28.31, 32.30. (OE. *fōda.*)

fol. See FUL, FOL(E).

folde, felde, *v.* to clasp 7.55, 13.40, to bind 7.12. (OE.Ang. *fáldan,* WS. *fealdan.*)

folde, *sb.* earth 2.42. (OE. *folde.*)

fol(e), *sb.* fool 24.9, *adj.* foolish 20.48, 21.14. (OF. *fol.*)

foleweþ, *3 pl.pres.* follow 13.48. (OE. *folgian.*)

folie, *sb.* folly, misdeeds 16.12, 21.37, 23.13. (OF. *folie.*)

folk, *sb.* people 10.57, 22.12 ; *gen.pl.* **folkes** 2.64. (OE. *folc.*)

fon, *v.* to receive 10.10. (OE. *fōn.*)

fonde, *v.* to have experience 32.4, use 10.21 ; *pp.* **fonde** 32.4. (OE. *fandian.*)

fo(o), vo, *sb.* enemy 2.40, 29.4, 27, Devil 10.53 ; *pl.* **fon** 2.47. (OE. *fāh,* adj., *gefā,* sb.)

for, fer, *prep.* for 28.5, concerning 6.13, on account of 21.14, because of 21.1, for the sake of 31.21, for fear of 12.21, in exchange for 9.33, in order to 20.14, to 15.22 ; *cj.* for, since, because 5.5, 20.44, 24.33. (OE. *for.*) See FORTE.

forbeode, *3 pl.pres.* to prevent, avert 2.26. (OE. *forbēodan.*)

fordred, *pp.* frightened 23.21. (OE. *for- + drǣdan.*)

fore, *prep.* on account of 25.18. (OE. *fore.*)

foreode, *3 sg.pa.t.* withstood 2.30. (OE. *forēode,* pa.t.) See FORGON.

foreward, *sb.* agreement, promise 10.10, 42. (OE. *foreweard.*)

forgon, *v.* to go without, forgo 11.35, 23.7. (OE. *forgān.*) See FOREODE.

forhaht, *pp.* despised 8.34. (OE. *for- + *hǣccean.*)

forhed, *sb.* forehead 7.22. (OE. *forhēafod.*)

forke, *sb.* forked stick 30.19. (OE. *forca.*)

forleose, *1 sg.pres.subj.* lose 26.15, 24. (OE. *forlēosan.*) See FORLORE.

forlete, *v.* to leave 21.19, lose 10.60, 22.6. (OE. *forlǣtan.*)

forlore, *ppl.adj.* condemned to destruction, ruined 27.30, 28.35. (OE. *forloren,* pp.) See FORLEOSE.

forsake, *v.* to refuse 4.19 ; *3 sg.pa.t.* **forsoc** 10.6. (OE. *forsacan.*)

forsoht, *pp.* sought out 3.20. (OE. *for- + sēcan.*)

forst, *sb.* frost 30.5. (OE. *forst.*)

forte, *prep.* to, in order to 4.18, 7.2, 8.13, (with passive infin.) 2.35, 14.29. (OE. *for + tō.*)

forþ, *adv.* forward 30.26, 37. (OE. *forþ.*)

forþfare, *v.* to die 13.90. (OE. *forþfaran.*)

forþren, *v.* to benefit 29.18. (OE. *fyrþr(i)an.*)

forwake, *pp.* worn out with lying awake 4.31. (OE. *for-* + *wacen,* pp. of *wæcnan.*)

forwleynt, *pp.* made proud 2.60. (OE. *forwlencean.*)

fot(e), *sb.* foot 14.76, 18.13 ; *pl.* fet 14.33, fete 6.32 ; *falle to fote, falle to fet(e),* humble oneself before 6.32, 33, 13.102. (OE. *fōt.*)

foul, *sb.* bird 4.3 ; *gen.pl.* **foules** 18.2. (OE. *fugol.*)

foule, *adj.* foul, unpleasant 10.53. (OE. *fūl.*)

founde(n), *v.* to go 20.52, to put to the test 12.27. (OE. *fúndian.*)

founde(n). See FYNDE.

fourme, *sb.* shape, form 15.59. (OF. *fourme.*)

fous, *adj.* eager 13.81. (OE. *fūs.*)

fre(ly). See FREO, FREOLY, *adj.*

fremede, *adj.* unfamiliar 8.1. (OE. *fremede.*)

frend, *sb.* friend 9.46, 22.37 ; *gen.sg.* **frendes** 31.24. (OE. *frēond.*)

freo, fre, *adj.* noble 18.17, 27.7, generous 9.31, beautiful 9.37, 14.8, free 21.49, forward, immodest 32.3. (OE. *frēo.*)

freoly, freoli, frely, *adj.* beautiful, excellent 7.45, 12.7, (used ironically) 10.57. (OE. *frēolic.*)

freoly, *adv.* nobly 12.40. (OE. *frēolīce.*)

frere, *sb.* friar 30.19. (OF. *frere.*)

freseþ, *3 sg.pres.* freezes 30.5. (OE. *frēosan.*) See FRORE.

friht, fryht, *sb.* wood 3.25, 8.1. (OE. *fyrhþ.*)

fro, *sb.* comfort, relief 29.51. (ON. *fró.*)

from, *prep.* from 3.27, free from 6.27. (OE. *from.*)

frore, *ppl.adj.* withered 2.63. (OE. *(ge)-froren,* pp.) See FRESEÞ.

frount, *sb.* forehead 14.15. (OF. *front.*)

ful, fol, vol, *adj.* full 20.61, 26.1, 29.7 ; *adv.* quite, very 2.54, 10.8, 26.9. (OE. *full.*)

fulle-flet, *sb.* useless encumbrance 13.16. (Stem of OE. *fyllan* + *flett,* floor.)

fur, *sb.* fire 9.41. (OE. *fȳr.*)

furmest, *adj. superl. as sb.* first 10.11. (OE. *fyrmest.*)

furst, *adj. and adv. superl.* first 2.15, 48, 10.26, 27.25. (OE. *fyrst.*)

furþe, *adj.* fourth 27.43. (OE. *fēorþa.*)

gabbe, *sb.* Falsehood (personified) 13.57 ; *pl.* **gabbes,** lies 13.73. (ON. *gabb,* OF. *gab.*)

gay, *adj.* gay, pleasant 14.40. (OF. *gai.*)

gale, *sb.* gaiety, merriment 3.26. (OF. *gale.*)

galle, *sb.* gall 29.12. (OE.Ang. *galla.*)

gaste, *v.* to lay waste, ruin 24.8. (OF. *gaster.*)

gates, *sb.pl.* way ; *go my gates,* go away 8.7. (ON. *gata.*)

geynest, *adj. superl.* kindest 4.37. (ON. *gegn.*)

gelde, *ppl.adj.* destitute 2.41, barren, profitless 13.43. (ON. *geldr.*)

gent, *adj.* noble, high-born 23.45. (OF. *gent.*)

gentil, *adj.* fair, gracious 3.3, 14.41. (OF. *gentil.*)

gere, *sb.* clothes 8.4. (ON. *gervi.*)

gernet, *sb.* garnet 3.4. (OF. *grenat.*)

gest, *sb.* guest 5.40. (OE.Ang. *gest,* ON. *gestr.*)

geþ. See GO(N).

gyle, *sb.* guile, treachery 8.48, Deceit (personified) 13.57. (OF. *guile.*)

gylofre, *sb.* clove, gillyflower 3.40. (OF. *gilofre.*)

gyngyure, *sb.* ginger 3.40. (OF. *gimgibre,* OE. *gingifer.*)

gynneþ, *3 sg.pres.* begin 13.37, (pa.t. constr. w. infin. without ' to ' as equiv. of simple pa.t.) did 27.44 ; *3 sg.pa.t.* **gon** 27.44 ; *3 pl.* **gonne** 10.60. (OE. *(on)-ginnan.*) See CON, *v.*²

Gyw, *sb.* Jew 29.29. (OF. *giu.*)

glad(e), *adj.* glad 20.2, beautiful 3.16. (OE. *glæd.*)

gladieþ, *3 sg.pres.* makes glad 15.52, 18.7. (OE. *gladian.*)

gladly, *adj.* beautiful 8.4. (OE. *glædlic.*)

gladshipe, *sb.* joy, gladness 9.5. (OE. *glædscipe.*)

glas, *sb.* glass 6.22. (OE. *glæs.*)

gle, *sb.* entertainment, sport 15.52; *pl.* **gleowes** 32.26. (OE. *glēo, glēow-.*)

gleem, *sb.* light 15.13. (OE. *glǣm.*)

glemede, *3 sg.pa.t.* gleamed, shone 8.3. (From prec.)

glemon, *sb.* minstrel 13.53. (OE. *glēomann.*)

gleowes. See GLE.

glewe, *v.* to make music or songs 9.6. (OE. *glēowian.*)

glyde, *v.* to glide; *by glyde*, overtake 23.6. (OE. *glīdan.*)

glystnede, *3 sg.pa.t.* shone 8.3. (OE. *glisnian.*)

glotonie, *sb.* Gluttony (personified) 13.53. (OF. *glotonie.*)

god, *sb.* God 8.44, 13.50; *gen.sg.* godes 9.49. (OE. *god.*)

god(e), **good**, *adj.* good 14.18, 30.29, 31.11; *as sb.* good, good thing 29.13, 23; *pl.* **godes** 13.42. (OE. *gōd.*)

godly, *adv.* beautifully 9.2. (OE. *gōd + -līce.*)

godnesse, *sb.* goodness 14.47. (OE. *gōdnes.*)

gold(e), *sb.* gold 3.4, 7.61, 8.3. (OE. *gold.*)

gome, *sb.*¹ person (man or woman) 3.26, 8.4, 48. (OE. *guma.*)

gome, *sb.*² pleasure, satisfaction 15.52; *pl.* **gomenes** 2.41, 32.26. (OE. *gomen.*)

go(n), *v.* to go 8.7, go away 2.51, pass 21.25, pass away 17.9, be 2.41, 9.49, walk 13.36, pierce 22.50; *3 sg.pres.* **geþ** 17.5, **goþ** 17.9, **gos** 21.27; *pp.* **go** 30.21, **gon** 9.5; *mony day go*, many days ago 30.21; *geþ al to noht*, passes away 17.5. (OE. *gān.*) See EODE.

gon(ne), **good**. See GYNNEÞ, GOD(E).

gore, *sb.* petticoat, gown; *vnder gore*, among women, alive 3.16, 4.37. (OE. *gāra.*)

gost, *sb.* spirit 26.33, Devil 31.6. (OE. *gāst.*)

goute, *sb.* gout 13.24. (OF. *goute.*)

grace, *sb.* grace, favour 21.2, 26.26. (OF. *grace.*)

graciouse, *adj.* gracious 14.40. (OF. *gracious.*)

gray, **grey**, *adj.* gray 7.16, 30.19. (OE. *grǣg.*)

gras, *sb.* grass, field 25.2. (OE. *græs.*)

graunte, *2 sg.imper.* grant 15.58, 16.17. (AN. *graunter.*)

graueþ, *3 sg.pres.* buries 17.11. (OE. *grafan.*)

grede, *1 sg.pres.* cry out 5.4. (OE. *grǣdan.*)

greete, **grey**. See GRETE, *v.*, GRAY.

grein, *sb.* grain, seed 17.11, bead of rosary 9.2. (OF. *grein.*)

gremede, *3 sg.pa.t.subj.impers.* angered; *lest hire gremede*, lest she became angry 8.7. (OE. *gremian.*)

grene, *adj.* green 3.37, 24.3, unripe 17.11, freshly made 31.28. (OE. *grēne.*)

gret(e), *adj.* large 7.16, great 16.11, sad 32.7. (OE. *grēat.*)

grete, **greete**, *v.* to greet 15.19, 32.31. (OE. *grētan.*)

greting, *sb.* greeting, welcome 9.49. (OE. *grēting.*)

greue, *sb.* thicket 3.37. (OE. *grǣfa.*)

grylle, *adj.* terrible, severe 24.34. (Cf. Du. *gril*, adj., OE. *grillan*, to provoke.)

grimly, *adj.* grim-looking, terrible 31.6. (OE. *grimlic.*)

grimly, *adv.* grievously 31.28. (OE. *grimlīce.*)

grys, *sb.* grey fur 3.16. (OF. *gris.*)

gro, *sb.* grey fur 3.16. (ON. *grár.*)

gromyl, *sb.* gromwell 3.37. (OF. *gromil.*)

grone, *sb.* seed 3.37. (Lat. *grānum.*)

grone, *1 sg.pres.* groan, sigh 5.4. (OE. *grānian.*)

grounde, *sb.* ground 13.97, 18.38. (OE. *grúnd.*)

gult, *sb.* guilt, transgression 20.9. (OE. *gylt.*)

gurdel, *sb.* girdle 7.61. (OE. *gyrdel.*)

ȝe, *pron. 2 pl.* you 7.60, 8.17 ; *acc.dat.* **ou** 7.79, 9.39 ; *gen.* **or** 8.17, 10.39 ; *ouself,* yourselves 7.60. (OE. *ȝē, ēow, ēower.*)

ȝeep, *adj.* prudent, wise 9.36. (OE. *ȝēap.*)

ȝef, ȝyf, *cj.* if 19.20, 21.36. (OE. *gyf, gef.*)

ȝef. See ȝEUE.

ȝeȝe, *I sg.pres.subj.* cry out 30.35. (OE. **ȝēgan,* cf. ON. *geyja.*)

ȝeynchar, *sb.* return, means of escape 12.35. (OE. *gegn-, ȝēancyr.*)

ȝer(e), *sb.* year 25.5 ; *to ȝere,* this year 12.21. (OE.Ang. *ȝēr.*)

ȝerne, *v.* to desire, long for 4.34, 10.58, entreat 8.27 ; *3 pl.pa.t.* **ȝyrnden** 10.58 ; *pp.* **yȝyrned** 4.34, **yȝyrnd** 13.95. (OE.Ang. *geornan,* WS. *girnan.*)

ȝerne, *adv.* eagerly, readily 16.21. (OE. *georne.*)

ȝet, *adv.* still 10.14, 58. (OE. *ȝīet.*)

ȝeue, *v.* to give 9.33 ; *2 sg.imper.* **ȝef** 16.2, **ȝeue** 15.7 ; *3 sg.pa.t.* **ȝef** 10.55. (OE. *giefan.*)

ȝyf. See ȝEF.

ȝynge, *adj. as sb.pl.* young people 27.22. (OE. *ging.*)

ȝyrnden. See ȝERNE, *v.*

ȝokkyn, *sb.* desire, craving 13.95. (From OE. **geoccian,* cf. *gicc(e)an.*)

ȝore, *adv.* for long 2.65, 4.34. (OE. *ȝēara.*)

habbe, haue(n), ha, *v.* to have, possess 7.56, 15.46, 27.47, (as auxiliary) 30.9 ; *2 sg.pres.* **haues** 32.13 ; *3 sg.* **haueþ** 6.1, **haþ** 6.52, **haht** 13.100 ; *I sg.pa.t.* **hade** 8.36 ; *3 sg.* **had** 32.4, **heuede** 1.4 ; *pp.* **yhad** 2.3. (OE. *habban.*) See NAÞ, NAUY.

hayward, haywart, *sb.* hayward 30.24, 27. (OE. *hege + wēard.*)

half, *adv.* half 9.37. (OE. *h(e)alf.*)

halle, *sb.* hall 6.70, 13.36. (OE. *h(e)all.*)

halt, *adj.* haughty 13.84. (OF. *halt.*)

haltinde, *pres.part.* limping 13.36. (OE. *h(e)altian.*)

hap, *sb.* destiny, good or bad fortune 2.19, 4.9, 21, 6.68, 69 ; *pl.* **happes** 2.44. (ON. *happ.*)

harde, *adj.* hard 20.6, unpleasant 21.34, 28.23. (OE. *heard.*)

harde, *adv.* violently 2.19. (OE. *hearde.*)

harmes, *sb.pl.* troubles, sorrows 2.43, 8.10. (OE. *hearm.*)

hate, *I sg.pres.* hate 24.1. (OE. *hatian.*)

hattren, *sb.pl.* clothes 30.6. (OE. *hæteru,* pl.)

haþ. See HABBE.

haþel, *sb.* splendid fellow 6.69 ; *pl.* **haþeles,** men, heroes 32.24. (OE. *æþelu,* infl. by *hæleþ.*) See AÞEL.

hauk, *sb.* hawk 6.28. (OE. *hafoc.*)

haue(n). See HABBE.

hawe, *sb.* awe 29.28. (ON. *agi.*)

he, *pron. 3 sg.masc.* he 10.2 ; *acc.dat.* **him** 32.14 ; *gen.* **his** 2.19, **hise** 18.39, **is** 2.28. (OE. *hē, him, his.*)

he, heo, hue, *pron. 3 sg.fem.* she 3.21, 9.49, 14.30 ; *acc.dat.* **hire** 3.10 ; *gen.* **hire** 5.40, **here** 9.30, **hyr** 23.46 ; *hire one,* alone 22.19. (OE. *hēo, hiere.*)

he, heo, hue, *pron. 3 pl.* they 6.27, 10.25, 58 ; *acc.dat.* **hem** 12.9 ; *gen.* **huere** 10.10, **hure** 12.16. (OE. *hēo, heora, him.*)

hed. See HEUED.

hede, *v.* to pay attention to 2.4, care for 3.48, 29.33. (OE. *hēdan.*)

hede, *sb.* heed, attention 7.42, 31.27. (From prec.)

hedy, *adj. as sb.* Blessed One (God or Christ) 2.3. (OE. *ēadig.*)

hegge, *sb.* hedge 30.8. (OE. *hecg.*)

heȝe, *sb.pl.* eyes 9.25. (OE. *ēage.*) See EȜE(N).

heh, heȝe, heyȝe, *adj.* high, noble 7.21, 13.30, 22.34 ; *superl.* **hest,** most important 2.4, (*as sb.pl.*) **heste** 13.20, 14.38 ; *an heh, vpon heh,* aloud 10.16, 30.35, aloft, above 7.25, 30.17. (OE.Ang. *hēh.*)

heyse, *sb.* ease 30.28. (OF. *aise.*)

helde, *sb.* grace, favour, kindness 8.9. (LOE. *hélde.*)

helde, *v.* to sink 13.37. (OE.Ang. *heldan.*)

hele, *sb.* cure 14.74. (OE. *hǣlu.*)

helle, *sb.* hell 2.46 ; *gen.* **helle** 27.29. (OE. *hell.*)

help, *sb.* help 15.48, 26.22. (OE. *help.*)

helpen, *v.* to help 10.9. (OE. *helpan.*)

hem. See HE, *pron. 3 pl.*

heme, *adj.* fitting, suitable 6.42. (OE. **hǣme,* cf. *hām.*)

hende, ende, *adj.* gracious, courteous 3.48, 6.28, beautiful 8.9 ; *as sb.* fair one 14.57, 32.12, *pl.* courteous persons 7.42 ; *comp.* **hendore** 3.48. (OE. *(ge)-hende.*)

hendelec, *sb.* courtesy 6.70. (Prec. + ON. *-leikr.*)

hendy, hendi, *adj.* gracious, fair 4.9, 39 ; *as sb.* fair one 3.49. (From HENDE ; cf. OE. *(list)-hendig.*)

hengest. See HONGE.

henyng, *sb.* insult 8.8. (From OE. *hēan,* adj.)

henne, *adv.* hence 2.20, 26.27. (OE. *heonane.*)

hente(n), *v.* to obtain, receive 6.42, take 2.76 ; *pp.* **hent** 6.69, **yhent** 4.9. (OE. *hentan.*)

heo, heouene. See HE, HEUENE.

heowe, *sb.* family 8.33, servant 32.24. (OE. *hīwan,* pl.)

her, *sb.,* hair 4.13. (OE. *hǣr.*)

her. See ER, *adv.*², HER(E), *adv.*

herde. See HERE, *v.*

her(e), *adv.* here 2.45, 7.84. (OE. *hēr.*)

here. See HE, *pron. 3 sg.fem.*

here, *v.* to hear 15.16 ; *3 sg.pa.t.* **herde** 28.41. (OE.Ang. *hēran.*) See YHERE.

heryen, *v.* to praise 13.100 ; *pp.* **heried** 23.46, **yheryed** 14.38. (OE. *herian.*)

herkne, *2 sg.imper.* listen 4.38. (OE. *hercnian.*)

hert(e), huerte, *sb.* heart 6.18, 13.37, 23.21 ; *gen.* **herte** 20.11, 31.35, **huerte** 14.74. (OE. *heorte.*)

hest(e). See HEH.

heste, *sb.* command 13.75. (OE. *hǣs.*)

hete, *v.* to call, cry 2.19, mention 6.67, promise 5.29 ; *pp.* **hyht** 5.29. (OE. *hātan.*)

heþe, *v.* to mock, scorn 8.10. (ON. *hǽða.*)

heu, hewe, *sb.* hue, colour 4.13, 12.37. (OE. *hēow.*)

heued, hed, *sb.* head 7.13, 18.15. (OE. *hēafod.*)

heuede. See HABBE.

heued-hount, *sb.* chief huntsman 13.85. (OE. *hēafod* + *hunta.*)

heuene, heouene, *sb.* heaven 4.10, 7.21 ; *gen.* **heuene** 2.14, **heouene** 6.18. (OE. *heofone.*)

heueriche, *sb.gen.sg.* the kingdom of heaven 26.24. (OE. *heofonrīce.*)

hewe, *pp.* hewn 30.23. (OE. *hēawan.*)

hewe, hi. See HEU, ICH.

hyd, *pp.* hidden, covered 9.55. (OE. *hȳdan.*)

hyde, *sb.* concealment 6.18. (From prec.)

hider, *adv.* hither 10.46. (OE. *hider.*)

hye, *v.* to hasten 30.35. (OE. *hīgian.*)

hyht, *sb.* height 3.5. (OE. *hīehþo.*)

hyht. See HETE.

hihte, *sb.* exertion, effort 30.11. (OE. *hīgþ.*)

him, hyr. See HE.

hyrd, *sb.* household, family 6.54, 8.34. (OE. *hīred.*)

hirdes, *sb.pl.* shepherds 27.36. (OE. *hirde.*)

hire. See HE, *pron. 3 sg.fem.*

hirmon, *sb.* servant, retainer 13.84. (OE. *hīredmann.*)

his(e). See HE, *pron. 3 sg.masc.*

hit, it, *pron. 3 sg.neut.* it 3.29, 4.10. (OE. *hit.*)

hoc, *sb.* hook 10.9. (OE. *hōc.*)

hode, *sb.* hood 14.19. (OE. *hōd.*)

holde, *v.* to keep, hold 3.5, 7.56, 29.6, hold, observe 10.39, to be faithful 8.23, consider, think 2.46, 29.29, respect 13.20, imprison 24.20, embrace 14.27 ; *1 sg.pa.t.* **huld** 13.75 ; *pp.* **holde** 29.6, **yholde** 13.20, **yholden** 3.5 ; *wiþ hem ich holde,* I defend them 6.54. (OE. *háldan.*)

holy, *adj.* holy 26.33, 27.59. (OE. *hālig.*)

hom, *sb.* home 2.45, 24.31. (OE. *hām.*)

hond(e), *sb.* hand 2.76, 5.14; *pl.* honde 20.5, honden 20.29; *haue on honde,* bring about, cause 5.14. (OE. *hand.*)

hondywerk, *sb.* work of the hands 16.20. (OE. *handgeweorc.*)

honge, *v.* to hang 22.45, to drip 22.25; *2 sg.pres.* hengest 22.25. (See NED. s.v. *Hang,* v.)

hongren, *v.* to be hungry, starve 8.33. (OE. *hyngran,* v., *hungor,* sb.)

honoures, *3 sg.pres.* honours, esteems 23.59. (OF. *honourer.*)

hope, *sb.* hope 23.27, 30.14. (OE. *hopa.*)

hope, *1 sg.pres.* hope 15.46. (OE. *hopian.*)

hord, *sb.* hoard, treasure 14.73. (OE. *hord.*)

hore, *1 sg.pres.* become grey 8.23, 13.93. (OE. *hārian.*)

hors(e), *sb.* horse 13.30, 24.12. (OE. *hors.*)

hosede, *ppl.adj.* wearing hose 30.37. (From OE. *hosa.*)

hot, *adj.* hot 9.41. (OE. *hāt.*)

hou, *adv.* how 10.54. (OE. *hū.*)

hous, *sb.* house 13.84, 23.19. (OE. *hūs.*)

howeþ, *3 sg.pres.* thinks 2.20. (OE. *hogian.*)

hue(m), huere. See HE.

huerte, huld. See HERT(E), HOLDE.

hupe, *2 sg.imper.* go 30.37; *1 sg.pres.subj.* huppe 8.42. (OE. **hyppan,* cf. *hoppian.*)

hure, *sb.* wage, pay 10.25. (OE. *hȳr.*)

hure. See HE, *pron. 3 pl.*

i, y. See ICH, IN.

ybend, yblessed, yboht, ybore(n), ybounde, ybrad, ybroht. See BEND, BLESSED, BEYE, BERE, BYNDE, BREDES, BRING(E).

ycayred, *pp.* separated 8.35. (ON. *keyra.*)

ycast. See CASTE(N).

ich, ych, i, y, hi, *pron. 1 sg.* I 2.14, 12.11, 13.64, 19.20, 24.30 ; *acc.dat.* me 13.29 ; *gen.* my 3.21, myn 23.21, myne 14.74 ; *myn one,* alone 9.9. (OE. *ic, mē, mīn.*) See MYSELF.

ichabbe, ichaue, *1 sg.pres.* I have 4.9, 5.28. (OE. *ic hæbbe, ic hafu.*)

icham, ycham, *1 sg.pres.* I am 4.8, 9.46. (OE.Ang. *ic am.*)

icherde, *1 sg.pa.t.* I heard 2.5. (OE.Ang. *ic hērde.*)

ichot, *1 sg.pres.* I know 3.1. (OE. *ic wāt.*)

ichulle, *1 sg.pres.* I will 4.19, 10.48. (OE. *ic wylle.*)

ycore. See CHEOSEN.

ycrouned, *pp.* crowned 28.45. (OF. *coroner.*)

ycud. See KYÞE.

ydel, *adj.* idle, without occupation 10.14. (OE. *īdel.*)

ydyht, ydon, yfalle, yfed. See DIHT, DO(N), FALLE(N), FEDE.

ygreyþed, *pp.* afflicted 13.24. (ON. *greiða.*)

y3yrn(e)d, yhad, yhent. See 3ERNE, HABBE, HENTE(N).

yhere, *v.* hear 8.9, 12.47. (OE.Ang. *gehēran.*)

yheryed, yholde(n), ylent, ylet, yleued. See HERYEN, HOLDE, LENT, LETE(N), LEUE(N).

ilke, *adj.* same, identical 20.58, 21.15. (OE. *ilca.*)

ille, ylle, *adv.* ill, badly 11.24, 17.10. (ON. *illr.*)

ylong, *adj.* due 25.21 ; *ylong on him,* caused by him 18.10. (OE. *gelang.*)

yloren. See LEOSE.

ymake, *adj.* becoming, comely 4.16. (OE. *gemæc.*)

ymaked. See MAKE(N).

in, y(n), *prep.* in 9.40, 30.18, into 2.55, 23.26, among 6.41, during 10.4, 14.39, at 24.23, 29.55, with 9.49, with respect to 3.23, 26, by reason of 9.20, clothed in 12.46, (following a rel. pron.) 7.70, 9.11. (OE. *in.*)

ynoh, *adj. and adv.* enough 1.4, 4.13. (OE. *genōh.*)

into, *prep.* into 23.26. (OE. *intō.*)

inwiþ, *prep.* within 13.38. (OE. *in + wiþ*.)

yplyht. See PLYHT.

is, ys, *3 sg.pres.* is 2.4, 7.7. (OE. *is*.) See NIS.

is, ysette. See HE, SETE, *v.*

ysped, *pp.* succeeded 30.22. (OE. *spēdan*.)

ystongen. See STONG.

yswongen, *pp.* flogged 21.44. (OE. *swingan*.)

it. See HIT.

ytake, ytold(e), ywarpe. See TAKE(N), TELLE, WARP.

ywedded, *pp.* married 8.39. (OE. *weddian*.)

ywynne, *v.* to obtain, win 32.14. (OE. *gewinnan*.) See WYNNE.

ywys, ywis(se), *adj.* true, certain 17.7 ; *adv.* indeed, certainly 6.12, 9.25 ; *sb.* certainty 15.3 ; *myd iwisse*, certainly 18.8. (OE. *gewis*, adj.)

ywraht, ywroht. See WURCHEÞ.

iay, *sb.* jay, magpie 14.41. (OF. *jay*.)

iaspe, *sb.* jasper 3.3. (OF. *jaspe*.)

ioie, ioye, *sb.* joy, pleasure 16.27, 17.5, source of joy 23.46. (OF. *joie*.)

ioyeþ, *3 sg.pres.* rejoices 3.50. (OF. *joir*.)

iolyf, *adj.* lively, gay 14.41. (OF. *jolif*.)

iolyfte, *sb.* gaiety, light-heartedness 23.54. (OF. *jolivete*.)

kare. See CARE, *sb.*

keyes, *sb.pl.* keys 13.58. (OE. *cǣg*.)

kelde, *sb.* cold, unpleasant situation 8.11. (OE.Ang. *celdu*, cf. WS. *cyldu*.)

kend, *pp.* taught 2.68. (OE. *cennan*.)

kene, *adj.* sharp 25.3, 30.6. (OE. *cēne*.)

kenede, *3 sg.pa.t.* gave birth to 8.5. (OE. *cennan*.)

kepe, *v.* to wait for 7.46, desire 8.8 ; *3 sg.pa.t.* **kepte** 8.8. (OE. *cēpan*.)

kynde, cunde, *sb.* characteristic quality 3.15, nature 20.35. (OE. *(ge)-cynde*.) See KUNDE.

king, kyng(e), *sb.* king 6.43, 15.1, 27.12. (OE. *cyning, cing*.)

kynne. See KUN(NE).

kyþe, *v.* to reveal 24.21 ; *pp.* **cud, ycud**, famous 3.38, 6.66. (OE. *cȳþan*.)

kneowe. See KNOWE.

knyht, *sb.* knight 3.7, 6.65. (OE. *cniht*.)

knowe, *v.* to know 2.68, reveal 7.65 ; *1 sg.pa.t.* **kneowe** 8.35 ; *pp.* **knowe** 29.30. (OE. *cnāwan*.)

kunde, cunde, *adj.* kind, good 29.26, well-born, well-bred 6.65. (OE. *(ge)-cynde*.) See KYNDE.

kun(ne), kynne, *sb.* family, kin 24.18, 35, descendants 20.15. (OE. *cynn*.)

lad. See LED(E).

ladde, *sb.* youth, fellow 30.36. (See NED.)

lahte, *3 sg.pa.t.* caught, seized 12.45. (OE. *lǣccan*.)

lay, *sb.*[3] lyric, song 5.27. (OF. *lai*.)

lay, *sb.*[2] religion, law 2.18, 29.5. (OF. *lei*.)

lay, *sb.*[3] light 27.33. (OE.Ang. *lēg*.)

layn. See LEȜE, *v.*[2]

largesse, *sb.* generosity 14.51. (OF. *largesse*.)

lasse, *adv.comp.* less 13.22. (OE. *lǣssa*, adj., *lǣs*, adv.)

last, *adv.superl.* last 10.26. (OE. *latost*.)

last(e), *sb.* vice, blame 6.27, 8.15, sin 13.8. (ON. *lǫstr*.)

laste, leste, *v.* to last, continue 5.30, 13.51. (OE. *lǣstan*.)

lasteles, *adj.* faultless 14.35. (ON. *lǫstr* + OE. *-lēas*, cf. ON. *lastalauss*.)

lat. See LETE(N).

late, *adv.* late 12.35, 29.4. (OE. *late*.)

latere, *adj.comp.* more recent 10.44. (OE. *lætra*.)

latymer, *sb.* interpreter 13.61. (OF. *latimier*.)

launterne, *sb.* lantern 14.24. (OF. *lanterne*.)

lauendere, *sb.* laundress 13.56. (OF. *lavandiere*.)

laueroc, lauercok, *sb.* lark 3.24, 9.52. (OE. *lāferce.*)

lawe, *sb.* law 30.36. (OE. *lagu,* from ON.)

lealte, *sb.* loyalty, faithfulness 14.54. (From OF. *leal,* adj.)

leche, *sb.* physician 23.35, 25.12. (OE. *lǣce.*)

lecherie, *sb.* Lechery (personified) 13.56. (OF. *lecherie.*)

led, *sb.* lead 21.13. (OE. *lēad.*)

led(e), *v.* to lead, conduct 14.69, 21.29, afflict 5.1 ; *3 sg.pa.t.* **lad** 10.23 ; *pp.* **lad** 5.1, **led** 23.24. (OE. *lǣdan.*)

ledy, ledies. See LEUEDI.

lees. See LES, *adj.*

lef, *sb.* leaf (of a tree) 12.3 ; *pl.* **leues** 11.14. (OE. *lēaf.*)

lef. See LEOF, LEUE, LEUE(N).

lefly, leofly, luefly, leflich(e), *adj.* beautiful 6.6, 7.31, 78, 14.14, pleasant 14.55. (OE. *lēoflic.*)

lefly, leuely, *adv.* well, pleasantly 9.19, favourably 12.47. (OE. *lēoflīce.*)

legges, *sb.pl.* legs 14.33. (ON. *leggr.*)

leȝe, *v.*[1] to tell lies 24.28. (OE. *lēogan.*)

leȝe, *v.*[2] to lie down 7.83 ; *1 sg.pres.* **lygge** 23.25 ; *3 sg.pres.* **liþ** 21.22, **liht** 12.44 ; *pp.* **layn** 13.8. (OE. *licgan.*)

leyde, *3 sg.pa.t.* laid, placed 1.3. (OE. *lecgan.*)

lele, *adj.* true 7.38. (OF. *leel.*) See LEALTE.

lemeþ. See LEOMEÞ.

lemmon, lemman, *sb.* lover (man or woman) 22.47, 24.16. (OE. *lēof + mann.*)

lene, *v.* to give, grant 13.67. (OE. *lǣnan.*)

leneþ, *3 sg.pres.* leans 30.19. (OE. *hleonian.*)

lengore, *adj. and adv.comp.* longer 7.44, 8.26, 13.51. (OE. *lengra,* adj., *leng,* adv.)

lent, ylent, *pp.* taken away 4.11, come 4.25. (OE. *lendan.*)

lenten, *sb.* spring 11.1. (OE. *lencten.*)

leode, *sb.* man, person 2.32 ; *pl.* **leode** 10.44. (OE. *lēod.*)

leof, luef, lef, *adj.* beloved 7.50, 8.48; as *sb.* dear one 24.16, 25.11; *comp.* **leuere** 7.46; *me wes luef,* I enjoyed 29.14 (OE. *lēof.*)

leofly. See LEFLY, *adj.*

leomeþ, lemeþ, lumes, *3 sg.pres.* shines, gleams 3.3, 7.8, 14.23. (From OE. *lēoma,* sb., cf. O.E. *gelēomod,* pp. and ON. *ljóma,* v.)

leor, lere, lure, *sb.* complexion 12.46, 14.23, cheek 7.78. (OE. *hlēor.*)

leose, *v.* to lose 31.8 ; *pp.* **yloren** 30.16. (OE. *(for)-lēosan.*)

lere. See LEOR.

leren, *v.* to teach 20.37. (OE. *lǣran.*)

les, *2 sg.imper.* loose, set free 5.12. (OE.Ang. *lēsan.*)

les, lees, *adj.* untrue, lying, false 13.73, 29.46. (OE. *lēas.*)

lest(e), *cj.* lest 2.43, 30.4. (OE. *þy lǣs þe.*)

leste, *adj.superl.* least 13.23. (OE. *lǣst.*)

leste. See LASTE, *v.*

lete(n), *v.* to allow 15.51, command 28.43, abandon 13.68, refrain 24.19 ; *2 sg.imper.* let 15.51, **lat** 20.18, lete 24.16 ; *3 sg.pa.t.* lette 28.43 ; *pp.* let 6.5, ylet 13.90. (OE. *lǣtan.*)

leue, *v.* to abandon 21.37, allow, cause, grant (foll. by infin.) 13.68 ; *2 sg.imper.* lef 13.68, leue 27.53. (OE. *lǣfan.*)

leue. See LEUE(N).

leuedi, leuedy, ledy, *sb.* lady 4.24, 5.11, 12.44 ; *pl.* **leuedis** 6.5, **ledies** 12.8. (OE. *hlǣfdīge.*)

leuely. See LEFLY, *adv.*

leue(n), *v.* to believe (constr. w. *(vp)on* before things, no prep. before persons) 8.25, 21.36; *2 sg.imper.* lef 5.27 ; *pp.* **yleued** 13.23 ; *to leue,* to be considered 10.45. (OE.Ang. *lēfan.*)

leuere, leues. See LEOF, *adj.*, LEF, *sb.*

lyare, *sb.* Liar, Falsehood (personified) 13.61. (OE. *lēogere.*)

libbe. See LYUE(N).

lif, lyf, *sb.* life 5.30, woman, person 14.21 ; *acc.dat.sg.* **lyue** 18.46, 23.43; *gen.sg.* **lyues** 2.61 ; *gen.pl.* **lyues** 18.48. (OE. *līf.*)

lygge, liht. See LE3E, *v.*²

lyht, *2 sg.imper.* shine on, illumine 26.17. (OE. *līhtan*, v.¹.)

liht, lyht, *2 sg.imper. and pp.* alight, come down 15.27, be born 6.19. (OE. *līhtan*, v.².)

liht, lyht(e), *sb.* light 3.3, 7.8 ; *in lyhte,* openly 14.70. (OE. *lēoht.*)

lyht(e), *adj.* light, bright 10.33, 11.14. (OE. *lēoht.*)

lyhtnesse, *sb.* brightness, light 27.34. (OE. *līhtnes.*)

lykeþ, likes, *3 sg.pres.* pleases 11.24, 29.20. (OE. *līcian.*)

likyng, *sb.* pleasure 2.18. (OE. *līcung.*)

lilie, *sb.* lily 11.17. (OE. *lilie.*)

lylie-flour, *sb.* lily 23.1. (OE. *lilie* + OF. *flour.*)

lylie-leor, *sb.* girl with lily-white cheeks 12.46. (OE. *lilie* + *hlēor.*)

lylie-, lilye-white, *adj.* white as a lily 3.12, as *sb.* 7.50. (OE. *lilie* + *hwīt.*)

lyn, *sb.* linen 12.46. (OE. *līn.*)

lynde, *sb.* lime tree, tree 12.3. (OE. *lind.*)

lippes, *sb.pl.* lips 7.38. (OE. *lippa.*)

lisse, *sb.* joy, delight 15.2, remission 20.59. (OE. *liss.*)

lystne. See LUSTNEÞ.

lit, lyt, *sb.* hue 6.6, 7.78. (ON. *litr.*)

liþ. See LE3E, *v.*²

lyþe, *2 sg.imper.* listen 27.5. (ON. *hlýða.*)

lyue(n), *v.* to live 4.19, 24.10 ; *1 sg.pres.* **libbe** 4.5. (OE. *libban.*)

lyues. See LYF.

lockes, lokkes, *sb.pl.* locks of hair 7.31, 14.14. (OE. *locc.*)

loft, *sb.* air ; *vpo loft,* alive 32.30. (OE. *loft.*)

loh, *3 sg.pa.t.* laughed 4.15, 7.17. (OE. *hl(i)ehhan,* pa.t. *hlōh.*)

loht. See LOÞ(E).

loke, *2 sg.imper.* take care, make sure 25.15. (OE. *lōcian.*)

lokkes. See LOCKES.

lome(n), lomes, *sb.pl.* tools, implements 10.15, 21, 29. (OE. *(ge)-lōma.*)

lond(e), *sb.* land, country 7.50, 12.19 ; *pl.* **londe** 5.11. (OE. *land.*)

long, *adj.* attributable to, on account of 5.10. (OE. *(ge)-lang.*) See YLONG.

long(e), *adj.* long 7.31, tall 7.10. (OE. *lang.*)

longe, *adv.* long, a long time 4.19. (OE. *lange.*)

longen, *v.* to long 18.23. (OE. *langian.*)

longyng, longing(e), *sb.* longing, yearning desire 4.25, 5.1, 15.55. (OE. *langung.*)

lord, louerd, *sb.* God 13.1, 29.26. (OE. *hlāford.*)

lore, *sb.* teaching, advice 8.25, 24.29. (OE. *lār.*)

losed, *pp.* brought low, ruined 29.3. (OE. *losian.*)

lossom, lossum, lussom, lussum, *adj.* lovely, pleasant 3.12, 7.27, 11.17 ; *as sb.* fair one 7.17 ; *comp.* **lussomore** 14.12. (OE. *lufsum.*)

lostlase, *adj.* listless, lazy 30.36. (ON. *losti* + OE. *-lēas.*)

lot, *sb.* behaviour 6.27, evil deed 13.68. (ON. *lát.*)

loþ(e), loht, *adj.* hateful 8.25, 13.41, 23.19. (OE. *lāþ.*)

loude, *adv.* loudly 21.22. (OE. *hlūde.*)

loue, *sb.* love 4.11, 10.60, 18.29, object of love 18.5, 32.14, Love (personified) 14.55, 63. (OE. *lufu.*)

loue, louye, louien, *v.* to love 5.19, 15.8, 18.24. (OE. *lufian.*)

loue-bene, *sb.* lover's petition 25.13. (OE. *lufu* + *bēn.*)

loue-bonde, *sb.pl.* bonds of love 15.24. (OE. *lufu* + ON. *band.*)

loueliche, *adj.* beautiful 14.32. (OE. *luflic.*)

loue-longinge, *sb.* lover's yearning 4.5. (OE. *lufu* + *langung.*)

louerd. See LORD.

loues, *sb.gen.sg.* of praise 29.27. (OE. *lof.*)

louye, louien. See LOUE, *v.*

lowe, *adv.* low 2.70, 29.32. (ON. *lágr*.)

lud, *sb.* language 4.4. (OE. *lýden*.)

luef, luefly, lumes, lure. See LEOF, LEFLY, *adj.*, LEOMEÞ, LEOR.

lussom(ore), lussum. See LOSSOM.

lust, *sb.* pleasure 23.7. (OE. *lust*.)

lustneþ, *1 pl.pres.* listen to, hear 2.61; *2 sg.imper.* **lystne** 9.38. (OE.Nhb. *lysna*.)

lut, *adj.* few 12.19. (OE. *lýt*.)

lutel, lvtel, *adj.* little 4.3, 21.30; *adv.* little 13.22, 31.1. (OE. *lýtel*.)

luþer(e), luthere, *adj.* base, hateful 13.8, 52, 73. (OE. *lýþre*.)

mad, *adj.* mad 5.2. (OE. *(ge)-mæded*.)

maht. See MAY, *v.*, MYHT, *sb.*

May, *sb.*[1] May 12.1. (OF. *mai*.)

may, mai, mey, *sb.*[2] maiden 3.9, 4.29, 8.44. (OE. *mæg*.)

may, mei, *v. 1 sg.pres.* can, may 13.28, must 7.23; *2 sg.* **maht** 24.20, **myht** 20.3, **mihtes** 25.11; *3 sg.* **may** 24.11, **mey** 8.45; *1 pl.* **mawen** 27.43; *2 pl.* **mowen** 7.60; *3 pl.* **mowe** 7.42; *1 pl.pres.subj.* **mowe** 16.26; *1, 3 sg.pa.t.* **myhte** 7.82, 29.25; (combining w. pers. pron.) **myhti** 8.40. (OE. *mæg*.)

maide(n), mayde(n), *sb.* maiden 5.3, 18.28, 20.48, 28.13; *pl.* **maidnes** 6.63. (OE. *mægden*.)

mayden-mon, *sb.* maiden, virgin 20.45. (OE. *mægdenmann*.)

maistry, maystry, *sb.* force 14.66; *for þe maystry,* in the highest degree, extremely 30.28. (OF. *maistrie, pour la maistrie*.)

make, *sb.* mate, lover 4.18, 33. (OE. *(ge)-maca*.)

make(n), *v.* to make 8.19, cause 24.24, cause to be 30.28; *1 sg.pres.* **makie** 22.42; *3 sg.pa.t.* **made** 6.14; *pp.* **mad** 2.1, **ymaked** 31.5. (OE. *macian*.)

man. See MON.

mandeþ, *3 sg.pres.* sends forth 11.16, 25. (OF. *mander*.)

marewe. See MOREWE.

margarite, *sb.* pearl 3.9. (OF. *margarite*.)

marreþ, *3 sg.pres.* injures 5.3. (OE. *merran*.)

mawe, *sb.* stomach 30.38. (OE. *maga*.)

mawen. See MAY, *v.*

me, *pron.* one 10.34, 12.17; *pl.* **men** 15.19. (Reduced from OE. *mann*.)

me. See ICH.

mede, *sb.*[1] reward 3.41, 10.36; *pl.* **mede** 2.2. (OE. *mēd*.)

mede, *sb.*[2] mead 23.32. (OE. *medo*.)

medycyn, medicine, *sb.* remedy 3.41, 23.30, 31. (OF. *medicine*.)

mey. See MAY, *sb.*[2] *and v.*

meyn, *sb.* strength 13.11. (OE. *mægen*.)

meind. See MENGEÞ.

meke. See MEOKE.

mele, *v.* to speak 7.37. (OE. *mælan*.)

men. See MON.

mene, *adj.* mean, undignified 6.44. (OE. *(ge)-mæne*.)

mene(n), *v.* to complain, lament 8.20, 23.14, 24.4. (OE. *mænan*.)

mengeþ, *3 sg.pres.* mingles 7.53; *pp.* **meind** 2.58. (OE. *mengan*.)

menske, *sb.* courtesy, honour 8.22. (ON. *mennska*.)

menske, *v.* to honour (' thee ' understood) 5.23. (From prec.)

menskful, *adj.* noble 14.7; *adv.* gracefully 14.31. (ON. *mennska* + OE. *-full*.)

meoke, meke, *adj.* meek, gentle 6.63, 28.15. (ON. *mjúkr*.)

merci(e), mercy, *sb.* mercy, compassion 3.41, 13.70, 32.18. (OF. *merci*.)

mere, *adj.* excellent, famous 3.9. (OE. *mære*.)

Mersh, *sb.* March 4.1. (OF. *marche*.)

mest(e), most, *adj. and adv. superl.* greatest 2.2, 13.66, 26.35. (OE. *mæst*, Nhb. *māst*.)

mete, *sb.* food, meat 13.44. (OE. *mete*.)

mete, *adj.* well-proportioned 7.73, *adv.* fitly 22.9. (OE. *mæte*.)

mete(n), *v.* to come across, find 13.65, 80; *1 sg.pa.t.* **mette** 7.44. (OE. *mētan*.)

methful, *adj.* moderate, gentle 6.51. (OE. *mæþfull*.)

mi. See ICH.

mid, myd, *prep.* by means of 8.45, 30.15, in exchange for 26.20, with, in 27.3. (OE. *mid.*)

midday, mydday, *sb.* noon, midday 10.7, 22.14. (OE. *middæg.*)

middel, myddel, *sb.* waist 4.16, 7.73. (OE. *middel.*)

middelerd, middelert, *sb.* earth 2.1, 13.2. (OE. *middan(g)eard,* altered by assoc. with prec.)

mye, *3 pl.pres.subj.* crumble, grate 30.39. (OF. *mier.*)

myht, miht, maht, *sb.* strength, power 3.8, 31, 7.19, mighty deed 29.1. (OE. *miht,* Ang. *mæht.*)

myht(e), mihtes. See MAY, *v.*

mihti, *adj.* powerful 6.51. (OE. *mihtig.*)

myhti, mykel. See MAY, *v.,* MUCHE.

milde, *adj.* gentle 18.21. (OE. *milde.*)

mildenesse, *sb.* gentleness 26.2. (OE. *milde + -ness.*)

mile, *sb.* mile 22.13. (OE. *mīl.*)

miles, *sb.pl.* animals 11.20. (W. *mil.*)

mylse, *sb.* mercy, forbearance 15.35, 26.29. (OE. *milts.*)

mynde, *adj.* mindful 20.34. (OE. *(ge)-mynde.*)

myn(e). See ICH.

mynge, *v.* to call to mind, mention 27.24. (OE. *myngian.*)

mynne. See MUNNE.

myrre, *sb.* myrrh 27.41. (OE. *myrre.*)

myself, miselue, *pron.* myself 18.11, 29.15. (OE. *(ic) mē self.*) See ICH.

misse, *v.* to lose 15.4, lose sight of 26.4, fail 27.58. (OE. *missan.*)

mythe, myþen, *v.* to conceal 2.59, 24.24. (OE. *mīþan.*)

mo, *comp.adj.* more 7.66, 10.52; *pron.* others 11.22, 28.47. (OE. *mā,* adv.)

mod(e), *sb.* mind 20.2, 24.5. (OE. *mōd.*)

moder, *sb.* mother 15.40, 18.28; *gen.sg.* **moder** 20.43. (OE. *mōdor.*)

mody, *adj.* as *sb.* high-spirited man 11.22. (OE. *mōdig.*)

molde, *sb.* earth 5.2, 6.29. (OE. *molde.*)

mon, man, *sb.* man 10.35, 21.27, lover 32.18, mankind 2.1; *gen.sg.* **monnes** 2.47; *pl.* **men** 25.14; *gen.pl.* **monne** 13.66. (OE. *mann.*) See ME, *pron.*

mondrake, *sb.* mandrake 3.31. (Lat. *mandragora,* infl. by DRAKE.)

mon(e), *sb.* moan, lament 2.17, 22.42. (OE. **mān,* cf. *mænan,* v.)

mone, *sb.* moon 3.31, 7.19. (OE. *mōna.*)

mone, *v.* to mention 25.20. (ON. *muna.*)

monge, *v.* to mingle 7.32, 14.16. (From OE. *gemang,* sb.)

moni, mony, *adj.* many 24.24, 25.6; *pl.* **monie** 14.16, **monye** 13.25. (OE. *manig.*)

monkyn, monkunne, *sb.* mankind 27.30, 31.35. (OE. *mancynn.*)

monkynde, monkunde, *sb.* mankind 20.8, 27. (OE. *mann + cynd,* cf. prec.)

more, *adj.comp.* greater 20.42, 27.47. (OE. *māra.*)

moren-mylk, *sb.* morning milk 7.77. (OE. *morgen+meolc.*) See MOREWE.

morewe, marewe, *sb.* morning 10.4, 20.56. (OE. *morgen, margen.*)

morewenyng, *sb.* morning 16.10, 23.11. (From prec.)

most. See MEST(E).

mot, *adj.* sorry 6.29. (OE. *mād.*)

mote, *3 sg.pres.* may, must 14.16; *3 sg.pa.t.subj.* moste 31.21; (coalescing with pers.pron.) **mosti,** if I could 7.1. (OE. *mōt,* pa.t. *mōste.*)

mouht. See MOUÞ.

mourne(n), *v.* to mourn, feel sorrow 4.36, 7.23; *pres.part.* mournynde 22.38. (OE. *múrnan.*)

mournyng, *sb.* grief, mourning 2.17, 16.11. (From prec.)

mous, *sb.* mouse 30.31. (OE. *mūs.*)

mouþ, mouth, mouht, *sb.* mouth 7.37, 9.27, 14.43. (OE. *mūþ.*)

mowe(n). See MAY, *v.*

muche, muchel(e), mykel, *adj.* great 7.19, 9.28, 24.15; *sb.* much 24.29; *adv.* very 2.17. (OE. *mycel.*)

muge, *sb.* nutmeg 3.31. (OF. *muge*.)

munne, mynne, *v.* to remember 8.20, 31.31, remind 13.3. (ON. *minna*, infl. by MYNGE.)

munnyng, *sb.* remembrance, memory 8.21. (From prec.)

munte, *2 sg.imper.* think 8.21. (OE. *myntan*.)

murgeþ, *3 sg.pres.* is pleasant 12.1; *3 pl.* gladden 11.20. (OE. *myrgan*.)

mury, *adj.* pleasing 7.37, 32.23; *superl.* murgest 6.64, 14.43. (OE. *myrige*.)

murþe, *sb.* joy, pleasure 2.58, 9.28. (OE. *myr(g)þ*.)

nadoun, 30.3. See NE, ADOUN.

nagulte, *3 sg.pa.t.* did not sin 31.12. (OE. *ne + agyltan*.)

naht, *adv.* not 20.35. (OE. *nāwiht*.) See NOHT, *pron.*, NOUT, *adv.*

naht. See NYHT.

nailed, nayled, *pp.* nailed 20.6, 21.43. (OE. *næglan*.)

nayl(l)es, *sb.pl.* nails 18.14, 22.31. (OE. *nægl*.)

nam, *3 sg.pres.* am not 10.45. (OE. *ne + am*.) See AM.

nam. See NOM.

namore, *sb.* nothing more 9.8, 13.70; *adv.* no more, no longer 2.59. (OE. *nā māre*.)

naþ, *3 sg.pres.* has not 10.38. (OE. *ne + hæfþ*.) See HABBE.

nauy, *1 sg.pres.* I have not 8.10. (OE. *ne + hafu + ic*.) See HABBE.

ne, *adv.* not 23.4; *ne . . . ne*, neither . . . nor 29.25. (OE. *ne*.)

nede, neode, *sb.* need, necessity 6.55, 20.46; *a nede*, of necessity 6.58. (OE. *nēod, nēd*.)

neʒyþ, *3 sg.pres.* approaches 21.26. (From OE. *nē(a)h*, adv.)

neh, *adv.* near 10.13, close together 7.26; *comp.* ner 25.7; *superl.* nest 15.48. (OE. *nē(a)h, nē(a)r, nē(a)hst*.)

nem(p)ne, *v.* to name 32.9, mention 7.79. (OE. *nemnan*.)

neode. See NEDE.

neose, *sb.* nose 7.28. (Cf. OE. *nosu*.)

ner. See NEH, NEUER.

nere, *3 sg. and pl.pa.t.subj.* were not 12.15, 17.7. (Cf. OE. *nǣron*, pa.t.pl.ind.) See WES.

nes, *3 sg.pa.t.* was not 8.4. (OE. *næs*.) See WES, NIS.

nest. See NEH.

neuer, ner, *adv.* never 6.56, 8.46. (OE. *nǣfre*.)

neuerʒete, *adv.* never 14.11. (OE. *nǣfre giet*.)

newe, *adj.* new 18.5; *adv.* anew 24.25; *an newe*, anew, again 8.31. (OE. *nēowe*.)

nyckenay, *1 sg.pres.* deny 6.55. (From OE. *ne ic* + ON. *nei*.)

nyʒe, *adj.* nine 8.32. (OE. *nigon*.)

niht, nyht, *sb.* night 5.40, 31.15; by night 31.17; *pl.* naht 8.32; *gen.sg. as adv.* nihtes, at night 4.22. (OE. *niht, næht*.)

nyhtegale, *sb.* nightingale 3.28, 25.1. (OE. *nihtegale*.)

nis, nes, *3 sg.pres.* is not 4.26, 9.5. (OE. *nis*.)

niþe, *sb.* Envy (personified) 13.59. (OE. *niþ*.)

no, *adj.* no 13.21. (OE. *nān*.) See NON(E).

noht, *pron.* nothing 12.31. (OE. *noht*.) See NAHT, *adv.*, NOUT, *adv.*

nolde. See NUL(LE).

nom, nam, *3 sg.pa.t.* took 10.6, went 27.51; *3 pl.* nome 10.25. (OE. *niman*.)

nome, *sb.* name 3.28, 29. (OE. *nama*.)

nome. See NOM.

non, noon, *sb.* ninth hour after sunrise 10.7, noon 7.14. (OE. *nōn*.)

non(e), *pron.* no one 8.44, none 12.38; *adj.* no 4.26, 8.10. (OE. *nān*.) See NO.

noon. See NON, *sb.*

norþ, *sb.* north 14.44. (OE. *norþ*, adv.)

norþerne, northerne, *adj.* northern 14.1, 3. (OE. *norþerne*.)

not, *1 sg.pres.* do not know 17.15. (OE. *nāt*.) See WYTE, *v.*[1]

note, *sb.* note of music 3.28. (OF. *note*.)

noþyng, *sb.* nothing 6.58, 29.52. (OE. *nān þing*.)

nou, now, *adv.* now 10.39, 20.31. (OE. *nū.*)

nout, noht, nowyht, *adv.* not, not at all 2.22, 66, 5.19. (OE. *nōwiht.*) See NAHT, *adv.*, NOHT, *pron.*

nouþer, *adv.* neither 29.54. (OE. *nōhwæþer.*)

now, nowyht. See NOU, NOUT.

nul(le), *1 sg.pres.* will not 6.38, 25.10 ; *2 sg.* **nult** 16.20 ; *3 sg.* **nul** 2.66 ; *1 pl.* **nulle** 31.27 ; *1, 3 sg.pa.t.* **nolde** 6.57, 8.28 ; *3 pl.* **nolde** 6.56. Also forms coalescing with pron. *1 sg.* **nuly** 5.19, **nullyt** 6.57 ; *3 sg.* **nulle** 30.35. (OE. *nyllan.*) See WIL(E), *v.*

nuste, *1 sg.pa.t.* did not know 14.11. (OE. *nyste.*) See WYTE, *v.*[1].

o. See O(N), *prep.*, ON(E), *pron. and adj.*, O(O), *adv.*

of, *prep.* of 15.1, 26.1, from 5.12, 6.72, with 2.7, 22.25, by 3.35, made of, consisting of 7.61, 14.10, on account of 23.22, with regard to 3.45, 8.24, on (after verb of pitying) 16.9, 20.43, for (after verb of beseeching) 20.59, 23.16 ; as equiv. of genitive : possessive 3.28, 27.25, partitive 5.20, 11.23, subjective 15.48, 32.5, objective 10.53, 28.5, adjectival 7.59, 14.47. (OE. *of.*)

oft(e), *adv.* often 6.7, 32.32. (OE. *oft.*)

ofþuncheþ, *3 sg.pres.* displeases 8.47. (OE. *ofþyncan.*)

oht. See OÞE.

ohte, *3 sg. and 1 pl.pa.t.* ought 18.18, 31.31. (OE. *āgan,* pa.t. *āhte.*)

o(n), *prep.* on, upon 4.15, 5.22, fixed on 23.27, 26.22, in 3.2, 4.4, as regards 4.13, 8.4, engaged in 23.12, about, concerning 16.12, 21.32, (following its case) 2.19, 22.40 ; *whet him ys on,* what is the matter with him 9.44. (OE. *on.*)

on, *adv.* on, onward 6.19, 7.35. (OE. *on.*)

onde, *sb.* enmity 5.18, Anger (personified) 13.59. (OE. *anda.*)

on(e), o, *pron.* one 2.45, 3.5, 12.11 ; *adj.* a single 5.40, a certain 23.11,

one 30.10, alone 20.26 ; *art.* a 14.58, 25.3 ; *myn one, hire one,* alone 9.9, 22.19. (OE. *ān.*)

onycle, *sb.* onyx 3.5. (OF. *onicle.*)

o(o), *adv.* always 11.7, 12.27. (OE. *ā.*)

opon, or. See VPON, 3E.

or(e), *cj.* or 23.26, 32. (Weakened from OÞER, *cj.*)

ore, *sb.* favour, grace 25.6, 32.17. (OE. *ār.*)

orn. See ERNE.

oþe, oht, *sb.* oath 8.43, 31.18. (OE. *āþ.*)

oþer, *adj.* other 1.2, 13.25, second 27.31 ; *pron.* others 10.28. (OE. *ōþer.*)

oþer, *cj.* or 9.52 ; *oþer . . . oþer,* either . . . or 30.15. (OE. *oððe,* infl. by *ōþer* or *āhwæþer.*) See OR(E), *cj.*

ou. See 3E.

oure, ous. See WE.

ouself. See 3E.

out, *adv.* out 2.18. (OE. *ūt.*)

ouer, *prep.* over 14.72, 30.26. (OE. *ofer.*)

ouerwerpes, *3 sg.pres.* is cast down 21.12. (OE. *oferweorpan.*)

owen, *adj.* own 4.18. (OE. *āgen.*)

papeiai, *sb.* parrot 3.21. (OF. *papegai.*)

Parays, *sb.* the garden of Eden 7.59, Paradise 26.2. (OF. *parais.*)

par amours, *adv. phrase* as a lover 24.26. (OF. *par amours.*)

paruenke, *sb.* periwinkle 3.13, 14.52. (AN. *pervenke.*)

passeþ, *3 sg.pres.* surpasses 3.13. (OF. *passer.*)

pees, *sb.* peace 10.39, Peace (personified) 14.62. (OF. *pais.*)

peyne, *sb.* punishment 18.40, suffering 20.17. (OF. *peine.*)

penaunce, *sb.* repentance 23.41. (OF. *penance.*)

peny, *sb.* coin 10.27, 56. (OE. *penig.*)

pycchynde, *pres.part.* making fast 30.13. (Obscure.)

pye, *sb.* magpie (used as good-humoured abuse) 30.37. (OF. *pie.*)

piete, *sb.* pity, compassion 23.52. (OF. *piete.*)

pyn(e), pine, *sb.* torment 3.21, 16.24, 26.31. (Cf. OE. *pīnian, v.*)

pyneþ, *3 sg.pres.* torments 20.17. (OE. *pīnian.*)

play, *sb.* pleasure 2.14, 27.2 ; *pl.* **plawes** 12.2. (OE. *plega,* Ang. *plæga, plaga.*)

plastre, *sb.* soothing remedy 23.41. (OF. *plastre.*)

plawes. See PLAY.

pley3yng, *sb.* exercise, pleasure 23.12. (From OE. *plegian, v.*)

pleyntes, *sb.pl.* complaints 14.63. (OF. *plainte.*)

plyht, yplyht, *pp.* promised 5.28, 12.22. (OE. *plihtan.*)

plowe-fere, *sb.* playfellow 13.55. (OE.Ang. *plaga + (ge)-fēra.*)

poer, *sb.* power, strength 14.62. (OF. *poer.*)

pope, *sb.* Pope 7.47. (OE. *pāpa.*)

poure, *adj.* poor 2.14. (OF. *povre.*)

preye, pre(y)3e, *v.* to beseech 26.3, (constr. w. ' of ') 25.13, invite 30.27. (OF. *preier.*)

presente, *v.* to present 27.40. (OF. *presenter.*)

primerole, *sb.* early spring flower, cowslip, field daisy 3.13. (OF. *primerole.*)

pris, *sb.* value, worth, estimation 3.13 ; *bereþ þe pris,* is most eminent 5.35. (OF. *pris.*)

proude, *adj.* proud 11.32. OE. *prūd,* from OF.)

prouesse, *sb.* prowess, excellence 14.52. (OF. *proece.*)

prude, *sb.* pride, splendour 5.35, Pride (personified) 13.55. (OE. *prȳdo.*)

putte, *1 sg.pa.t.* made 14.63. (OE. **putian* ; cf. *putung,* sb.)

queme, *v.* to please 2.66, 26.27. (OE. *cwēman.*)

quene, *sb.* queen 15.43, 23.4. (OE. *cwēn.*)

quibebe, *sb.* cubeb 3.38. (OF. *cubebe.*)

rad, *adj.* quick, ready 12.16. (OE. *hræd.*)

rad, rafte. See REDE, *v.,* REUE, *v.*

raht, *3 sg.pa.t.subj.* should give 10.34. (OE. *ræcan.*)

rayleþ, *3 sg.pres.* puts on, arrays 11.13. (OF. *reiller.*)

ran. See ERNE.

red(e), reed, *sb.* advice 8.29, teaching 21.36, help 15.57, course of action 12.16. (OE. *rǣd.*)

red(e), *adj.* red 3.11, 7.38. (OE. *rēad.*)

rede, *v.* to advise, guide 5.24, bring 5.8, read 7.39, say 6.60, express 13.14, guess 3.30 ; *pp.* **rad** 5.8. (OE. *rǣdan.*)

redes, *3 sg.pres.* is red 7.36. (OE. *rēadian.*)

reed. See RED(E), *sb.*

rees, *sb.* rashness, recklessness 29.42. (OE. *rǣs.*)

reynes, *sb.pl.* reins 6.16. (OF. *regne.*)

reyse, *2 sg.imper.* raise 29.32. (ON. *reisa.*)

rekene, *adj.* ready, prompt, straightforward 3.42. (OE. *recen.*)

reode, *sb.* reed 2.28. (OE. *hrēod.*)

reowe, rewe, *v.* to regret 31.13, to have pity 5.7, 24.13, to grieve 32.20. (OE. *hrēowan.*)

resoun, *sb.* sense, wisdom 3.42, 6.61. (OF. *reson.*)

rest(e), *sb.* rest 2.28, 5.17. (OE. *rest(e).*)

reste, *3 sg.pa.t.reflex.* remained 14.20. (OE. *restan.*)

resting, *sb.* peace, rest 5.14. (From prec.)

reue, *3 sg.pres.subj.* rob, deprive 4.33 ; *3 sg.pa.t.* **rafte** 6.15. (OE. *rēafian.*)

rewe. See REOWE.

riche, *sb.* kingdom 26.35. (OE. *rīce.*)

riche, *adj.* splendid 7.11. (OE. *rīce,* OF. *riche.*)

richesse, *sb.* wealth 6.15. (OF. *richesse.*)

ryde(n), *v.* to ride 6.16, 7.1 ; *1 sg.pa.t.* **rod** 27.1. (OE. *rīdan.*)

ryf, *adj.* abundant 6.15. (OE. **rīfe,* ON. *rífr.*)

ryht, *adj.* true 3.4, 6.61, right 2.76. (OE. *riht.*)

ryht, riht, *adv.* 3.30, 24.17. (OE. *riht(e)*.)

ryhtes, *sb.pl.* justice 29.38. (OE. *riht*.)

ryhtfulnesse, *sb.* virtue, integrity 14.48. (Late OE. *rihtful* + *-ness*.)

ryhtwyse, *adj.* righteous 2.77. (OE. *rihtwīs*.)

rykening, *sb.* estimation, distinction 6.62. (From OE. *(ge)-recenian*.)

rym, *sb.* verse 6.62. (OF. *rime*.)

ryngeþ, *3 sg.pres.* resounds 11.12. (OE. *hringan*.)

rys, *sb.* twig, small branch 3.11, 5.32. (OE. *(gelēaf)-hrīs*.)

ryse, *1 sg.pres.* (*for fut.*) to rise 20.51 ; *3 sg.pa.t.* **ros** 20.55. (OE. *rīsan*.)

ro. See RO(O), *sb.*[1] and *sb.*[2].

robes, *sb.pl.* robes, clothes 8.16. (OF. *robe*.)

rod. See RYDE(N).

rod(e), *sb.* cross 14.20, 29.17. (OE. *rōd*.)

rode, *sb.* rosy hue 7.11, 11.13, complexion 3.11, 5.32. (OE. *rudu*.)

romaunʒ, *sb.pl.* romances 7.39. (OF. *romanz*.)

ron. See ERNE, ROUN(E), *sb.*

ro(o), *sb.*[1] rest, peace 6.41, 8.30, 29.49. (ON. *ró*.)

ro(o), *sb.*[2] roe 5.17, 10.50. (OE. *rā*.)

rooles, *adj.* restless 10.50. (ON. *ró* + OE. *-lēas*.)

ros. See RYSE.

rose, *sb.* rose 3.11, 5.32, 7.11. (OE. *rose*.)

roser, *sb.* rose-bush 7.36. (AN. *roser, cf. OF. *rosier*.)

rote, *sb.* root 6.61, 15.10, 29.45. (ON. *rót*.)

roun(e), ron, *sb.* speech 4.38, song 11.2, poetry 6.62. (OE. *rūn*.)

roune, *v.* to speak privately 6.41, whisper 3.30. (OE. *rūnian*.)

rouþe, *sb.* sorrow, distress 5.8 ; *pl.* **rouþes,** repentance 13.14. (From OE. *hrēowan*, v.)

rowe, *sb.* row, line 7.64, position, place 2.76. (OE. *rāw*.)

ruby, rubie, *sb.* ruby 3.4, 14.48. (OF. *rubi*.)

rude, *adj.* as *sb.pl.* violent people 6.41. (OF. *rude*.)

sad, *adj.* sated, weary 2.7, 5.5. (OE. *sæd*.)

sahte, *adj.* at peace, reconciled 12.48, 13.5. (OE. *sæht*.)

say(en), seye, seyn, seien, sugge, *v.* to say 7.82, 13.10, 19.19, 20.25, 21.39, 29.50 ; *1 sg.pres.* **sai** 2.12, **sugge** 2.38 ; *2 sg.* **seist** 24.13 ; *3 sg.* **seiþ** 10.37 ; *3 pl.* **says** 25.14 ; *1 sg.pa.t.* **seyde** 29.46 ; *3 sg.* **sayde** 10.16 ; *3 pl.* **saide** 10.59, **seyden** 7.72 ; *pp.* **seid** 6.10. (OE. *secgan*.)

sake, *sb.* sin, guilt 2.13, sake 4.24, 20.33. (OE. *sacu*.)

sale, *sb.* hall, palace 3.23. (OE. *sæl*.)

salte, *adj.* salt 15.20. (OE. *sealt*.)

saneþ, *3 sg.pres.* heals 3.34. (Lat. *sānāre*.)

saphyr, *sb.* sapphire 3.2. (OF. *safir*.)

sare. See SORE, *adv.*

sauge, *sb.* sage 3.18. (OF. *sauge*.)

sauhting, *sb.* agreement, covenant 2.7. (Cf. OE. *seaht*, sb., *sehtan*, v.)

sauue, *v.* to heal 3.20. (OF. *sauver*.)

sauour, *sb.* scent 23.2. (OF. *savour*.)

sawes, *sb.pl.* speeches 6.30, 13.10. (OE. *sagu*.)

schule. See SHAL.

scole, *sb.* school 24.29. (OE. *scōl*.)

scourges, *sb.pl.* whips, scourges 21.44. (AN. *escurge*.)

se, seo, suen, sene, *v.* to see, look at 5.6, 7.60, 27.54, 29.39, to watch over 7.82 ; *2 sg.pres.* **sys** 3.18 ; *3 sg.* **syht** 3.19 ; *1, 3 sg.pa.t.* **seh** 13.33, 15.40 ; *2 sg.* **seʒe** 28.29 ; *3 pl.* **seʒen** 7.72 ; *1, 3 sg.pa.t.subj.* **seʒe** 7.15, 82 ; *pp.* **seie** 27.35, **sene** 15.44. (OE. *sēon*.)

se. See SO, *adv.*

seche, *v.* to seek 25.10, attack 14.59 ; *2 sg.pa.t.* **sohtes** 16.21 ; *3 sg.* **sohte** 10.4 ; *pp.* **soht** 14.59. (OE. *sēcan*.)

sedewale, *sb.* setwall, valerian 3.40. (AN. *zedewale*, cf. OF. *citoual*.)

see, *sb.* sea 9.35. (OE. *sǣ*.)

seete. See SETE, *adj.*

seʒe(n), seh. See SE, *v.*

seid, seyde(n). See SAY(EN).

seie. See SE, *v.*

seye, seien, seyn. See SAY(EN).

seint, *pp.* sunk, plunged 2.56. (OE. *sencan.*)

seint(e), *adj.* holy 26.13 ; *sb.* saint 22.38. (OF. *seint.*) See SONTES.

seist, seiþ. See SAY(EN).

sek, *adj.* ill 23.47. (OE. *sēoc.*)

selde(n), *adv.* seldom 5.5, 32.35. (OE. *seldan.*)

selleþ, *3 pl.pres.* betray 22.57 ; *pp.* **solde,** sold 29.36. (OE. *sellan.*)

selþe, *sb.* happiness 6.71, 12.48. (OE. *sǣlþ.*)

seluer, *sb.* silver 3.2. (OE. *seolfor.*)

seme(n), *v.* to befit, beseem 6.44, 45, appear 2.13 ; (coalescing with pers.pron.) *I sg.* **semy** 13.15. (ON. *sóma.*)

semly, *adj.* fair 3.2, 4.6 ; *as sb.* fair one(s) 3.19, 5.6, 6.44 ; *superl.* **semlokest** 4.6. (Cf. ON. *sómiligr.*)

send, *v.* to send 12.43 ; *2 sg.imper.* **sent** 5.15 ; *3 sg.pa.t.* **sende** 10.8 ; *pp.* **sent** 4.10. (OE. *sendan.*)

sene, *adj.* visible, plain 17.13. (OE.Ang. *(ge)-sēne.*)

sene. See SE, *v.*

sent. See SEND.

seo. See SE, *v.*

serewe, *v.* to be sad 26.7, grieve 13.96. (Cf. OE. *sorgian.*) See SOREWE, *sb.*

seruen, *v.* to serve 6.44, 23.42. (OF. *servir.*)

set. See SETE, *v.*

sete, seete, *adj.* easy in mind, content 23.40, 32.35. (Cf. OE. *andsǣte.*)

sete, *2 sg.imper.* set, place 15.10, 30.26 ; *pp.* **set** 6.7, **ysette** 7.43. (OE. *settan.*)

seþþe, *adv.* later 2.15, 15.60 ; *cj.* since 6.24. (OE. *seoþþan.*)

shake, *v.* to move 30.11. (OE. *scacan.*)

shal, *I sg.pres.* shall, will, must 24.4 ; *2 sg.* **shalt** 24.10 ; *3 sg.* **shal** 9.19 ; *I pl.* **shule** 2.71, **schule** 30.32, **shulen** 23.29 ; *3 pl.* **shule** 12.18 ; *I, 3 sg.pa.t.* **shulde** 20.4, 27.27 ; *I pl.* **shulde** 31.19 ; *3 pl.* **shulden** 15.19 ; *I pl.pa.t.subj.* **shulde** 21.33. (OE. *sceal.*)

sham(e), shaped. See SHOME, SHUP.

sheddest, *2 sg.pa.t.* sheddest 15.32, 20.65. (OE. *scēadan.*)

sheld, *sb.* protector 20.60. (OE. *sceld.*)

shene, *adj.* beautiful 15.41, 26.17. (OE. *scēne.*)

shereþ, *3 sg.pres.* changes direction 30.4. (OE. *sceran.*)

shild(e), *2 sg.imper.* protect 17.14, 23.19, 28.3. (OE. *scildan.*)

shoddreþ, *3 sg.pres.* trembles 30.4. (Cf. MLG. *schoderen.*)

shome, sham(e), *sb.* shame, disgrace 24.11, 15, 28.3. (OE. *scamu.*)

shon, *3 sg.pa.t.* shone 6.20, 9.2. (OE. *scīnan.*)

shoures, *sb.pl.* pains, especially of child-birth 23.55. (OE. *scūr.*)

shulde(n). See SHAL.

shuldre, *sb.pl.* shoulders 14.28. (OE. *sculdor.*)

shule(n). See SHAL.

shup, *3 sg.pa.t.* made, created 12.14 ; *pp.* **shaped,** decreed 8.44. (OE. *scieppan.*)

shupping, *sb.* decree 8.45. (From prec.)

syde, *adj.* ample 8.16. (OE. *sīd.*)

side, syde, *sb.* side 6.21, 21.7. (OE. *sīde.*)

syht, *sb.* sight 13.106 ; *on syht,* to look at 3.2, 14.6. (OE. *sihþ.*)

syht. See SE, *v.*

syk(e), *sb.* sigh 25.6, sighing 9.48. (OE. *sice.*)

sike, syke, *v.* to sigh 18.20, 22.28. (OE. *sīcan.*)

syker, *adv.* certainly 13.72. (OE. *sicor.*)

sykyng, *sb.* sighing 14.60, 64. (From OE. *sīcan,* cf. *sīcettung.*)

sylk, *sb.* silk 7.76. (OE. *sioloc.*)

syng(e), *v.* to sing 4.4, 9.19. (OE. *singan.*)

synke, *v.* to sink 8.16. (OE. *sincan.*)

synne, sys. See SUNNE, SE, *v.*

sitten, *v.* to sit 30.30, to apply 6.8 ; *3 sg.pres.* **syt** 30.7. (OE. *sittan.*)

syþe, *sb.* time 2.55. (OE. *sīþ.*)

siweþ, *3 sg.pres.* follows 13.29. (OF. *sevir.*)

skrinkeþ, *3 sg.pres.* withers 23.1. (OE. *scrincan.*)

slake, *1 sg.pres.* become weak 14.83. (OE. *slacian.*)

slawen. See SLO(N).

sleye, *adj.* skilful 22.32. (ON. *slǽgr.*)

slep, *sb.* sleep 14.83, Sleep (personified) 13.62. (OE. *slǽp.*)

sleuthe, *sb.* Sloth (personified) 13.62. (OE. *slǽwþ.*)

slyt, *3 sg.pres.* falls 30.3. (OE. *slīdan.*)

slo(n), *v.* to strike, beat 8.40, kill 14.65, 24.20; *3 sg.pa.t.subj.* **slowe** 8.40; *pp.* **slawen** 27.45. (OE.Nhb. *slān.*)

sloweste, *adj.superl.* slowest 30.12. (From OE. *slǽw.*)

smal, *adj.* slender 4.16, 7.62; *pl.* **smalle,** few, unimportant 29.10. (OE. *smæl.*)

smerte, *v.* to smart 22.48, feel pain 18.19. (OE. *smeortan.*)

smyþes, *sb.pl.* smiths 22.32. (OE. *smiþ.*)

smok, *sb.* smock 9.54. (OE. *smȯc.*)

smulleþ, *3 pl.pres.* smell 23.33. (Obscure.)

so, swo, se, *adv.* thus 6.46, 13.50, so, to such an extent 9.36, 19.19, 22.26, as, like 4.32, 22.17; *cj.* as 21.13; *so . . . as,* as . . . as 26.23. (OE. *swā.*) See ALSO.

soffre, *2 sg.imper.* allow 26.14, suffer 21.17. (OF. *soffrir.*)

soft(e), *adj.* soft 7.76, gentle 18.21. (OE. *sōfte.*)

soht(e), sohtes. See SECHE.

solas, *sb.* comfort 27.14. (OF. *solas.*)

solde. See SELLEÞ.

solsecle, *sb.* marigold 3.20, 14.53. (OF. *solsecle.*)

some. See SUM.

somer, *sb.* summer 23.3, 24.3. (OE. *sumor.*)

somme. See SUM.

sonde, *sb.* message 5.15, errand 6.45. (OE. *sand.*)

son(e), *adv.* forthwith 2.7, quickly 10.8. (OE. *sōna.*)

sone, *sb.* son 27.45. (OE. *sunu.*)

song, *sb.* song, poetry 6.7. (OE. *sang.*)

sonne, *sb.* sun 6.22, 9.35. (OE. *sunne.*)

sonnebeem, sonnebem, *sb.* sunbeam 7.7, 14. (OE. *sunnebēam.*)

sontes, *sb.pl.* saints 13.106, 27.56. (OE. *sanct.*) See SEINT(E).

sor, *sb.* pain, grief 23.37. (OE. *sār.*)

sor(e), *adj.* grievous 14.67, sad 31.18. (OE. *sār.*)

sore, sare, *adv.* sorely 4.35, 17.3. (OE. *sāre.*)

sorewe, serewe, *sb.* pain, sorrow 13.33, 23.36; *gen.sg.* **serewe** 2.56. (OE. *sorg.*) See SEREWE, *v.*

soreweful, *adj.* distressing, lamentable 20.54. (OE. *sorgful.*)

sorewyng, *sb.* grief 14.60. (OE. *sorgung.*)

sory, *adj.* sad 18.20, 24.22. (OE. *sārig.*)

sotel, *adj.* open, revealed 2.12. (OE. *sweotol, s(w)utol.*)

soteleþ, *3 pl.pres.* are revealed 2.11. (OE. *sweotolian, swutelian.*)

soþ, *adj.* true 6.59, 16.22. (OE. *sāþ.*)

soule, *sb.* soul 2.38; *gen.sg.* **soule** 2.25, 15.29. (OE. *sāwol.*)

sound(e), *adj.* healed 23.40, 31.5. (OE. *(ge)-súnd.*)

sour, *adj.* sour, bitter 32.34. OE. *sūr.*)

souþ, *adv. and sb.* south 14.44, 15.47. (OE. *sūþ,* adv.)

spaclyche, *adv.* quickly, soon 8.29. (ON. *spakr* + OE. *-līce,* cf. ON. *spakliga.*)

speche, *sb.* speech 7.30, 25.9. (OE. *spǣc.*)

speke, *v.* to speak 29.40. (OE. *specan.*)

spere, *sb.* spear 21.42, 22.49. (OE. *spere.*)

spices, *sb.pl.* spices 7.30. (OF. *espice.*)

spille, *v.* to perish 21.33. (OE. *spillan.*)

sponne, *sb.* span 7.44. (OE. *spann.*)

spradde. See SPREDES.

spray, *sb.* small branch, twig 4.2. (Obscure.)

spredes, *3 sg.pres.* spreads 7.30; *3 sg.pa.t.* **spradde,** shed 21.9. (OE. *sprǣdan.*)

springe, *v.* to grow 4.2, begin 20.56; *3 sg.pa.t.* **sprong** 28.11. (OE. *springan.*)

staf, *sb.* staff 13.34. (OE. *stæf.*)

stake, *sb.pl.* stakes 30.13. (OE. *staca.*)

stalle, *sb.* stall for horses 13.35. (OE. *steall.*)

stark, *adj.* powerful, mighty 23.4. (OE. *stearc.*)

stede, *sb.* horse, steed 7.48, 13.34; *pl.* **steden** 13.35. (OE. *stēda.*)

ster(re), *sb.* star 26.17, 27.35. (OE. *steorra.*)

steuenyng, *sb.* assignation, meeting 12.33. (From OE. *stefnan,* v.)

sty, *sb.* path 30.26. (OE. *stīg.*)

stille, *adj.* still, quiet 24.17; *adv.* softly 11.21, 24.33, continually 22.9, firmly 24.35. (OE. *stille.*)

stiþ, *adv.* firmly, violently 29.21. (OE. *stīþe.*)

styþe, *adj.* strong 13.35; *superl.* **styþest** 7.48. (OE. *stīþ.*)

styþye, *sb.* excellent person 6.17. (From prec.)

stod(e). See STONDE.

stonde, *v.* to stand 10.18, to be, exist 32.2; *3 sg.pres.* **stont** 7.68, **stond** 22.18; *1, 3 sg.pa.t.* **stod** 29.21, 28; *2 sg.* **stode** 28.25; *1 pl.* **stod** 24.23; stod aȝeyn, opposed 29.21. (OE. *standan.*)

ston(e), *sb.* stone, rock 22.18, gem 7.68. (OE. *stān.*)

stong, *3 sg.pa.t.* (*for pres.*) pierced 18.4; *pp.* **stongen** 20.29, **ystongen** 21.42. (OE. *stingan.*)

stont. See STONDE.

stou, *sb.* place 28.25. (OE. *stōw.*)

stounde, *sb.* period of time 13.94, 21.30; harde stounde(s), times of suffering 21.34, 28.23. (OE. *stúnd.*)

stour, *adj.* strong, stalwart 23.4. (MLG. *stûr.*)

stout, *adj.* stately, magnificent 14.40. (OF. *estout.*)

streynþe, streinþe, *sb.* strength 2.27, 15.7. (OE. *strengþu.*)

strem, *sb.* stream 11.21. (OE. *strēam.*)

stryd. See STRIT.

strif, stryf, *sb.* contention, dispute 6.17, 9.10. (OF. *estrif.*)

strikeþ, *3 sg.pres.* flows 11.21. (OE. *strīcan.*)

strit, *3 sg.pres.* strides 30.1; *2 sg.imper.* **stryd** 30.26. (OE. *strīdan.*)

stronge, *adj.* strong 22.31, severe 18.35. (OE. *strang.*)

stude, *sb.* place 16.6. (OE. *styde.*)

stunt, *2 sg.imper.* put an end to 13.94; *3 sg.pa.t.* **stunte** 6.17. (OE. *styntan.*)

sturne, *adj.* angry, violent 6.17. (OE. *styrne.*)

such, *adj.* such 8.14. (OE. *swylc.*)

sucre, *sb.* sugar 3.34. (OF. *sucre.*)

suen, suere See SE, *v.*, SWERE.

suert, *sb.* sword 20.11. (OE. *sweord.*)

suete, suetyng. See SWETE, SWET-ING.

suetly, *adj.* lovely 14.27. OE. *swēte + -lic,* cf. *swētlīce,* adv.)

suetnesse, *sb.* sweetness, beauty 14.53. (OE. *swētnes.*)

sugge, suyre, suyþe. See SAY(EN), SWYRE, SWYÞE.

sully, *adv.* exceedingly 2.57, 14.6. (OE. *syllīce.*)

sum, *adj.* some, a certain 30.24; *pl.* **some** 2.39, **somme** 10.31. (OE. *sum.*)

sunful, *adj.* sinful 2.7, 29.36. (OE. *synfull.*)

sunne, synne, *sb.* sin 13.6, 21.22; *gen.sg.* **sunne** 2.55; *pl.* **sunne** 10.54; *gen.pl.* **sunnes** 20.59. (OE. *synn.*)

swannes. See SWON.

swere, suere, *v.* to swear 12.24, 22.56; *3 pl.pa.t.* **swore** 10.28. (OE. *swerian.*)

swete, suete, *adj.* sweet, pleasant 11.5; *as sb.* fair one 14.75; *adv.* sweetly 23.33. (OE. *swēte.*)

sweting, suetyng, *sb.* dear one 14.2, 36. (From prec.)

swyke, *1 sg.pres.* leave off, cease 13.28. (OE. *swīcan.*)

swyke, *sb.* deceiver, traitor 12.25. (OE. *swica.*)

swyre, suyre, *sb.* neck 4.28, 14.27. (OE. *swīra.*)

swyþe, suyþe, *adv.* very, very much 7.43, 10.17. (OE. *swiþe.*)

swo. See so.

swon, *sb.* swan 4.28 ; *gen.sg.* **swannes** 7.43. (OE. *swan.*)

swore. See SWERE.

swote, *adj.* sweet, gentle 15.11 ; *as sb.* fair one 14.75. (OE. *swōt.*) See SWETE.

ta. See TO, *prep.*

tahte, *3 sg.pa.t.subj.* taught 12.39. (OE. *tǽcan.*)

take(n), *v.* to take, receive 4.17, accept 27.11, capture 24.19, follow 30.9 ; *3 sg.pa.t.* **toc** 1.1, **tok** 27.11 ; *pp.* **take** 24.11, **ytake** 24.19, **taken** 30.24 ; *take an hond,* undertake 8.23. (ON. *taka.*)

tale, *sb.* tale, story 3.22, 7.9. (OE. *talu.*)

te, *v.* to go 15.51. (OE. *tēon.*)

teht. See TEÞ.

tele, *sb.* calumny 6.35. (OE. *tæl.*)

telle, *v.* to tell, narrate 4.27, to inform 9.39, to mention 2.48, to esteem, value 13.22 ; *1, 3 sg.pa.t.* **tolde** 2.48, 7.9 ; *pp.* **told** 6.37, **ytold** 3.32, **ytolde** 13.22. (OE. *tellan.*)

teme, *v.* to vouch 6.38. (OE.Ang. *tēman.*)

te(o)ne, *v.* to grieve 25.4, to be angry 30.39. (OE. *tēonian.*)

teres, tern, *sb.pl.* tears 20.20, 22. (OE. *tēar.*)

teþ, teht, *sb.pl.* teeth 7.40, 30.39. (OE. *tēþ,* pl.)

tyde, *sb.* time, season 23.3. (OE. *tīd.*)

tide, *v.* to befall 6.38. (OE. *tīdan.*)

tiding, tydynge, *sb.* news 28.41, event 6.38. (OE. *tīdung.*)

til, *cj.* until 6.3. (OE.Nhb. *til.*)

time, tyme, *sb.* time 20.50, 23.23. (OE. *tīma.*)

tyttes, *sb.pl.* breasts 7.58. (OE. *titt.*)

to, *sb.* toe 7.63. (OE. *tā.*)

to, *adv.* too, besides 7.26, 12.16, 22.31. (OE. *tō.*)

to, ta, *prep.* to, towards, into 3.19, 10.23, as, for 2.40, as far as 7.63, to, in order to 2.73, (following its case) 29.53, (as sign of infin.) 10.10, (with inflected infin.) 27.52, 54, (with passive infin.) 10.45. (OE. *tō.*) See FORTE.

toc. See TAKE(N).

to-day, *adv.* to-day 10.47, 32.9. (OE. *tō dæg.*)

to-drawe, *3 sg.pres.subj.* tear to pieces 30.34. (OE. *tō + dragan.*)

toforen, *prep.* in front of 30.10. (OE. *tōforan.*)

tok, told(e). See TAKE(N), TELLE.

tonge, *sb.* tongue 6.36, 26.32. (OE. *tunge.*)

tortle, *sb.* turtle-dove 3.22, 9.3. (OE. *turtle.*)

to-tereþ, *3 pl.pres.* tear to pieces 30.6. (OE. *tō-teran.*)

toune, *sb.* town ; *in toune,* in the world 6.37, alive 4.29. (OE. *tūn.*)

tour, *sb.* tower, castle 3.22, 32.23. (OF. *tūr.*)

toward, *prep.* towards 8.42. (OE. *tōweard.*)

tre, *sb.* cross 20.6, 21.43, 22.4. (OE. *trēo.*)

tresor, *sb.* wealth, treasure 23.39. (OF. *tresor.*)

treuþe, trouþe, *sb.* faith, truth 5.28, 12.20. (OE. *trēowþ.*)

trewe, *adj.* faithful, true 3.22. (OE. *trēowe.*)

triacle, *sb.* remedy 3.32. (OF. *triacle.*)

tricherie, *sb.* deceit, perfidy 12.21. (OF. *tricherie.*)

trichour, *sb.* deceiver 12.22, 31, 39. (OF. *tricheur.*)

trikeþ, *3 sg.pres.* hangs down 7.63. (Cf. OE. *strican* ?)

trone, *sb.* heaven 3.32, 13.4. (OF. *trone.*)

trous, *sb.* bundle 30.15, 25. (OF. *trousse.*)

trouþe. See TREUÞE.

trowe, *3 sg.pres.* believes, knows 30.9 ; (coalescing with pers.pron.) *1 sg.pres.* **trowy** 12.38. (OE. *treow(i)an, trūwian.*)

trowe, *sb.* trust, belief 29.27. (From prec.)

trusti, *adj.* trustworthy, reliable 13.4. (Cf. ON. *traustr,* adj.)

tuo, *adj.* two 7.59, 22.27. (OE. *twā.*) See ATWO.

turne, *v.* to turn, direct 18.32. (OE. *tyrnan, turnian.*)

twybyl, *sb.* two-edged axe 30.15. (OE. *twibill.*)

þah, *cj.* though 2.70. (OE. *þah.*)

þarefore. See ÞERFORE.

þareto, *adv.* in addition, besides 3.14. (OE. *þærtō.*)

þart, 2 *sg.pres.* thou art 30.38. (OE. *þū eart.*)

þat, *dem.pron.* that 2.14, 8.47 ; *rel.pron.* that, who 6.26, 8.24, that which 6.56, he who 13.95, those who 20.38 ; *dat.sg.* to whom 10.55 ; *dem.adj.* that 3.19, 6.69 ; *art.* the 32.11 ; *cj.* that 2.61, 14.77, so that 21.3, until 8.23 ; *þat . . . ys,* whose 23.10, *þat . . . yn,* in which 7.70, *þat . . . to,* for whose sake 26.16. (OE. *þæt.*)

þe, *art.* the 3.40, 5.36, (before comp.) 25.7, 27.17. (OE. *þe,* earlier *sē.*)

þe. See ÞOU, *pron.*

þeȝes, *sb.pl.* thighs 14.33. (OE. *þēoh.*)

þei, þey, *pron.* they 22.9, 24.19. (ON. *þeir.*)

þen, *cj.* than 7.44, 8.26. (OE. *þanne, þænne.*) See ÞENNE.

þenche, þenke(n), *v.* to think 21.4, 29.52, 32.8 ; *1, 3 sg.pa.t.* **þohte** 10.1, 16.12. (OE. *þencan, þōhte.*)

þenne, *adv.* then 8.33, 29.40 ; *as sb.* that time 2.22. (OE. *þanne, þænne.*) See ÞEN.

þeo. See ÞO, *adj. and pron.*

þeode, *sb.* people, nation ; *in þeode,* among men 2.24. (OE. *þēod.*)

þer, *adv.* there 7.68, 30.16, where 12.17, 26.35. (OE. *þǣr.*)

þerfore, þarefore, *adv.* therefore 15.19, 28.39. (OE. *þǣr + fore.*)

þerfro, *adv.* away from it 29.6. (OE. *þǣr + ON. frá.*)

þeryn, *adv.* therein 15.27. (OE. *þǣrin.*)

þerled. See ÞURLED.

þerof, *adv.* with regard to that 21.24. (OE. *þǣrof.*)

þeues, *sb.pl.* thieves 22.27. (OE. *þēof.*)

þewes, *sb.pl.* virtues, good qualities 2.12. (OE. *þēaw.*)

þi. See ÞOU, *pron.*

þider, *adv.* thither 10.8, 23.48. (OE. *þider.*)

þin(e). See ÞOU, *pron.*

þing(e), *sb.* thing, creature, person 9.23, 27.6. (OE. *þing.*)

þynkeþ. See ÞUNCHEÞ.

þynne. See ÞUNNE.

þis, *adj. and pron.* this 2.60, 5.37, these 6.40, 12.2. (OE. *þis,* neut.)

þiself, *pron.* thyself 3.18. (OE. *þū þē self,* infl. by ÞI in ME.) See ÞOU, *pron.*

þo, þeo, *adj.* those 14.61 ; *pron.* they, them 2.27, 5.20. (OE. *þā.*)

þo, *adv.* then 1.4, 20.55, when 10.2, 28.17. (OE. *þā.*)

þoht(e), *sb.* thought 9.15, 31.7, Grief (personified) 14.60. (OE. *þoht.*)

þohte. See ÞENCHE, ÞUNCHEÞ.

þole, þolie(n), *v.* to suffer, endure 4.35, 18.25, 24.34. (OE. *þolian.*)

þonk, *sb.* thought, pleasure 8.18. (OE. *þanc.*)

þornes, *sb.pl.* thorns 30.6, 14. (OE. *þorn.*)

þoro, *adj.* complete, perfect 27.33. (OE. *þurh.*) See ÞOURH.

þou, *pron.* thou, you 15.6 ; *acc.dat.* **þe** 8.12 ; *gen.* **þi** 5.15, **þin** 6.68, **þine** 4.24. (OE. *þū, þē, þīn.*) See ÞISELF.

þou, *cj.* although 20.45. (ON. **þóh,* later *þó.*)

þourh, þurh, *prep.* through 6.20, by means of 6.51, 23.30, on account of 20.63, 23.45. (OE. *þurh.*)

þourhout, *adv.* completely 18.4, 20.29. (OE. *þurhūt.*)

þourhsoht, þurhsoht, *pp.* thoroughly examined 29.15, pierced 13.78. (OE. *þurhsēcan.*)

þowen, *pp.* flourishing 2.24. (OE. *þēon.*)

þral, *sb.* slave 23.44. (OE. *þræl.*)

þrat. See ÞRETE(Þ).

þre, þreo, *adj.* three 2.23, 9.33. (OE. *þrēo.*)

þrestelcoc, þrestelcok, sb. song-thrush 9.51, 11.7. (OE. þrostle + cocc; vowel infl. by ME. thrushe/threshe, from OE. þrysce.) See ÞRUSTLE.

þrete(þ), 3 pl.pres. accuse, rebuke 2.21, 23, threaten 14.65; 3 sg.pa.t. þrat 14.65. (OE. þrēatian.)

þreteþ, 3 sg.pres. contends 11.7. (ON. þræta.)

þridde, adj. third 20.51, 27.37. (OE. þridda.)

þryftes, sb.pl. lot, fortune 13.9. (ON. þrift.)

þryuen, þriuene, ppl.adj. outstand-ing 2.24, 3.23, virtuous 2.21, beautiful 9.16. (ON. þrifinn.)

þro, sb. strife 3.23. (ON. þrá.)

þro, adj. excellent 9.16. (ON. þrár.)

þroh, sb. coffin, grave 1.3. (OE. þrūh.)

þrowe, sb. time 2.72. (OE. þrāg.)

þrustle, sb. thrush 3.23. (OE. þrostle.)

þuncheþ, þunkeþ, þynkeþ, 3 sg.pres.impers. seems 9.47, 13.49, 21.26; 3 sg.pa.t. þohte 7.15. (OE. þyncan, þūhte.)

þunne, þynne, adj. thin 31.34, slight 8.18, unhappy 13.9; as sb. thin, poor clothes 8.15. (OE. þynne.)

þurh, þurhsoht. See ÞOURH, ÞOURHSOHT.

þurled, þerled, pp. pierced 18.13, 23.10. (OE. þyrlian.)

þus, adv. thus 7.23, 9.20. (OE. þus.)

vch(e), adj. each 6.67, 7.8. (OE.VP. ylc.)

vmbe(n), prep. about, around 7.62; vmbe stounde, vmbe þrowe, vmbe while, at times 2.72, 12.33, 13.63. (OE. ymbe.)

vnbliþe, adj. sad 6.3. (OE. unbliþe.)

vnbold(e), adj. afraid, timid, back-ward 29.40, 41. (OE. unbáld.)

vndefong. See VNDERFONGE.

vnder, sb. third hour of the day, about 9 a.m. 10.5. (OE. undern.)

vnder, prep. under 2.10, 13.39; vnder bis, vnder felde, vnder gore, on earth, alive 2.39, 3.16, 17. (OE. under.)

vnderfynde, 1 sg.pres. perceive, understand 12.6. (OE. under- + findan.)

vnderfonge, v. to receive 15.59; 2 sg.imper. vndefong 18.50. (OE. underfōn, pp. -fangen.)

vnderstonde, v. to understand, know 15.22. (OE. understandan.)

vndertoc, 3 sg.pa.t. received 10.12. (OE. under- + ON. taka.)

vndo, 2 sg.imper. open 15.27. (OE. undōn.)

vndreh, adj. unwilling 10.17. (OE. un- + ON. drjúgr.)

vnfete, adj. not well-disposed 10.57. (OE. un- + OF. fait.)

vnglad, adj. sad 5.4. (OE. unglæd.)

vngreyþe, adj. unprepared 29.8. (OE. un- + ON. greiðr.)

vnholde, adj. disastrous 2.44. (OE. unhold.)

vnlahfulliche, adv. unlawfully 14.70. (OE. un- + lagu + fullīce.)

vnmete, adj. excessive 2.17. (OE. unmǣte.)

vnmihti, adj. weak, powerless 2.2. (OE. unmihtig.)

vnne, 1 sg.pres. wish 9.45. (OE. unnan.)

vnreken, adj. uneasy, unpleasant 29.42, 49. (OE. un- + recen.)

vnsaht, adj. dissatisfied, displeased 10.31. (Cf. OE. unseht.)

vnsemly, adj. unseemly, unbecoming 6.8. (OE. un- + ON. sœmiligr, or earlier form of ON. úsœmiligr.)

vnsete, adj. unbecoming, evil 2.15, 13.74; as sb. evil 10.51. (Cf. OE. andsǣte.) See SETE, adj.

vntoun, adj. evil 6.37. (Cf. OE. ungetogen.)

vntrewe, adj. unfaithful 12.29; as sb. unfaithful person(s) 6.35, 32.35. (OE. untrēowe.)

vnwynne. See VNWUNNE.

vnwis, adj. foolish 21.23. (OE. unwis.)

vnwraste, adj. evil, unreliable 8.17. (OE. unwrǣst.)

vnwrþ, adj. unworthy 29.53. (OE. unweorþ, unwurþ.)

vnwunne, vnwynne, sb. grief, sorrow 2.50, 13.13. (OE. un- + wynn.)

vp, *adv.* up 22.15, 29.32. (OE. *up.*)

vpo(n), opon, apon, *prep.* on 20.51, 30.35, with regard to 3.17, of, concerning 25.16, 31.27, in 12.16, 32.30, (after verb of seeing) 3.19, 7.13. (OE. *up + on.*)

vr(e), vs. See WE.

vachen, *v.* to fetch 8.31. (OE. *feccan, fæccan.*)

valle. See FALLE(N).

vilore, *adj.comp.* baser, viler 29.29. (From OF. *vil.*)

virgyne, *sb.* virgin 23.28. (OF. *virgine.*)

vo, vol. See FO(O), FUL.

wayle, *sb.* beautiful or excellent person 9.1, 50. (ON. *val.*) See WALE, *v.*

waynoun, *sb.* good-for-nothing, scoundrel 13.17. (ONF. *waignon.*)

wayted, *pp.* watched, spied upon 24.18. (ONF. *waitier.*)

wayteglede, *sb.* one who sits watching the fire 13.17. (Prec. + OE. *glēd.*)

wake, *v.* to lie awake 4.22, 14.84, to waken 14.42. (OE. *wacian.*)

wakeneþ, *3 sg.pres.* arouses 17.1. (OE. *wæcnan.*)

wale, *v.* to choose 7.2. (From ON. *val,* sb.) See WAYLE, *sb.*

walke, *v.* to toss about restlessly 24.6; *1 sg.pa.t.* **welk,** walked 29.43. (OE. *wealcan.*)

walle, *sb.pl.* walls 13.38. (OE. *weall.*)

wan. See WON, *adj.*

war, *adj.* cautious 5.34. (OE. *wær.*)

war, *sb.* defence; *on war,* on one's guard 12.34. (OE. *waru.*)

war, *2 sg.imper.reflex.* beware 12.25. (OE. *warian.*)

warne, werne, *v.* to restrain 20.22, protect 7.69. (OE. *wearnian, wiernan.*)

warp, *3 sg.pa.t.* rescued 6.48; *pp.* **ywarpe,** devised, destined 2.65. (OE. *weorpan.*)

was. See WES.

water, *sb.* water 4.32, 7.70. (OE. *wæter.*)

waxe, *1 sg.pres.* grow, become 5.2; *3 sg.pa.t.* **wax** 7.18. (OE. *weaxan.*)

we, *pron.* we 2.69; *acc.dat.* **vs** 2.52, **ous** 13.83; *gen.* **vr** 2.25, **vre** 13.101, **oure** 12.14. (OE. *wē, ūs, ūre.*)

wed, *sb.* pledge 30.24, 32. (OE. *wedd.*)

wede(s), *sb.pl.* clothes, garments 2.10, 30.8. (OE. *wǣd(e).*)

wees, weete. See WES, WETE, *adj.*

wey, *sb.* way, path 26.4; *adv.* away 20.7, 24.9. (OE. *weg.*)

weylaway, weylawey, weylawei, *interj.* alas! 22.20, 24.13, 25. (OE. *weg lā weg.*)

wel, *adv.* well 4.16, very 3.4; *wel were me,* I should be happy 7.57. (OE. *wel.*)

wel. See WEL(E).

welde, *v.* to control 2.35, to possess 7.3. (OE.Ang. **weldan,* cf. WS. *wieldan.*)

wel(e), weole, *sb.* happiness, good fortune 6.50, 9.45, 11.11. (OE. *we(o)la.*)

welk. See WALKE.

welkne, *sb.* sky 32.34. (Cf. OE. *wolcen.*)

welle, *sb.* spring, well 26.29. (OE.Ang. *wella.*)

welle, *1 sg.pres.* boil (fig.), suffer 9.40. (OE. Ang. *wellan.*)

wende, *v.* to go away 18.49, to turn 4.22, to change 24.21; *3 sg.pres.* **went** 2.16; *3 sg.pa.t.* **wende** 23.12; *pp.* **went** 6.49. (OE. *wendan.*)

wene, *v.*[1], *1 sg.pres.* think, expect 24.6, 25.2. (OE. *wēnan.*)

wene, *v.*[2] to attract 13.63, 64. (OE. *wenian.*)

went, weole. See WENDE, WEL(E).

weolewe, *1 sg.pres.* wither, waste away 13.79. (Cf. OE. *wealwian.*)

weore. See WERE, *v.*

wepeþ, *3 sg.pres.* weeps 22.29; *pres.part.* **wepynde** 22.39. (OE. *wēpan.*)

weping(e), wypinge, *sb.* weeping 6.1, 20.7, 22.3. (From prec.)

were, weore, *v.* to wear 8.14, 15; *1 sg.pa.t.* **werede** 13.31. (OE. *werian.*)

were(n). See WES.

wery, *adj.* weary, tired 4.32, 27.39. (OE. *wērig.*)

werk, *sb.* grief 6.26, work 10.23, 32, deed 6.2, 15.30. (OE. *weorc.*)

werne. See WARNE.

werryng, *sb.* strife, contention 2.33. (From ONF. *werre.*)

wes, was, *1 sg.pa.t.* was 24.22, 29; *2 sg.* **were** 15.15; *3 sg.* **wes** 2.73, **wees** 10.42, **was** 6.24; *1 pl.* **weren** 2.67; *3 pl.* **were** 10.29; *1, 2, 3 sg.pa.t.subj.* **were** 7.4, 8.22, 9.51; *1 pl.* **weren** 12.48; *3 pl.* **were** 12.13. (OE. *wæs, wæron,* etc.) See NES, NERE.

west, *sb. and adv.* west 5.37, 12.10, 15.47. (OE. *west,* adv.)

wete, weete, *adj.* wet, moist 22.8, 32.33. (OE. *wæt.*)

wete, *v.* to make wet 6.26, to become wet 7.70, to weep 21.18; *pp.* **wet** 6.1. (OE. *wætan.*)

whal, *sb.* whale 7.40; *gen.sg.* **whalles** 7.67, 9.1. (OE. *hwæl.*)

wham, what. See WHO, WHET.

when, *adv.* when 7.49; *when þat,* when 30.31. (OE. *hwenne.*)

whener, *adv.* whenever 30.17. (OE. *hwenne + æfre.*)

wher, *adv.* wherever 16.6, 24.14. (OE. *hwær.*)

wher. See WHEÞER.

wherso, *adv.* wherever, 23.47. (OE. *(swā) hwær swā.*)

whet, what, *pron.* what, which 9.44, 20.16; *adj.* which 13.26, 20.38. (OE. *hwæt.*)

wheþer, wher, *cj.* whether 15.47, 30.13. (OE. *hweþer.*)

whi, why, *interr.adv.* why 8.25, 13.50, 31.27; *interj.* why 10.38. (OE. *hwi.*)

whider, *adv.* whither 17.15, 23.24. (OE. *hwider.*)

whil(e), whyle, *sb.* time 13.54; *adv.* formerly 13.18, 52, for a time 4.35; *cj.* while 5.30, 9.6. (OE. *hwil.*)

whilen, whylen, *adv.* formerly 23.2, 24.22. (OE. *hwilum,* dat.pl. of prec.)

whit(e), whyt(e), *adj.* white 5.31, 7.35, 40, 9.50; *comp.* **whittore** 4.28, 7.77. (OE. *hwit.*)

who, *pron.* who 8.5, 22.28, whoever 12.9; *dat.sg.* **wham** 7.23. (OE. *hwā, hwām.*)

whose, *pron.* whoever 3.30, 9.38. (OE. *(swā) hwā swā.*)

whuch, *adj. and pron.* which 7.3, 12.42. (OE. *hwylc.*)

wycche, *sb.* witch 8.46. (OE. *wicce.*)

wicked(e), wycked, wikked, *adj.* wicked, evil 2.35, 6.2, 25, 29.44. (From prec.)

wyde, *adj.* broad, wide 12.28, 21.10. (OE. *wid.*)

wyde, *adv.* far and wide 6.14. (OE. *wide.*)

wif, wyf, *sb.* woman 6.13, 9.12, 23.50, wife, married woman 20.48, 27.48; *gen.sg.* **wyues** 2.34; *pl.* **wyue** 2.33. (OE. *wif.*)

wyht, *adv.* quickly 11.36. (ON. *vigt.*)

wyht, *sb.* creature 12.23. (OE. *wiht.*)

wihtstonden, *v.* to resist 2.27. (OE. *wiþstandan.*)

wyke, *1 sg.pres.* become weak or spiritless 22.53. (OE. *wican.*)

wikked. See WICKED(E).

wil. See WIL(LE), *sb.*

wilde, wylde, *adj.* wild, untamed 2.16, 12.5, wanton, pleasure-loving 7.2. (OE. *wilde.*)

wil(e), wol(e), *1 sg.pres.* desire, will, wish 8.11, 11.35, 21.18, 26.5; *2 sg.* **wolt** 13.86; *3 sg.* **wol** 9.21, **wole** 2.27, **wyle** 21.36; *3 sg.pres.subj.* **wolle** 4.17; *1, 3 sg.pa.t.* **wolde** 2.50, 7.3; *1 pl.* **wolde** 6.50. (OE. *willan,* pa.t. *wolde.*)

wyle, *sb.* sorcerer, wizard 8.46. (OE. *wigela.*)

wil(le), *sb.* will, pleasure 8.6, 24.36, lust 2.34; *gen.sg.* **wille** 13.18. (OE. *willa.*)

wymmon, wymman, wommon, *sb.* woman 5.34, 37, 27.49; *pl.* **wymmen** 4.11. (OE. *wifmann.*)

wyn, *sb.* wine 23.32. (OE. *win.*)

wynd, *sb.* wind 14.1, 3. (OE. *wind.*)

wyndou, *sb.* window 24.23. (ON. *vindauga.*)

wynȝord, *sb.* vineyard 10.2. (OE. *wīngeard.*)

wynne, *v.* to obtain, win 24.20. (OE. *winnan.*) See YWYNNE.

wynne. See WUNNE.

wynter, *sb.* winter 11.8, 17.1. (OE. *winter.*)

wypinge. See WEPING(E).

wys, *adj.* wise, cautious 3.45, 5.34 ; *superl.* **wisist** 3.27. (OE. *wīs.*)

wysse, *3 sg.pres.subj.* teach 26.3. (OE. *wissian.*)

wiste. See WYTE, *v.*[1]

wyt, *sb.* understanding 6.2. (OE. *wit.*)

wyte, *v.*[1] to know 8.5 ; *1, 3 sg.pres.* **wot** 6.25, 30.7 ; *2 sg.* **wost** 20.44 ; *1, 3 sg.pa.t.* **wiste** 9.15, 29.13. (OE. *witan.*) See NOT, NUSTE.

wyte, *v.*[2] *1 sg.pres.* blame 9.12 ; *to wyte,* blameworthy 29.5. (OE. *wītan.*)

wite, *v.*[3] *2 sg.imper.* guard 15.28. (OE. *witan.*)

wyter, *adj.* wise 4.26. (ON. *vitr.*)

wytnesse, *sb.* testimony 27.36. (OE. *witnes.*)

wiþ, wyþ, *prep.* with 18.14, 32.6, together with 11.1, 27.53, among 7.6, 13.20, by 5.1, 24.7, by means of 3.3, 10.9, in comparison with 3.26, like, resembling 2.28, 5.17, in exchange for 26.16, towards 13.5, 31.17, against 12.25, 30.39. (OE. *wiþ,* infl. by senses of *mid.*)

wiþinne, *prep.* within 7.65, 8.32, 21.30. (OE. *wiþinnan.*)

wiþoute(n), *prep.* outside 2.46, without 7.75. (OE. *wiþūtan.*)

wyues. See WIF.

wlyteþ, *3 pl.pres.* chirp, warble 11.11. (Imitative.)

wo, *sb.* woe, misery 13.47 ; *as adj.* sorrowful 9.18, 21.15. OE. *wā.*)

wod(e), *adj.* mad, senseless 22.55, 26.14, 28.7. (OE. *wōd.*)

wode, *sb.* wood 11.12, 24.31, 27.2. (OE. *wudu.*)

wode-gore, *sb.* forest 24.31. (OE. *wudu + gāra.*)

woderoue, *sb.* woodruff 11.9. (OE. *wudurofe.*)

wodewale, *sb.* a singing bird 3.24. (Cf. MLG. *wedewale.*)

woh, *sb.* wrong, harm 1.1. (OE. *wōh.*)

wol. See WIL(E), *v.*

wolc, *sb.* hawk 3.24. (Cf. W. *gwalch.*)

wolde, *sb.* power, control 13.18, 29.34. (OE. *(ge)-wáld.*)

wolde, wole, wolle, wolt. See WIL(E), *v.*

wommon. See WYMMON.

won, *sb.* riches 2.49, world 14.9, dwelling 12.28. (ON. *ván.*)

won, wan, *adj.* pale, wan 4.23, 26.9. (OE. *wann.*)

wonde, *v.* to refuse, hesitate 5.19, 10.24. (OE. *wandian.*)

wonder, wounder, *sb.* wonder, marvel 7.81, 20.30, 22.44, 30.3 ; *adv.* wonderfully 7.80, 11.32, 31.16. (OE. *wúndor.*)

wondes. See WOUNDE(N).

wondryng, *sb.* unsettled course, distress of mind 9.40. (From OE. *wandrian.*)

wone, *sb.* lack 6.2. (OE. *wana.*)

woneþ, *3 sg.pres.* lives, dwells 5.37 ; *pp.* **woned,** accustomed 13.10. (OE. *wunian.*)

wonges, *sb.pl.* cheeks 4.23, 6.1, 13.13. (OE. *wang.*)

wonte, *v.impers.* to lack 11.34. (ON. *vanta.*)

word, *sb.* word 14.71, 24.7. (OE. *word.*)

wore, *sb.* troubled pool 4.32. (OE. *wār,* sandy shore.)

woren, *v.* to disturb, confuse 2.50. (OE. *wōrian,* intr.)

worhliche. See WORLY.

world, *sb.* world 4.26, 7.57. (OE. *world.*)

worly, worhliche, wurhliche, *adj.* splendid 12.10, 14.9, 42 ; *adv.* beautifully 9.13. (OE. *weorþlic, wurþlic.*)

wormes, *sb.pl.* worms 11.31. (OE. *wyrm.*)

worse, *adv.comp.* worse 20.21. (OE. *wyrs.*)

worst, wrst, *adj.superl.* worst 2.33, 29.16. (OE. *wyrsta.*)

worþeþ, *3 sg.pres.* becomes (constr. w. ' to ') 7.71. (OE. *weorþan.*)

wosshe, *2 sg.imper.* wash 20.20. (OE. *wascan.*)

wost, wot. See WYTE, *v.*[1]

wounded, *pp.* wounded 9.25. (OE. *wúndian.*)

wounde(n), woundes, wondes, *sb.pl.* wounds 18.39, 20.53, 21.10, 24.30. (OE. *wúnd.*)

wounder. See WONDER.

woweþ, *3 sg.pres.* woos 12.41. (OE. *wōgian.*)

wowyng, *sb.* love-making 4.31. (OE. *wōgung.*)

wraht. See WURCHE.

wrakeful, *adj.* wicked, sinful 2.10. (OE. *wracu* + *-ful.*)

wraþþelees, *adj.* without anger 10.48. (OE. *wrǣþþu* + *-lēas.*)

wrecche, *sb.* wretch 8.39. (OE. *wrecca.*)

wrieþ, *3 pl.pres.* go 13.45. (OE. *wrīgian.*)

wroht, *adj.* angry 13.45, 31.16. (OE. *wrāþ.*)

wroht(e). See WURCHE.

wrong(e), *adj.* wrong, untrue 6.12; *adv.* ill, unjustly 6.13 ; *sb.* wrong, injustice 18.47, 32.6. (Late OE. *wrang.*)

wrot, *3 sg.pa.t.* wrote 10.3. (OE. *wrītan.*)

wroþe, *adv.* evilly, badly 8.39. (OE. *wrāþe.*)

wrst. See WORST.

wunne, wynne, *sb.* joy 8.14, 13.12 ; *gen.pl.* wynne 11.11, **wunne** 11.35. (OE. *wynn.*)

wurche, *v.* to cause 10.49, to make 7.80, to do 12.32, to work 10.35, to act, behave 13.76, to write 6.11 ; *1 sg.pa.t.* **wroht** 13.76, **wrohte** 6.13 ; *3 sg.* **wraht** 10.35, **wrohte** 10.2 ; *pp.* **wroht** 6.11, **wrohte** 23.20, **ywroht** 7.80, **ywraht** 14.34. (OE. *wyrcan,* pa.t. *worhte.*)

wurhliche. See WORLY.

wurþe, *adj.* worthy, deserving 8.22. (OE. *wyrþe.*)

wurþes, *sb.pl.* equivalents 9.32. (OE. *weorþ, wurþ.*)

ANGLO-NORMAN GLOSSARY

ay, *1 sg.pres.* have, possess 19.4.
alme, *sb.* soul 28.30.
amour, *sb.* sake 28.16.
auera, *3 sg.fut.* will have 28.48.
baroun, *sb.* man, noble, 28.42.
beal, bele, *adj.* beautiful 19.9, 11.
beyser, *v.* to kiss 19.16 ; *3 sg.pret.*
 beysa 28.18.
bele. See BEAL.
cel, *dem.adj.* this 28.2.
ciel, *sb.* heaven 28.40.
come, *cj.* as 19.14.
cora, *3 sg.pret.* ran, flowed 28.34.
couent, *3 sg.pres.impers.* it is neces-
 sary 19.7.
creatour, *sb.* Creator, God 28.12.
cum, *cj.* as if 19.10.
dame, *sb.* lady 19.9.
de, *prep.* from 28.4, 6, 30, 34, of
 28.10.
descenda, *3 sg.pret.* descended 28.38.
dieu, *sb.* god 19.2.
doint, *3 sg.pres.subj.juss.* give 19.15 ;
 3 sg.pret. **dona** 28.22.
donque, *adv.* then 28.18.
doucour, *sb.* sweetness, graciousness
 28.10.
duel, *sb.* grief 19.3.
e, *cj.* and 28.4, 10.
ele, *pron.* she 19.9.
en, *prep.* in 28.8, 32, into 28.38, 40.
enfern, *sb.* Hell 28.38.
est, *3 sg.pres.* is 19.9.
feloun, *sb.* evil-doer 28.4.
fere, *v.* to do 19.16.
fitʒ, *sb.* son 28.28.
flur, *sb.* flower, 19.12.
fourma, *3 sg.pret.* made 28.20.
fu, *3 sg.pret.* was 28.42 ; *3 sg.pret.subj.*
 fust 19.10, 28.32.
gente, *adj.* lovely, fair 19.9.
Gyw, *sb.* Jew 28.22.
grant, *adj.* great 28.48.
greua, *3 sg.pret.impers.* grieved 28.24.
il, *pron.* he 28.36.
ie, *pron.* I 19.4.
ioyous, *adj.* glad, happy 28.42.

la, *pron.* her 19.4.
la, *def.art.fem.* the 28.16.
le, *pron.* him 28.24, it 28.36.
le, *def.art.masc.* the 28.22, 34.
li, ly, *pron.* him 28.18, 22, her 19.7, 8.
ly, *def.art.masc.* the 28.4, 12.
lune, *sb.* moon 19.14.
mal, *adj.* evil 28.4.
me, *pron.* me 28.6.
me. See ME(S), *cj.*
meneʒ, *2 pl.imper.* (*with sg. meaning*)
 lead 28.6.
merour, *sb.* mirror 19.3.
me(s), *cj.* but 28.24, 36.
mi, *sb.* middle ; *en mi,* in the middle
 of 19.18.
moi, *pron.* me 19.2.
molt, *adv.* very 28.42.
mon, *poss.adj.* my 19.18.
mound, *sb.* world 28.32.
mounta, *3 sg.pret.* ascended 28.40.
Naʒaroun, *adj.* of Nazareth 28.44.
ne, *adv.* not 19.4.
nostre, *poss.adj.* our 28.46.
nus, *pron.* us 28.20.
oieʒ, *2 pl.imper.* (*with sg. meaning*)
 hear 28.2.
ore, *adv.* now 28.8.
oreysoun, *sb.* prayer 28.2.
ostel, *sb.* abode 19.18.
pardoun, *sb.* pardon 28.48.
partaunt, *pres.part.* leaving 28.30.
pendant, *pres.part.* hanging 28.28.
pensaunt, *ppl.adj.* sorrowful, 28.26.
plein, *adj.* full 28.10.
poi, *adv.* little 28.24.
prisoun, *sb.* prison 28.8.
pucele, *sb.* virgin, maid 28.26.
puis, *adv.* then 28.40.
pur, *prep.* for 28.16, 46.
pus, *1 sg.pres.* can 19.8.
qe, *cj.* that 19.6.
qe. See QUE.
quant, *adv.* when 19.13.
que, qe, *rel.pron.* who 28.20, 32,
 which 28.22.
rechata, *3 sg.pret.* redeemed 28.36.

123

redempcioun, *sb.* redemption 28.46.
sang, *sb.* blood 28.34.
seint, *adj.* holy, blessed 28.14.
semblant, *sb.* appearance 19.11.
si, *adv.* so 19.9.
si, *cj.* if 19.4.
socour, *sb.* help 28.14.
soi, *I sg.pres.* know 19.6.
souerein, *adj.* supreme 28.12.
su, *I sg.pres.* am 19.13.
sue, *poss.adj.* his 28.16.

tiel, *adj.* such 19.2.
tient, *3 sg.pres.* holds 19.2.
ton, *poss.adj.* thy 28.28.
tot, *adv.* very, quite 28.26.
tous, *adj.pl.* all 28.20.
tresoun, *sb.* wrong-doing 28.6.
vey, *I sg.pres.* see 19.13 ; *2 sg.pret.*
  veites 28.28.
vile, *sb.* town, city 19.18.
viuaunt, *pres. part.* living 28.32.
vostre, *poss.adj.* your 28.14.

INDEX OF PROPER NAMES

INDEX OF FIRST LINES

SELECT BIBLIOGRAPHY

Books are listed in chronological order within each section.

EDITIONS CONTAINING LYRICS FROM MS. HARLEY 2253

RITSON, J., ed. *Ancient Songs from the Time of King Henry the Third to the Revolution.* London, 1790. (Nos. 4, 11, 12, 14, 17, 25, 30.)

WRIGHT, T., ed. *The Political Songs of England from the Reign of John to that of Edward II.* Camden Society, 1839. Contains the political songs of MS. Harley 2253, not included in the present edition.

WRIGHT, T., ed. *Specimens of Lyric Poetry composed in England in the Reign of Edward the First.* Percy Society, 1842. (Nos. 2–32.)

WÜLCKER, R. P., ed. *Altenglisches Lesebuch, erster Teil.* Halle, 1874. (Nos. 4, 11, 14, 17, 20, 25, 27, 28.)

BÖDDEKER, K., ed. *Altenglische Dichtungen des MS. Harl. 2253.* Berlin, 1878. (Nos. 2–18, 20–32.)

CHAMBERS, E. K., and SIDGWICK, F., ed. *Early English Lyrics.* London, 1907. (Nos. 4, 11, 17, 23, 24, 25, 28.) Contains a valuable essay on ' Some Aspects of Mediaeval Lyric ' and a useful bibliography.

PATTERSON, F. A., ed. *The Middle English Penitential Lyric.* New York, 1911. (Nos. 3, 16, 23, 29.)

MURRAY, HILDA M. R., ed. *The Middle English Poem, Erthe upon Erthe, printed from Twenty-four Manuscripts.* EETS, 1911. (No. 1.)

SISAM, K., ed. *Fourteenth Century Verse and Prose*, with Glossary by J. R. R. Tolkein. Oxford, 1922. (Nos. 4, 11.)

SAMPSON, G., ed. *The Cambridge Book of Prose and Verse.* Cambridge, 1924. (Nos. 4, 5, 9, 11, 14, 15, 17, 18, 20, 22, 24–28.)

BROWN, CARLETON, ed. *Religious Lyrics of the XIV Century.* Oxford, 1924. (Nos. 13, 15, 16, 17, 23, 27.) New edition revised by G. V. Smithers, 1952.

BROWN, CARLETON, ed. *English Lyrics of the XIII Century.* Oxford, 1932. (Nos. 2–6, 10–12, 14, 21, 24, 25, 28–32.) Referred to in the present edition as Brown XIII.

GREENE, RICHARD LEIGHTON, ed. *The Early English Carol.* Oxford, 1935. (No. 14.)

MOSSÉ, FERNAND. *Manuel de l'Anglais du Moyen Age: II Moyen-Anglais.* 2 vols. Paris, 1949. (Nos. 14, 25.) Translated by J. A. Walker: *A Handbook of Middle English.* Baltimore, 1952.

DICKINS, BRUCE and R. M. WILSON, ed. *Early Middle English Texts.* Cambridge, 1951. (Nos. 14, 20, 24, 25, 30.)

KAISER, ROLF, ed. *Alt- und Mittelenglische Anthologie.* Zweite Auflage. Berlin, 1955. (Nos. 3, 4, 5, 9, 11, 12, 14, 24, 25, 30, 31, 32.)

GREENE, RICHARD LEIGHTON, ed. *A Selection of English Carols.* Oxford, 1962. (No. 14.)

DAVIES, R. T., ed. *Medieval English Lyrics: A Critical Anthology.* London, 1963. (Nos. 4, 9, 11, 14, 20, 22, 23, 24, 25, 27, 30.)

BENNETT, J. A. W. and SMITHERS, G. V. ed. *Early Middle English Verse and Prose,* with a Glossary by Norman Davis, second edition, Oxford, 1968. (Nos. 5, 7, 8, 9, 12, 14, 24, 25, 30.)

EDITIONS OF OTHER EARLY ENGLISH LYRICS

WRIGHT, THOMAS and J. O. HALLIWELL, ed. *Reliquiae Antiquae.* 2 vols. London, 1841–3.

FURNIVALL, F. J., ed. *Political, Religious and Love Poems.* EETS., 1866.

FURNIVALL, F. J., ed. *Hymns to the Virgin and Christ.* EETS., 1867.

MORRIS, RICHARD, ed. *An Old English Miscellany.* EETS., 1872.

HORSTMANN, C., and FURNIVALL, F. J., ed. *The Minor Poems of the Vernon MS.* EETS., 1892–1901.

HORSTMANN, C., ed. *Yorkshire Writers,* 2 vols. London, 1895–6.

KAIL, J., ed. *Twenty-six Political and other Poems.* EETS., 1904.

HEUSER, W., ed. *Die Kildare Gedichte.* Bonn, 1904.

PADELFORD, F. M., ed. *Early Sixteenth Century Lyrics.* Boston, 1906.

DYBOSKI, R., ed. *Songs, Carols, &c., from Richard Hill's Balliol MS.* EETS., 1907.

PERRY, G. G., ed. *Religious Pieces in Prose and Verse from the Thornton MS.* Revised edition. EETS., 1913.

DAY, MABEL, ed. *The Wheatley MS.* EETS., 1917.

WHITING, E. K., ed. *The Poems of John Audelay.* EETS., 1931.

BROWN, CARLETON, ed. *Religious Lyrics of the XVth Century.* Oxford, 1939.

ROBBINS, ROSSELL HOPE, ed. *Secular Lyrics of the XIVth and XVth Centuries.* Oxford, 1952.

ROBBINS, ROSSELL HOPE, ed. *Historical Poems of the XIVth and XVth Centuries.* New York, 1959.

STUDIES OF THE LYRICS OF MS. HARLEY 2253

KÖLBING, E. 'Altenglische Dichtungen des MS. Harl. 2253' in *Englische Studien,* ii (1879), 499–517. A long review of Böddeker's edition.

SCHLÜTER, A. 'Über die Sprache und Metrik . . . des MS. Harl. 2253' in *Herrigs Archiv,* lxxi (1884), 153, 357.

GIBSON, J. A. *The Lyrics of MS. Harley 2253.* London University M.A. Dissertation, 1914. Typescript.

BROOK, G. L. 'The Original Dialects of the Harley Lyrics' in *Leeds Studies in English,* ii (1933), 38–61.

SISTER MARY IMMACULATE. 'A Note on "A Song of the Five Joys"' in *Modern Language Notes,* lv (1940), 249–54. (No. 27.)

MERONEY, HOWARD. 'Man Must Fight Three Foes' in *Modern Language Notes,* lviii (1943), 109–113. (No. 2.)

MENNER, R. J. 'The Man in the Moon and Hedging' in *Journal of English and Germanic Philology*, xlviii (1949), 1–14. (No. 30.)

SCHOECK, R. J. 'Alliterative Assonance in Harley MS. 2253' in *English Studies*, xxxii (1951), 68–70.

DEGGINGER, STUART H. L. '"A Wayle Whyt ase Whalles Bon"—Reconstructed' in *Journal of English and Germanic Phililogy*, liii (1954), 84–90. (No. 9.)

BREWER, D. S. 'The Ideal of Feminine Beauty in Medieval Literature, especially "Harley Lyrics", Chaucer, and Some Elizabethans' in *Modern Language Review*, l (1955), 257–69.

STEMMLER, THEO. *Die englischen Liebesgedichte* des MS. Harley 2253. Bonn, 1962.

STUDIES DEALING WITH THE MIDDLE ENGLISH LYRIC

CHAMBERS, E. K. *The Mediaeval Stage*, 2 vols. Oxford, 1903.

HEIDER, OTTO. *Untersuchungen zur mittelenglischen erotischen Lyrik (1250–1300)*. Halle, 1905.

MÜLLER, A. *Mittelenglische Geistliche und Weltliche Lyrik des XIII Jahrhunderts*. Halle, 1911.

KER, W. P. *English Literature, Medieval*. London, 1912.

SANDISON, H. E. *The 'Chanson d'Aventure' in Middle English*. Bryn Mawr, 1913.

COHEN, HELEN LOUISE. *The Ballade*. New York, 1915.

MEDARY, MARGARET P. 'Stanza-Linking in Middle English Verse' in *Romanic Review*, vii (1916), 243–70.

BROWN, ARTHUR C. L. 'On the Origin of Stanza-Linking in English Alliterative Verse' in *Romanic Review*, vii (1916), 271–83.

JONES, WILLIAM POWELL. *The Pastourelle, a Study of the Origins and Tradition of a Lyric Type*. Cambridge, Mass., 1931.

WEHRLE, WILLIAM O. *The Macaronic Hymn Tradition in Medieval English Literature*. Washington, D.C., 1933.

SINGER, SAMUEL. *Die religiöse Lyrik des Mittelalters (Das Nachleben der Psalmen)*. Bern, 1933.

MALONE, KEMP. 'Notes on Middle English Lyrics' in *English Literary History*, ii (1935), 58–65.

ROBBINS, R. H. 'The Earliest Carols and the Franciscans' in *Modern Language Notes*, liii (1938), 239–45.

WILSON, R. M. *Early Middle English Literature*. London, 1939.

ROBBINS, ROSSELL HOPE. 'The Authors of the Middle English Religious Lyrics' in *Journal of English and Germanic Philology*, xxxix (1940), 230–8.

MENNER, R. J. 'Notes on Middle English Lyrics' in *Modern Language Notes*, lv (1940), 243–9.

CHAMBERS, E. K. *English Literature at the Close of the Middle Ages*. Oxford, 1945. A volume of the Oxford History of English Literature.

BAUGH, A. C., ed. *A Literary History of England*. New York, 1948.

WOLPERS, THEODOR. 'Geschichte der englischen Marienlyrik im Mittelalter' in *Anglia*, lxix (1950), 3–88.

MOORE, ARTHUR K. *The Secular Lyric in Middle English*. Lexington, Kentucky, 1951.

KANE, GEORGE. *Middle English Literature: A Critical Study of the Romances, the Religious Lyrics, Piers Plowman*. London, 1951.

SPITZER, LEO. '*Explication de Texte* Applied to Three Great Middle English Poems' in *Archivum Linguisticum*, iii (1951), 1–22, 137–65.

WILSON, R. M. *The Lost Literature of Medieval England*. London, 1952.

STEINBERG, S. H., ed. *Cassell's Encyclopaedia of Literature*, 2 vols. London, 1953.

WOOLF, ROSEMARY. *The English Religious Lyric in the Middle Ages*. Oxford, 1968.

METRE

KASTNER, L. E. *A History of French Versification*. Oxford, 1903.

SCHIPPER, JAKOB. *History of English Versification*. Oxford, 1910.

KALUZA, MAX. *A Short History of English Versification*, translated by A. C. Dunstan. London, 1911.

THE LATIN BACKGROUND

WADDELL, HELEN. *The Wandering Scholars*. London, 1927.

RABY, F. J. E. *A History of Christian-Latin Poetry to the Close of the Middle Ages*. Oxford, 1928.

WADDELL, HELEN, ed. *Medieval Latin Lyrics*. London, 1929.

RABY, F. J. E. *A History of Secular Latin Poetry in the Middle Ages*, 2 vols. Oxford, 1934.

BRITTAIN, F. *The Mediaeval Latin and Romance Lyric*. Cambridge, 1937.

DRONKE, PETER. *The Medieval Lyric*. London, 1968.

FRENCH AND PROVENÇAL BACKGROUND

BARTSCH, K. *Altfranzösische Romanzen und Pastourellen*. Leipzig, 1870.

CHAYTOR, H. J. *The Troubadours of Dante*. Oxford, 1902. Contains a brief outline of Provençal grammar, selections, and glossary.

CHAYTOR, H. J. *The Troubadours*. Cambridge, 1912.

PARIS, GASTON. *La Littérature française au moyen âge* (XIe–XIVe siècle). Cinquième édition. Paris, 1914.

ANGLADE, J. *Les Troubadours, leurs vies, leurs œuvres, leur influence*. Nouvelle édition. Paris, 1919.

CHAYTOR, H. J. *The Troubadours and England*. Cambridge, 1923.

FARAL, EDMOND. *Les Arts Poétiques du XIIe et du XIIIe Siècle*. Paris, 1924.

JEANROY, A. *Les Origines de la Poésie Lyrique en France au Moyen-Age*. Troisième édition. Paris, 1925.

AUDIAU, J. *Les Troubadours et l'Angleterre.* Nouvelle édition. Paris, 1927.

AUDIAU, J., et LAVAUD, R. *Nouvelle Anthologie des Troubadours.* Paris, 1928.

ABBOTT, C. C., ed. *Early Mediaeval French Lyrics.* London, 1932.

JEANROY, A. *La Poésie Lyrique des Troubadours,* 2 vols. Paris, 1934.

BÉDIER, JOSEPH et HAZARD, PAUL, ed. *Histoire de la littérature française illustrée. Nouvelle édition, refondue et augmentée sous la direction de P. Martino.* 2 vols. Paris, 1948–9.

COURTLY LOVE

ANDREAS CAPELLANUS. *De Arte Honeste Amandi,* ed. E. TROJEL. Copenhagen, 1892. Translated by John J. Parry, *The Art of Courtly Love.* New York, 1941.

COHEN, GUSTAVE. *Chrétien de Troyes et son œuvre.* Paris, 1931.

LEWIS, C. S. *The Allegory of Love: a Study in Medieval Tradition.* Oxford, 1936.

PAINTER, SIDNEY. *French Chivalry: Chivalric Ideas and Practices in Mediaeval France.* Baltimore, 1940.

DENOMY, A. J. ' An Inquiry into the Origins of Courtly Love ' in *Mediaeval Studies,* vi (1944), 175–260.

GILSON, ÉTIENNE. *La Théologie mystique de Saint Bernard.* Paris, 1947. Appendix IV (pp. 193–215) on ' Saint Bernard et l'Amour Courtois '.

MUSIC

BECK, JEAN. *La Musique des Troubadours.* Paris, 1910.

GALPIN, F. W. *Old English Instruments of Music.* Revised edition. London, 1932.

REESE, GUSTAVE. *Music in the Middle Ages.* New York, 1940.

BUKOFZER, MANFRED F. ' *Sumer is icumen in* ': *a Revision.* Berkeley, California, 1944.

HUGHES, ANSELM, ed. *Early Medieval Music up to 1300.* Oxford, 1954. Vol. 2 of the New Oxford History of Music.

GROVE'S *Dictionary of Music and Musicians.* Fifth edition ed. by ERIC BLOM, 9 vols. London, 1954.

BIBLIOGRAPHIES

WELLS, J. E. *A Manual of the Writings in Middle English.* New York, 1916. Nine supplements have been issued. The latest, published in 1951, lists work published before the end of 1945.

BROWN, CARLETON, and ROBBINS, R. H. *The Index of Middle English Verse.* New York, 1943.

BATESON, F. W., ed. *The Cambridge Bibliography of English Literature,* Vol. I. Cambridge, 1940. Vol. V, *Supplement,* 1957.

RENWICK, W. L., and ORTON, HAROLD. *The Beginnings of English Literature to Skelton 1509.* Second edition. London, 1952.